AF098740

Haunted America: A True Ghost Stories Collection book of the Nation's Most Terrifying Haunted Locations

Subtitle: A Horror Stories Collection of Real-Life Hauntings, Unexplained Phenomena, and Paranormal Encounters from across the U.S., featuring haunted houses, battlefields, hotels, and graveyards.

James Corbin Carter

Copyright © 2025 **James Corbin Carter** All rights reserved.

No part of this book may be reproduced in any form or by any electronic or mechanical means, including information storage and retrieval systems, without written permission from the author, except for the use of brief quotations in a book review.

Disclaimer

The stories, locations, and historical accounts presented in *The Haunted History of America: True Ghost Stories from Every State* are based on **a combination of historical research, firsthand accounts, folklore, and local legends.** While **every effort has been made to verify the accuracy of historical details**, many of the ghost stories and paranormal experiences described within remain **unverified and subject to personal interpretation**.

This book is intended **for entertainment, historical interest, and cultural exploration only**. The authors and publishers **do not make any claims regarding the authenticity of supernatural phenomena, nor do we take responsibility for any interpretations, beliefs, or experiences that readers may have after visiting any of the locations mentioned**.

Furthermore, we **strongly advise readers to respect all locations, public and private, and to follow all local laws and guidelines** when visiting historical or allegedly haunted sites. Trespassing, vandalism, or any illegal activity in pursuit of paranormal experiences is **strictly discouraged and entirely the responsibility of the individual**.

The authors and publishers **assume no liability for any experiences, injuries, legal consequences, or supernatural encounters that may arise from readers visiting or investigating the sites mentioned in this book**. While many locations are open to the public through official tours and historical programs, **always seek permission when necessary and approach each site with respect for its history and its significance**.

Whether one believes in ghosts or not, the stories in this book serve as **a reflection of American history, folklore, and cultural fascination with the unknown**. The past lingers in many ways—through memories, through stories, and perhaps, for some, through something more.

Explore at your own risk.

Contents

Part 1
Introduction: The Ghosts of America's Past

The Allure of the Paranormal	3
Historical Context: How America's Past Shapes Its Hauntings	9
Methodology: Separating Legend from Reality	15
What to Expect in This Book	23

Part 2
State-by-State Hauntings
Each chapter will focus on a specific state, detailing one or more notable hauntings.

Alabama	31
Alaska	43
Arizona	59
Arkansas	69
California	81
Colorado	95
Connecticut	103
Delaware	111
Florida	119
Georgia	127
Hawaii	135
Idaho	143
Illinois	151
Indiana	159
Iowa	167
Kansas	175
Kentucky	183
Louisiana	193
Maine	201

Maryland	211
Massachusetts	225
Michigan	233
Minnesota	241
Mississippi	249
Missouri	257
Montana	269
Nebraska	275
Nevada	283
New Hampshire	291
New Jersey	297
New Mexico	305
New York	313
North Carolina	319
North Dakota	325
Ohio	333
Oklahoma	341
Oregon	349
Pennsylvania	357
Rhode Island	367
South Carolina	377
South Dakota	383
Tennessee	389
Texas	395
Utah	405
Vermont	411
Virginia	419
Washington	427
West Virginia	437
Wisconsin	449
Wyoming	455

Part 3
Conclusion: The Ghosts We Leave Behind

Reflections on America's Haunted Legacy	467
How to Explore Hauntings Safely & Respectfully	487

Part 1

Introduction: The Ghosts of America's Past

The Allure of the Paranormal

Ghost stories have captivated us for centuries. They are whispered around campfires, passed down through generations, and immortalized in books and film. They linger in the eerie corridors of abandoned mansions, drift through fog-laden graveyards, and stand silent in the ruins of once-thriving towns. But why do we keep telling these stories? Why do we seek out haunted places, listen for footsteps in empty hallways, and stare into the dark, hoping—or perhaps dreading—to see something staring back?

The allure of the paranormal is not just about the ghosts themselves. It's about what they represent: fear, mystery, history, and the ever-haunting question of what happens after death.

The Thrill of Fear, Mystery, and the Unknown

Fear is one of the most powerful emotions we experience, and it has an almost paradoxical grip on us. While our instincts tell us to avoid danger, many of us actively seek out experiences that simulate fear—watching horror movies, exploring haunted houses, or reading chilling tales of ghostly encounters. This controlled fear is thrilling. It sends adrenaline coursing through our veins, heightens our senses, and gives us the excitement of the unknown without any real danger.

But beyond the excitement, ghost stories tap into something even deeper: mystery. Humans are natural storytellers, and we are drawn to the unexplained. We don't like loose ends or unanswered questions, yet the supernatural defies easy explanations. Hauntings leave us with lingering puzzles—who are these spirits? Why do they remain? What do they want? And the most unsettling question of all: could it happen to *me*?

The paranormal is alluring precisely because it straddles the line between possibility and impossibility. For every scientific explanation, there's an experience that defies logic. And in a world where so much can be explained, the unknown remains intoxicating.

America's Deep-Rooted Tradition of the Supernatural

The United States is a nation built on stories. From the oral traditions of Indigenous tribes to the ghostly superstitions of early settlers, the paranormal has always been part of our cultural fabric. Every region has its own signature hauntings, shaped by history, folklore, and the people who lived—and died—there.

- **New England** is steeped in Puritan fear and colonial-era ghosts. The Salem Witch Trials left an indelible mark, and stories of vengeful spirits and lingering witches still circulate today.

- **The South** is haunted by echoes of the Civil War, where countless soldiers met their end on bloody battlefields. Antebellum mansions, slave quarters, and abandoned plantations hold secrets that refuse to stay buried.

- **The Midwest** is a land of eerie urban legends and haunted roads, where phantom hitchhikers and ghostly cries fill the night air.

- **The West**, with its rugged frontier past, is filled with spectral cowboys, haunted mining towns, and spirits of pioneers who never made it to their final destination.

From the Headless Horseman of Sleepy Hollow to the restless ghosts of Gettysburg, these stories endure not just because they are terrifying, but because they reflect the struggles, fears, and dreams of the people who came before us.

The Rise of Paranormal Pop Culture

Our fascination with the supernatural has only grown in the modern era. What was once relegated to folklore and campfire tales has become mainstream entertainment. The rise of **ghost-hunting reality shows** like *Ghost Hunters*, *Paranormal Witness*, and *The Dead Files* has turned casual believers into passionate investigators. Paranormal tourism is booming, with visitors flocking to haunted hotels, asylums, and historic sites in hopes of capturing a glimpse of the otherworldly.

The internet has further fueled the fire. Social media is flooded with eerie videos, unexplained photographs, and spine-chilling personal accounts of hauntings. Platforms like YouTube, TikTok, and Reddit are digital campfires where modern ghost stories are shared in real time. Paranormal podcasts dissect famous hauntings, while entire online communities are dedicated to analyzing ghostly encounters and debating the authenticity of paranormal evidence.

It's no longer just about believing in ghosts—it's about experiencing them.

Where History and the Paranormal Collide

What makes ghost stories especially compelling is their deep connection to history. A ghost is never just an apparition—it's a fragment of the past refusing to be forgotten.

Hauntings often take root in places where trauma, tragedy, or unresolved events occurred. A battlefield where soldiers fought to the death. A hospital where patients suffered and died. A prison where inmates endured a lifetime of misery. These places become more than just historical sites; they become **echoes of the past**, charged with the energy of those who lived—and perished—there.

Some hauntings serve as grim reminders of injustices:

• The spirits of enslaved people still heard weeping in former plantations.

• The ghosts of prisoners still pacing their cells in abandoned penitentiaries.

• The spectral soldiers reliving their final moments in places like Gettysburg and Antietam.

These aren't just ghost stories; they are history *manifesting itself*. In this way, ghost stories act as time capsules, preserving the emotions, fears, and unresolved narratives of generations past.

But are these hauntings real? Are ghosts truly lingering in the shadows, or do these stories persist because we, as humans, are desperate to connect with the past?

Do You Believe?

There are those who scoff at ghost stories, dismissing them as nothing more than overactive imaginations and coincidences. Others swear they've felt something unexplainable—an icy touch on their skin, a whisper in an empty room, the fleeting shadow of something *watching*.

Whether you are a skeptic, a believer, or simply someone who enjoys a good eerie tale, one thing is undeniable: ghost stories endure. They have survived for centuries, passed down in whispers and written into history, and they will continue to be told long after we are gone.

Because, in the end, the allure of the paranormal isn't just about ghosts.

It's about us. Our fears. Our history. And the mysteries we may never solve.

So as you turn the page and embark on this journey through America's most haunted places, ask yourself:

Do you believe in ghosts?

Or do they simply believe in *us*?

Historical Context: How America's Past Shapes Its Hauntings

Ghosts do not appear without a story. They are the echoes of history, imprints left behind by those who lived, fought, suffered, and died. The haunted places of America are not just eerie tourist attractions or legends meant to entertain—they are windows into the past, whispering tales of war, tragedy, and unresolved mysteries.

Every spirit, every shadowy figure, every unexplained knock in the dead of night is rooted in something real: a moment frozen in time, a sorrow left unfinished, a secret buried just beneath the surface.

To understand hauntings, we must first understand history.

Where the Past Refuses to Rest

America's landscape is a vast and layered tapestry of triumph and turmoil. The nation was born in revolution, shaped by conflict, and built on the backs of those who endured hardship. With every war, every tragedy, every whispered injustice, the past has left its fingerprints. And sometimes, those fingerprints manifest as hauntings.

Ghosts are often tied to places where history was written in blood and grief:

- **Battlefields where soldiers took their final breath.**
- **Graveyards where the forgotten remain nameless.**
- **Asylums where the misunderstood were abandoned.**
- **Hotels where guests checked in—but never left.**

These sites are not merely locations; they are **portals to the past**, places where time does not move forward as easily as it does elsewhere. The restless spirits that linger in these spaces are more than just flickering shadows—they are reminders of the people who came before us, the ones who never had a chance to say goodbye.

The Haunted Regions of America: How Culture Shapes the Paranormal

While every state has its ghosts, the way we interpret hauntings is shaped by regional history and cultural narratives. Each part of America has its own relationship with the supernatural, deeply rooted in its past.

The Northeast: Colonial Spirits and Witch Trials

The ghost stories of the Northeast are steeped in America's earliest history. This is the land of **the Salem Witch Trials**, where paranoia and fear led to the execution of the innocent. It is a place of **colonial graveyards**, where headstones lean with age, and spirits from the Revolutionary War still patrol cobblestone streets.

In towns like **Sleepy Hollow**, folklore and reality intertwine, blurring the line between myth and truth. The spirits of Puritan settlers, sailors lost at sea, and accused witches cast long shadows over New England's fog-drenched cemeteries and crumbling mansions.

The South: Civil War Ghosts and Echoes of the Past

The American South is a region haunted by its own history. **Civil War battlefields** are among the most paranormally active places in the country—Gettysburg, Antietam, and Chickamauga are still filled with the restless spirits of soldiers who never left the fight.

But it's not just the war that lingers. The South is home to sprawling **plantations**, where the ghosts of enslaved people are said to roam, forever tied to the land they were forced to toil. In cities like New Orleans, where **Voodoo, mysticism, and folklore** converge, the supernatural is not just legend—it is woven into everyday life.

From the phantom horsemen of the Mississippi Delta to the mournful spirits of Savannah's historic district, the South's ghosts are deeply entwined with its painful past.

The Midwest: Urban Legends and Forgotten Souls

In the heart of the country, ghost stories take on a different tone—one of isolation, open roads, and forgotten towns. The Midwest is home to some of the most chilling **urban legends**, from the vanishing hitchhiker to the spectral woman in white.

Abandoned **mental asylums** and **prisons** dot the landscape, filled with the tormented echoes of those who were once confined within their walls. The old slaughterhouses of Chicago, the desolate farmlands of Kansas, the ghost towns of North Dakota—each tells a story of the past refusing to fade away.

The West: Frontier Phantoms and Desert Hauntings

The ghosts of the Wild West are as untamed as the land itself. Boomtowns that once bustled with gold miners and outlaws now stand in eerie silence, their remnants haunted by spirits of gunslingers who died in duels at high noon.

From the haunted streets of **Tombstone, Arizona**, to the spectral miners of **Virginia City, Nevada**, the West is a land of **restless spirits** and **unfinished business**. And in the vast, empty deserts, where mirages and reality blur, some believe that spirits roam free, forever wandering beneath the burning sun.

The Power of Folklore: How Stories Keep Hauntings Alive

Ghost stories are more than just eerie tales; they are part of our **cultural memory**. Oral traditions, passed down through generations, ensure that spirits never fade from existence.

Before the written word, legends were spoken, whispered around fires, shared in hushed voices on darkened porches. These stories serve a purpose—they warn, they explain the unexplainable, and they remind us of the past.

Every culture has its own version of the supernatural:

- The **Cherokee tell of the Little People**, spirits that inhabit the mountains.

- The **Gullah people of the South speak of "haints," restless souls who can be warded off by blue-painted doors.**

- The **Mexican legend of La Llorona**, the Weeping Woman, has spread across the Southwest, her cries warning children not to stray too far from home.

These stories endure not just because they terrify us, but because they connect us to those who came before us. Ghosts, in many ways, are the past's way of ensuring it is never forgotten.

History, Hauntings, and the Echoes of the Past

The ghosts of America are not random; they are tied to the moments that shaped the nation. They are the echoes of soldiers who fell in battle, the victims of injustice who never found peace, and the lonely souls who met tragic ends.

Some believe that hauntings are merely figments of imagination, tricks of the mind. Others insist that ghosts are real, tangible remnants of history refusing to let go.

Whichever you believe, one thing is certain:

The past is never truly dead.

It lingers. It watches. It waits.

And sometimes, it reaches out.

Methodology: Separating Legend from Reality

Ghost stories thrive in the space between truth and folklore, between history and myth. They are passed down through generations, whispered in the dark, and written into the very fabric of a place. But how do we separate a genuine haunting from a well-told tale? How do we sift through centuries of storytelling to uncover the real events that gave birth to these lingering spirits?

In exploring America's most haunted locations, we have sought to balance **historical fact with firsthand experiences, local legend with documented evidence**. Every story in this book has been chosen not simply because it is chilling, but because it carries a deeper connection to the past.

Some hauntings are the result of tragic history. Others have been shaped over time, evolving with each retelling until the original story is barely recognizable. And then there are those rare cases—where the line between legend and reality is razor-thin, where the unexplained defies logic, and where even skeptics struggle to dismiss the eerie phenomena reported by countless witnesses.

This section explores the **process of distinguishing truth from folklore, the role of evidence, and the people who dedicate their lives to investigating the paranormal.**

How Stories Were Chosen: Balancing History, Eyewitness Accounts, and Local Legends

For every haunted house or battlefield that has become famous for its ghosts, there are dozens more with stories known only to locals. Some hauntings are well-documented, with historical records and multiple eyewitness accounts supporting their eerie reputations. Others are born from folklore, passed down as cautionary tales or thrilling legends with little factual basis.

To create a **comprehensive and credible** collection of ghost stories, the stories chosen for this book had to meet certain criteria:

• **A strong historical connection** – The most compelling hauntings are rooted in real events: battles, murders, shipwrecks, epidemics, or other significant tragedies. We sought locations where history itself suggests a reason for spirits to linger.

• **Eyewitness testimonies** – While personal accounts are subjective, repeated reports over generations—from locals, tourists, and even skeptics—lend credibility to a haunting.

• **Archival and newspaper records** – Many hauntings stem from real events that left a paper trail: death certificates, old news articles, court records, and first-hand reports of tragedies.

- **A connection to local folklore** – Even when a story is unverifiable, its longevity in local culture speaks to something deeper—whether a true haunting or a psychological imprint that refuses to fade.

By focusing on locations where history, legend, and firsthand experiences converge, we aim to present not just ghost stories, but **hauntings that tell a deeper truth about America's past.**

The Importance of Credible Sources: Archival Research, Newspaper Reports, and Firsthand Testimonies

Paranormal accounts are notoriously difficult to verify. Unlike traditional historical research, ghosts do not leave behind artifacts or written records—at least, not in ways that science can currently measure. Instead, we must rely on a combination of **historical documentation, witness testimony, and investigative research** to determine which stories have substance beyond legend.

Archival Research and Historical Records

Many of America's most famous hauntings have direct ties to tragic events. **Civil War battlefields, abandoned hospitals, and centuries-old mansions** all come with a documented past. Old newspapers, census records, and personal diaries often reveal forgotten tragedies—murders, unexplained deaths, or mass casualties—that may explain why certain places are said to be haunted.

For example, in the case of **the Myrtles Plantation in Louisiana**, stories of ghostly apparitions and tragic deaths have been told for generations. Some of these stories have been exaggerated or debunked, but historical records confirm that the plantation has been the site of multiple deaths, making it fertile ground for ghostly folklore.

Newspaper Reports and Eyewitness Accounts

Contemporary news reports are often the first step in verifying a haunting. Many infamous ghost stories began as unexplained news events—strange occurrences in hotels, odd happenings in graveyards, or chilling encounters in historic buildings.

In some cases, newspapers from the 19th and early 20th centuries reported ghost sightings as genuine news stories. For instance, **the Brown Lady of Raynham Hall**, one of the most famous ghost photographs ever taken, was widely reported in newspapers, sparking debate among skeptics and believers alike.

Firsthand Testimonies

While personal accounts can be unreliable, they remain one of the most compelling aspects of ghost stories. Some hauntings are **experienced repeatedly by different people over the course of decades**—and while a single sighting may be dismissed, multiple reports from unrelated witnesses lend weight to the claims.

For example:

- In **the Queen Mary (Long Beach, CA),** visitors have reported hearing phantom footsteps and seeing shadowy figures for years, aligning with documented deaths aboard the ship.

• At **Gettysburg Battlefield,** reenactors and tourists alike claim to have encountered ghostly soldiers, even speaking with men who later vanished.

The consistency of these reports, often from skeptics or those unfamiliar with the history, is what makes them so difficult to dismiss.

Myth, Exaggeration, and Well-Documented Paranormal Activity

Not all ghost stories hold up to scrutiny. Some are **purely legend**, crafted over time by locals to add intrigue to a place. Others are **embellished versions of true events**, where minor details are exaggerated until the original story is barely recognizable.

Distinguishing the credible from the exaggerated requires careful investigation.

• **Myths and Urban Legends** – Many ghost stories are based on popular folklore, but when investigated, have no historical basis. The infamous **"Crybaby Bridges"** found across America—where an infant is said to have drowned and can still be heard crying—often lack any record of an actual tragedy.

• **Exaggerated Hauntings** – Some locations become famous through sheer storytelling, even if the evidence is thin. For example, **The Bell Witch of Tennessee** is one of the most well-known hauntings in the U.S., but the details of the story change dramatically depending on the source.

- **Well-Documented Paranormal Activity** – Some hauntings stand out because of **historical documentation, photographic evidence, and scientific investigations.** The **Stanley Hotel** in Colorado, inspiration for *The Shining*, has been the subject of multiple paranormal investigations, with numerous guests and staff reporting unexplained activity.

A critical approach allows us to explore these stories while **separating folklore from genuine mystery.**

The Role of Ghost Hunters, Historians, and Skeptics in Paranormal Research

The study of hauntings does not belong to one field—it is a **collaboration between historians, ghost hunters, scientists, and skeptics.** Each plays a role in investigating claims of paranormal activity.

- **Ghost Hunters** – Equipped with electromagnetic field detectors (EMF), thermal cameras, and EVP (Electronic Voice Phenomena) recorders, ghost hunters attempt to capture evidence of spirits.

- **Historians** – They provide context, verifying whether deaths, battles, or disasters actually took place at a haunted site. Without historical accuracy, even the scariest ghost story loses credibility.

- **Skeptics** – Skeptics help weed out hoaxes, illusions, and psychological factors that contribute to hauntings, ensuring that what remains is truly unexplained.

It is through the interplay of these perspectives that we get closer to answering the ultimate question: **Are ghosts real?**

Fact, Fiction, and the Unexplained

History and hauntings are intertwined. Some ghost stories are **born from fact**, while others are **shaped by folklore** until they take on a life of their own.

But what cannot be denied is that **people have seen, heard, and felt things that defy explanation**.

What causes a place to hold onto the past so tightly that it refuses to let go?

The answer, like the ghosts themselves, remains just beyond our reach.

And that is what makes the mystery so compelling.

What to Expect in This Book

Ghost stories have always been more than just tales told in the dark. They are reflections of history, whispers from the past, and reminders that some places hold onto their secrets long after those who lived there are gone.

In this book, you will embark on a **state-by-state journey through America's most haunted locations**, traveling from the shadowy streets of colonial towns to the eerie expanse of abandoned asylums, from the bloodstained soil of battlefields to the silent corridors of historic hotels where footsteps still echo—long after the guests have checked out.

Some of these stories are famous, etched into the fabric of American folklore. Others are known only to locals, whispered from generation to generation, growing more chilling with every retelling.

But they all have one thing in common: **they refuse to be forgotten.**

A Journey Through America's Haunted History

Each chapter of this book is dedicated to a different state, unearthing its **most chilling and compelling hauntings**. Some stories will take you to well-known paranormal hotspots—places that have drawn ghost hunters, historians, and skeptics alike. Others will introduce you to **hidden gems of the supernatural**, eerie locations that have remained just beneath the surface, waiting for those brave enough to uncover their mysteries.

Along the way, you'll explore:

• **The restless ghosts of Civil War battlefields,** where soldiers still march and gunfire echoes through the night.

• **Haunted mansions and abandoned asylums,** where tragedy and mystery intertwine.

• **Historic hotels where guests check in, but some never leave.**

• **Phantom ships lost at sea, still appearing on the horizon centuries after they vanished.**

• **Lonesome highways where hitchhikers disappear into thin air, their stories leaving behind only questions.**

Each location will be explored through a blend of **historical research, firsthand accounts, and local lore**, painting a vivid picture of why these places may be haunted—and what it means for those who still encounter the unexplained.

True Stories of the Unexplained

The stories in this book are not fiction. They are drawn from **eyewitness testimonies, historical records, and well-documented investigations**. Some have been studied by paranormal researchers using modern technology—capturing EVP recordings, detecting anomalies, and documenting chilling encounters. Others have endured purely through **word of mouth, preserved by the people who swear they've seen things that cannot be explained.**

In reading these stories, you'll encounter:

• **Spirits seen by dozens of witnesses, described the same way by people who have never met.**

• **Objects moving on their own, doors slamming without explanation, and cold spots where no draft should exist.**

• **Unsettling disappearances, ghostly apparitions, and unexplained phenomena that defy logic.**

• **Tales of tragic love, betrayal, and revenge—emotions so strong they seem to leave an imprint on the places where they unfolded.**

Some of these hauntings are **terrifying, sending even the bravest ghost hunters running for the exits**. Others are **heartbreaking**, reminding us that not all spirits are malevolent—some simply never found their way home.

Infamous Hauntings and Hidden Horrors

While this book will cover **some of the most well-known haunted places in America**, it also dives into **the lesser-known, spine-tingling locations that have remained in the shadows.**

Expect to encounter:

- **The infamous ghosts of the Queen Mary in California,** where spectral voices still call out in the night.

- **The haunted halls of the Stanley Hotel in Colorado,** the inspiration for *The Shining*.

- **The restless spirits of the Myrtles Plantation in Louisiana,** where the past never truly died.

- **The ghostly soldiers of Gettysburg,** who still relive the battle they never escaped.

- **And many more chilling tales, some you may have heard of—and others that will be entirely new to you.**

For every well-documented haunting, there are dozens more that have **never made headlines but are no less eerie**. Some of the most unsettling ghost stories are the ones whispered between locals, stories that **never reached national fame but are just as chilling as any Hollywood horror film**.

Are These Places Truly Haunted?

That, dear reader, is for you to decide.

This book does not seek to convince you that ghosts exist. Instead, it offers **stories, history, and evidence**—leaving the final conclusion in your hands. As you turn the pages, ask yourself:

- Are these places haunted, or are they merely rich with history that refuses to fade?

• Are ghost sightings a trick of the mind, or do spirits truly walk among us?

• Can certain places absorb **the energy of the past**, replaying moments over and over, like an old record stuck on repeat?

• Or do these tales reflect **our own deepest fears, our longing for answers, and our fascination with what lies beyond death?**

The world is full of mysteries, some of which will never be explained. Perhaps ghosts exist in the space between **what we know and what we refuse to believe**.

So as you read, keep an open mind. Let yourself step into the shadows, walk the silent hallways, and listen for the whispers of the past.

Because whether you believe in ghosts or not...

They may believe in you.

Part 2
State-by-State Hauntings

Each chapter will focus on a specific state, detailing one or more notable hauntings.

Alabama

The Red Lady of Huntingdon College

(Montgomery, AL)

Tucked away in Montgomery, Alabama, Huntingdon College is a picturesque campus with ivy-covered walls and a rich history dating back to the mid-19th century. But beneath its scholarly charm lies a legend that has chilled students for generations—the tale of **Martha, the Red Lady of Huntingdon College**.

Her story is one of isolation, sorrow, and an eerie afterlife that refuses to fade.

The Lonely Student in Red

The legend of the **Red Lady** begins with a young woman named **Martha**, a student who once resided in **Pratt Hall**. Martha was not like the other students—she was quiet, withdrawn, and seemed to struggle with loneliness. Coming from a wealthy family, she arrived at Huntingdon with all the material comforts money could buy. But money could not purchase friendship, nor could it erase the overwhelming sense of solitude that followed her through the corridors of the dormitory.

Woman's College of Alabama, Montgomery Ala., April 17th, 1918 digital file from intermediary roll film copy (No known restrictions on publication. No renewal found in Copyright Office)

Some say she desperately wanted to fit in, but no one took the time to truly know her. Others believe she was battling inner demons that no one understood. Whatever the case, Martha became increasingly reclusive, her presence barely acknowledged by those around her.

She was often seen wearing a **striking red robe**, a bold color that stood out against the drab hues of the dormitory halls. Perhaps it was a reflection of her emotions—anger, passion, despair—or perhaps it was simply a personal choice. But after her death, it became the symbol of her ghostly presence.

One fateful night, the weight of her loneliness became unbearable. In the quiet of her room, surrounded by the red glow of her lamp, Martha **ended her own life**. The details vary—some say she slashed her wrists, others claim she hanged herself—but the outcome remains the same. Her absence was not immediately noticed, but when it was, it was too late.

What no one knew then was that **Martha never truly left.**

The Glowing Red Apparition

Soon after Martha's tragic death, strange occurrences began to unfold in Pratt Hall. Students reported **seeing flashes of red light in the hallways**, flickering and vanishing in an instant. Doors would **slam shut on their own**, and an unshakable **feeling of being watched** crept over those who wandered the dormitory alone at night.

Then came the sightings.

Students swore they had seen a **glowing red apparition moving through the hallways**. At first, it was nothing more than a fleeting shadow, but over time, the form became clearer—a woman, cloaked in **a blood-red robe**, silently drifting past stunned witnesses. Some claimed they heard **soft sobbing** echoing through the halls when no one was there. Others reported an overwhelming **chill in the air**, as if an unseen presence had brushed past them.

The encounters became so frequent that Martha was no longer just a sad story from the past—**she became a legend**.

Even today, students and faculty at Huntingdon College speak of the **Red Lady** with a mixture of fear and reverence. Some say she appears only to those who experience deep loneliness, as if she recognizes the pain she once felt. Others believe she simply lingers in the place where she took her final breath, forever trapped between the world of the living and the dead.

A Chilling Campus Tradition

Over the decades, the story of the **Red Lady of Huntingdon College** has become one of **Alabama's most famous hauntings**, frequently discussed in paranormal circles and whispered among students. While Pratt Hall is no longer used as a dormitory, the legend persists, and sightings of Martha have not ceased.

Ghost hunters and thrill-seekers still visit the campus, hoping for a glimpse of the glowing red figure or to hear the soft cries of a spirit that never found peace. But for those who call Huntingdon home, the Red Lady is more than just a ghost story—she is a **reminder of the loneliness that can haunt the living just as much as the dead**.

So if you ever find yourself walking the quiet halls of Huntingdon College at night, be careful. If you see a **flash of red light** in the darkness or feel a sudden chill in the air, you may not be alone.

Martha may still be there, waiting. Watching.

And perhaps, hoping that this time, someone will notice her.

The Hole That Will Not Stay Filled: The Legend of Bill Sketoe

(Newton, AL)

Some ghosts linger in the form of **apparitions**, haunting the places where they once lived and died. Others **make their presence known in stranger ways**—in objects that move on their own, in whispers carried on the wind, or in something far more unsettling: a physical scar left on the land itself.

Such is the case of **Bill Sketoe**, a man whose tragic death has been etched into Alabama's soil for over a century. His story is one of injustice, vengeance, and a mystery that has defied logic for generations.

For in the woods near **Newton, Alabama**, there is a hole.

And no matter how many times it has been filled, **it refuses to stay that way.**

The Hanging of Bill Sketoe

The legend begins in the final years of the **Civil War**, a time when brother fought against brother, and suspicion could mean the difference between life and death.

Bill Sketoe was a **Methodist minister**, a respected man known for his kind heart and unwavering faith. But in the chaos of war, kindness could be mistaken for treason. He was accused of **aiding Unionists**, providing shelter and supplies to those who resisted the Confederacy. Whether or not the accusations were true has been lost to history—what remains undisputed is what happened next.

A group of **Confederate soldiers, acting as vigilantes, captured Sketoe** and led him deep into the woods near the banks of the Choctawhatchee River. There, beneath the towering trees, they prepared to execute him by **hanging him from a sturdy branch**.

But there was one problem.

Bill Sketoe was **a tall man**—so tall, in fact, that when the noose was placed around his neck and the soldiers tried to hang him, his feet **still touched the ground**.

Frustrated and impatient, the executioners quickly **dug a hole beneath his feet**, ensuring that his body would drop far enough to complete the grim task. And there, with the Alabama sun beating down and the wind rustling through the trees, **Bill Sketoe's life came to an end.**

Or so they thought.

The Hole That Would Not Stay Filled

After the deed was done, the soldiers left the area, satisfied that justice—**or revenge**—had been served. They believed that Sketoe's story had ended.

But nature, it seemed, **had other plans.**

Soon after the hanging, something strange began to happen. **The hole that had been dug beneath Sketoe's feet would not stay filled.** Locals attempted to cover it with dirt, rocks, and debris, but no matter how many times they tried, the hole **would reappear**, as if the earth itself refused to forget what had happened there.

For over a **century**, the mysterious depression in the ground baffled those who lived near Newton. Some said it was **Sketoe's spirit**, refusing to rest, a silent protest against the injustice of his death. Others believed the land had been cursed by the wrongful hanging, forever marked by the tragedy.

Even when floodwaters washed through the area, reshaping the landscape, the hole endured—**an eerie, unexplainable scar in the earth.**

A Haunting Without a Ghost

Unlike many ghost stories, **there are no reports of a spectral figure roaming the woods** near Newton. No glowing apparitions, no disembodied voices whispering in the trees. Bill Sketoe has never been seen **walking the site of his execution**.

And yet, his presence is undeniable.

His ghost does not manifest in the form of **a traditional haunting**—instead, it lingers in the very soil where he took his final breath. The persistent, **unyielding hole** is his mark, a reminder that some injustices cannot be buried.

For over 100 years, the phenomenon continued, perplexing scientists, historians, and townsfolk alike. Even those who did not believe in ghosts struggled to explain it. Could it have been the result of **erosion**? A trick of the terrain? Some peculiar geological anomaly?

Perhaps.

Or perhaps **Bill Sketoe never left.**

The Fate of the Mysterious Hole

In the **20th century**, the landscape surrounding the site was altered when the area was dredged for flood control. The legendary hole, which had mystified generations, was finally **covered for good**—or so it seemed.

Though the physical evidence may now be gone, the story remains, passed down through time like a warning, a reminder that **the past does not always stay buried.**

Even today, the tale of **Bill Sketoe's hole** is one of Alabama's most famous supernatural legends. Visitors still come to Newton, **searching for the place where the earth once refused to stay filled.** Some claim to feel an inexplicable chill in the air. Others say they hear **the rustling of leaves and the faint creak of a rope swinging in the breeze.**

But whether you believe in ghosts or not, one thing is certain:

Some marks on history cannot be erased.

And in the woods of Newton, Alabama, one man's final moments left behind something that even time itself could not cover.

The Haunting of Sweetwater Mansion

(Florence, AL)

Some houses wear their history like a veil—silent, dignified, and untouched by time. Others seem to absorb the past, allowing its echoes to seep into the walls, lingering long after those who lived there have turned to dust.

Sweetwater Mansion, one of Alabama's most famous antebellum homes, belongs to the latter.

With its towering spires, intricate details, and overgrown grounds, Sweetwater Mansion stands as a symbol of the region's rich history, while its eerie ambiance continues to captivate visitors and enthusiasts of the supernatural

With its grand columns and weathered brick exterior, the mansion stands as a relic of the early 1800s, a reminder of the wealth and prestige of the Old South. But behind its stately facade lies **a darker story**, one filled with whispered voices, unexplained apparitions, and a chilling vision of **a funeral that had not yet happened.**

It is a place where history refuses to rest.

A House with a Haunting Past

Sweetwater Mansion was built in **the early 1800s** for **General John Brahan**, a veteran of the War of 1812 and a prominent landowner. As the years passed, the home became the backdrop for a century of family triumphs and tragedies, standing through the Civil War, Reconstruction, and beyond.

But it was during the dark days of the **Civil War** that the mansion's most infamous legend took shape—a tale so eerie that it continues to chill those who hear it.

The Casket in the Room

The most well-known ghostly encounter at Sweetwater Mansion occurred when a **caretaker was tending to the house** alone one evening. Walking through one of the dimly lit rooms, the caretaker suddenly stopped.

There, in the center of the room, stood **a casket draped in solemn mourning cloth**. The sight was unnerving, but what made it even more unsettling was that **the caretaker swore the body of a Confederate soldier lay inside.**

The caretaker blinked. The casket remained.

Moments later, the vision faded—gone as if it had never been there at all. But the unease it left behind did not disappear so easily. The caretaker fled, **shaken to the core**.

At the time, no funeral had taken place in the mansion. There was no reason for a casket to be in that room. The vision seemed impossible—until, some time later, the **future caught up to the past.**

A Funeral Foretold

It was eventually discovered that **a funeral had indeed taken place inside Sweetwater Mansion during the Civil War**—but not at the time the caretaker had seen it.

The funeral was held for **Billy Patton, the son of the mansion's owner**, whose body was laid in state **in the very same room** where the ghostly casket had appeared.

Was the caretaker's vision **a glimpse of a moment trapped in time**, an imprint of grief so powerful that it bled through the years? Or was it something more—a warning, an omen of a tragedy yet to come?

Either way, the incident solidified **Sweetwater Mansion's reputation as one of the most haunted places in Alabama**.

Ghosts That Refuse to Leave

The sighting of the phantom casket is not the only chilling encounter tied to Sweetwater Mansion. Over the years, visitors and staff alike have reported a string of **unexplained phenomena**:

- **Shadowy figures moving through empty hallways.**
- **Disembodied voices whispering in hushed tones.**
- **Doors slamming shut with no one around.**
- **The feeling of unseen eyes watching from the upper floors.**

Some say they have seen the **apparition of a Confederate soldier**, still standing guard over the house as if the war had never ended. Others claim to hear **the echoes of distant footsteps**, as if those who once called Sweetwater home are still there, pacing the halls long after their time.

Even those who don't believe in ghosts admit that there is something unsettling about the house—**a presence, a weight in the air**, as if the past is just beneath the surface, waiting to be acknowledged.

A Mansion Frozen in Time

Sweetwater Mansion stands today as a historic landmark, its walls holding secrets that may never be fully uncovered. Paranormal investigators, history enthusiasts, and ghost hunters continue to visit, drawn by the stories and the mystery that surrounds the house.

But whether or not one believes in ghosts, one fact remains:

Something happened at Sweetwater Mansion.

Something so powerful that **it imprinted itself onto time itself**, replaying over and over like a scene from a history that refuses to be forgotten.

And if you listen closely enough, you just might hear it—the distant murmur of voices, the echo of footsteps from another era, and the whispers of a house that remembers everything.

Because **some spirits do not leave.**

Some stories are never truly over.

And some houses… **never let go.**

Alaska

The Abandoned Town of Portlock: Alaska's Vanishing Settlement

(Portlock, AK)

Deep in the **rugged wilderness of Alaska**, where towering mountains meet icy waters and the forests stretch endlessly into the unknown, lies a town that no longer exists.

Portlock, once a bustling **cannery town on the southern edge of the Kenai Peninsula**, should have had a long and prosperous future. It had everything a thriving settlement needed—rich fishing waters, an industry that supported families, and a tight-knit community of people carving out a life in one of the most untamed places in America.

And yet, by the **1950s, it was abandoned**.

Not faded over time like so many boomtowns that simply ran out of resources, but **abruptly and mysteriously deserted**, as if something had driven its people away in fear.

According to local legends, something *did*.

For decades, whispers of **an unknown terror lurking in the forests** plagued the town—something watching from the shadows, something hunting those who wandered too far from home. **Bodies were found mutilated, people vanished without a trace, and an overwhelming sense of dread hung over the settlement.**

The people of Portlock did not leave because the fish stopped coming.

They left because they were afraid **they would never leave at all.**

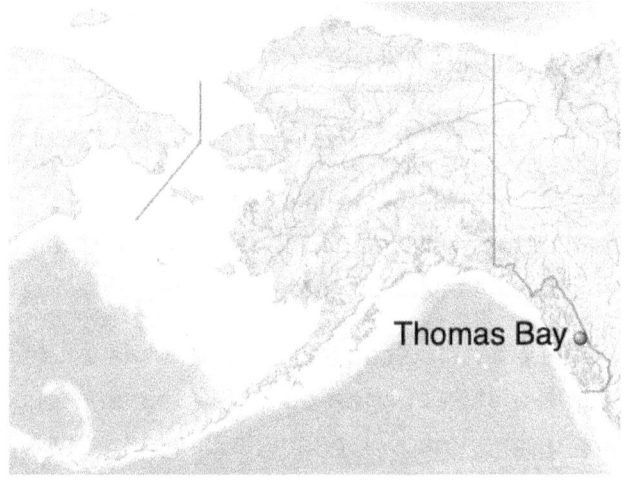

Thomas Bay aka "The Bay of Death" located in Southeast Alaska

A Town with a Dark Reputation

The town of **Portlock** was founded in the **early 1900s**, named after British Captain Nathaniel Portlock, who had explored the

Alaskan coast in the late 18th century. Like many other settlements in Alaska at the time, it was built around **fishing and canning**, industries that brought jobs, families, and the hope of a prosperous life.

But almost from the beginning, Portlock had **a sinister undertone**.

Stories circulated among the Native Alutiiq people long before settlers arrived, warning of a creature known as **Nantiinaq**—a **Bigfoot-like being**, said to be larger than any man, covered in thick dark fur, and possessing unnatural strength. Unlike the Sasquatch legends of the lower 48 states, **Nantiinaq was not just a shy forest dweller—it was a predator.**

And as the years passed, it seemed the warnings were more than just folklore.

Unexplained Deaths and Vanishings

By the **1920s and 1930s**, reports of **strange disappearances and horrifying discoveries** began to surface. Hunters and loggers would venture into the dense woods surrounding Portlock—some of them never returned.

- The few who were found had suffered **violent, gruesome deaths**, their bodies **mangled and torn apart** in ways that no animal in the region was known to do.

- Stories spread of men being **stalked by something unseen**, hearing heavy footsteps in the forest, feeling an **intense, unshakable sense of being watched**.

- Some who claimed to have survived encounters spoke of **a towering creature standing on two legs**, lurking in the mist, moving faster than any man should be able to.

One horrifying discovery cemented the town's fear:

A group of loggers working **deep in the woods** found **huge footprints—far larger than any human's—pressed into the earth**. The prints led to the battered, lifeless body of a man, whose injuries were so severe that **they could not have been caused by a bear or any known predator**.

Then the disappearances increased.

More and more men **vanished while hunting, fishing, or traveling alone.** Some bodies were found, others were simply **gone**, lost in the wilderness without a trace. The air of fear grew **so thick** that some people refused to go into the woods at all.

And then, the town made a decision that defied all logic—**they left.**

The Town That Walked Away

By the **1940s**, Portlock was **slowly being abandoned**. Entire families packed up and left without hesitation, choosing to leave behind their homes and livelihoods rather than risk becoming the next victim.

By the **1950s**, the town was **completely deserted**.

No final battle, no dramatic event—just a town that had lived in **fear for too long**, finally giving in.

What had happened in those final years? Did the people of Portlock witness something so terrifying that it **drove them to flee** without looking back? Or had the slow trickle of deaths and disappearances simply reached a breaking point?

Even today, no one knows for sure.

A Place Frozen in Fear

The remains of Portlock **still exist**, but they stand as a ghost town in the truest sense—**empty, untouched, and avoided.**

- **Visitors report an unsettling silence**, as if the land itself remembers what happened there.

- **Some claim to have seen large, shadowy figures moving through the trees.**

- Others describe the unmistakable feeling of being **watched from the forest**—an unseen presence, waiting.

Many believe that **Nantiinaq still roams the area**, guarding its territory, keeping humans away just as it did decades ago.

Skeptics argue that **the disappearances were simply the harsh reality of life in the Alaskan wilderness**—bears, accidents, exposure to the elements. But the locals who lived there, those who walked away from everything they had built, would tell you otherwise.

They would tell you **something unnatural lived in those woods.**

And they would tell you that **some places are not meant for the living.**

So if you ever find yourself near the ruins of Portlock, standing in the shadow of the dense Kenai forests, listening to the wind as it moves through the trees—ask yourself:

Is something watching?

And if it is, will it let you leave?

The Legend of Thomas Bay: Alaska's "Bay of Death"

(Thomas Bay, AK – Northeast of Petersburg)

Some places seem cursed from the very beginning.

Nestled in the wilds of southeastern Alaska, **Thomas Bay** is a remote, mist-shrouded place, untouched by time and heavy with an eerie silence. To the unknowing eye, it appears as any other breathtaking stretch of Alaskan wilderness—rugged cliffs, thick forests, and icy waters stretching as far as the eye can see.

But those who know its history call it something else.

They call it **"The Bay of Death."**

And for good reason.

A place of **tragedy, mystery, and chilling encounters**, Thomas Bay has earned a reputation as one of Alaska's most haunted and **feared** locations. Some believe it is simply a site of **natural disaster and misfortune**, while others insist that something **far more sinister** lurks in the dense, unforgiving wilderness.

The 1750 Disaster: When the Earth Turned Against the People

The legend of Thomas Bay begins long before written history, in the oral traditions of the indigenous **Tlingit people**. They tell of a time when the land itself **betrayed them**, a tragedy so great that it left its mark forever.

In **1750**, a catastrophic **landslide** struck the area, a massive collapse of rock and earth that **buried an entire village**, killing hundreds in an instant.

It happened without warning.

The sound must have been deafening—a thunderous roar as the mountainside gave way, sending an unstoppable wave of destruction down into the valley below. **Homes, families, and entire lives were swallowed whole**, vanishing beneath tons of debris. Those who survived could only watch in horror as their loved ones and their history were wiped from existence.

From that moment on, Thomas Bay was seen as a cursed place—a land where **the spirits of the dead remained trapped**, forever lingering beneath the rubble.

For many, the bay was **never the same again**.

But that was only the beginning.

The "Devil's Country": A Warning from the Wilderness

If the 1750 disaster left the land haunted by spirits, what happened next **suggested something far more physical—and terrifying—was still out there.**

Fast forward to the **early 1900s**, when a man named **Harry D. Colp**, a prospector searching for gold, came across a story that would **solidify Thomas Bay's reputation as one of the most feared places in Alaska.**

Colp wrote about an acquaintance—an unnamed man—who had ventured deep into **the wilderness of Thomas Bay** in search of gold. What he found instead **sent him fleeing in terror, vowing never to return.**

The Beasts of the Bay: The Strange, Ape-Like Creatures

According to Colp's account, the prospector had spent the day **exploring the remote terrain**, eventually stumbling upon a **strange rock formation** that seemed out of place in the dense forest. The moment he approached, an unsettling feeling washed over him—as if he were being watched.

Then, he saw **them**.

Emerging from the shadows of the trees were **strange, ape-like creatures**, **larger than any man**, covered in **dark, shaggy hair** with **glowing eyes that burned through the mist**.

The creatures **did not walk like bears**—they **moved like men**.

Panic surged through the prospector's body as the creatures **rushed toward him, emitting guttural, inhuman noises**. In pure terror, he dropped his gear and ran, crashing through the underbrush with **the sounds of his pursuers close behind**.

By the time he reached his boat, he was out of breath, **his body shaking uncontrollably**. The creatures had not followed him onto the water, but their presence, their **unnatural existence**, had left an imprint on his soul.

The man **never returned to Thomas Bay**.

And he was not the only one to tell such a story.

The Bay That Watches

After Colp's chilling account was published, more stories emerged from those who had dared to **venture into the forests of Thomas Bay**. Hunters, loggers, and prospectors spoke of:

- **Unexplained movements in the trees**—large, shadowy figures lurking just out of sight.
- **Eerie, guttural noises** echoing through the wilderness, unlike any known animal.

- **Massive footprints** left in the mud, far too large for any human or bear.

- **The overwhelming feeling of being watched**, as if unseen eyes followed every step.

The Tlingit people, whose ancestors had survived the 1750 landslide, were not surprised by these stories. **They had long believed that Thomas Bay was home to dark spirits—creatures that were not meant to be seen by man.**

They warned outsiders **not to go there alone**.

Not to stay after dark.

Not to disturb whatever lay hidden within the trees.

Some believe that the creatures are the restless **souls of those buried in the landslide**, transformed into something neither fully human nor fully spirit. Others speculate that **Thomas Bay hides something even older**, an unknown species that has remained undiscovered, lurking in the shadows for centuries.

Whatever the truth may be, one thing is certain:

No one who has seen the creatures of Thomas Bay ever returns the same.

A Place of Mystery, Fear, and the Unknown

Today, **Thomas Bay remains largely uninhabited**—a wild, untamed land where nature reigns supreme. Few venture deep into its forests, and those who do **speak in hushed tones about what they feel there.**

- Some **refuse to camp overnight**, claiming they hear **whispers in the wind**.

- Others report **seeing strange shapes in the mist**, too fast, too large, and too unnatural to be a trick of the eye.

- Many **refuse to talk about what they've experienced at all**.

The land remembers.

Whether it is **the weight of tragedy from the 1750 disaster**, the presence of **something not yet understood**, or **the power of a legend that refuses to die**, Thomas Bay is a place **where the past is still alive—and watching.**

If you ever find yourself near **the Bay of Death**, staring into the thick, ancient forests, ask yourself this:

Are the spirits of the lost still lingering there?

Or is something else **waiting in the trees**, watching... and deciding if you should leave?

The Haunted Alaskan Hotel and Bar: Juneau's Most Chilling Lodging

(Juneau, AK – Established 1913)

Some hotels welcome guests. Others **never let them leave.**

In the heart of **Juneau, Alaska**, where mist rolls in from the Gastineau Channel and the mountains loom like silent watchers, stands a hotel with **a history as dark as its mahogany bar.**

The **Alaskan Hotel and Bar**, established in **1913**, is the **oldest operating hotel in the city**. On the surface, it is a charming relic of a bygone era—**Victorian architecture, antique furnishings, and a bar where stories of gold rush days are still shared over whiskey and beer.** But beneath its historic elegance lies **something far more unsettling.**

For over a century, **guests and staff have reported strange occurrences**—whispers in empty hallways, doors creaking open on their own, flickering lights, and a chilling sense of being watched.

And then there's **her**.

A woman, **draped in sorrow and shadow**, who has been seen wandering the halls, **forever searching for something... or someone.**

A Hotel with a Haunted History

The Alaskan Hotel was built during a time of **gold fever and lawlessness**. The Klondike Gold Rush had drawn thousands to Alaska, turning quiet outposts into booming towns practically overnight. Many arrived hoping to strike it rich, but just as many found themselves **trapped in a world of hardship, danger, and desperation.**

Like many establishments of the era, the hotel had a reputation for more than just comfortable lodging. Some say it once **doubled as a brothel**, catering to lonely miners who came in from the cold with pockets full of gold and hearts full of longing.

And **one such woman**, legend has it, never truly left.

The Lady of Room 315

The most infamous ghost of the **Alaskan Hotel** is said to be **the spirit of a woman who once lived—and died—within its walls.**

According to local lore, **a young woman** came to Juneau with her husband, who sought fortune in the goldfields. She waited at the hotel while he set off to **make his claim, promising to return with wealth beyond their dreams.**

But fortune never came.

Weeks turned into months. Then, months into years. The man **never returned.**

Alone and desperate, the woman had no choice but to **turn to the only work available to women in her position—prostitution.** Some say she **fell into despair**, broken by the cruel realities of her new life. Others whisper that her end was far more violent—that she was **murdered by an unknown assailant in one of the hotel rooms.**

Her tragic fate left something behind—**a restless spirit, trapped in the place where she suffered.**

Unexplained Occurrences and Hauntings

The **paranormal activity** at the Alaskan Hotel has been documented for decades, reported by both **guests and staff**. While no official record exists of the woman's death, **something strange** undeniably lingers in the hotel's historic corridors.

Common experiences include:

- **A female apparition drifting through the hallways**—often near **Room 315**, where she is believed to have lived.

- **Whispers and soft crying** heard in the dead of night, especially when no one is nearby.

- **The feeling of an unseen presence standing at the foot of the bed**, watching, waiting.

- **Doors unlocking on their own, footsteps echoing in empty rooms.**

- **Objects moving mysteriously, sometimes disappearing entirely.**

One **bartender** reported seeing a **woman in an old-fashioned dress walking through the bar, only to vanish before his eyes.** Others have described a **sudden, overwhelming sense of sadness** upon entering certain areas of the hotel, as if stepping into **a lingering echo of despair.**

Even skeptics admit that there is something *unsettling* about the Alaskan Hotel. Some claim it is simply **the power of suggestion**—that the stories have created an atmosphere of unease. But others insist that **they have felt her presence**, a whisper from the past that refuses to fade.

A Hotel That Holds Its Secrets

Unlike many "haunted" hotels that **capitalize on their ghostly reputations**, the Alaskan Hotel does not turn its paranormal past into a tourist attraction. It remains **a fully**

operational hotel and bar, a favorite among travelers, locals, and those who seek a taste of old Alaska.

But for those who stay the night, **the spirits of the past may be closer than they think.**

If you ever find yourself in **Room 315**, pay attention to the silence.

Listen to the creak of the wooden floors, the way the air suddenly chills, the faint scent of **perfume lingering in an empty space**.

And if you wake to find **a shadowy figure at the edge of your bed**, do not be afraid.

She is only searching—still waiting for the man who never came home.

Some ghosts **do not haunt in anger**.

Some simply **never stop waiting.**

Arizona

The Copper Queen Hotel: Arizona's Grand Haunting

(Bisbee, AZ – Established 1898-1902)

Some hotels hold onto their history like a cherished memory, preserving their past in photographs and old guest registries. Others, like the **Copper Queen Hotel**, hold onto something else—**their ghosts.**

Nestled in the historic **mining town of Bisbee, Arizona**, the **Copper Queen Hotel** has stood for well over a century, watching as fortunes were made and lost, as the town around it changed, and as guests came and went. But not all of them left.

Regal and timeless, the hotel is **Arizona's longest continuously operated hotel**, built between **1898 and 1902 by the Phelps Dodge Corporation** to host wealthy investors, mine executives, and travelers drawn to the booming copper industry. It was a beacon of luxury in an otherwise rugged frontier town, a place where the elite could sip whiskey and smoke cigars while looking out over the dusty streets below.

But beneath its grand chandeliers and antique furnishings, **something lingers.**

Over the decades, **whispers of spirits** have become as much a part of the Copper Queen's identity as its lavish decor. Guests and staff alike have reported **strange sounds, eerie sensations, and ghostly figures appearing in the dead of night.**

And among the hotel's many lingering spirits, **one name is whispered more than any other—Julia Lowell.**

The Tragic Ghost of Julia Lowell

Of all the spirits said to roam the Copper Queen, **Julia Lowell's** story is perhaps the most haunting.

As legend tells it, Julia was **a beautiful woman in her 30s**, believed to have been a **prostitute who used the hotel to meet clients**. Though she lived a life on the fringes of respectability, she was not without hope—because **Julia fell in love.**

But love was not kind to Julia.

She **confessed her feelings** to one of her regular clients, hoping that he would see her as more than just a fleeting pleasure. But instead of love, she was met with **rejection**.

Heartbroken and humiliated, Julia **took her own life in the hotel**, her final moments lost to history.

But if death was supposed to be an escape, it did not free her from her sorrow. **Her spirit remains within the Copper Queen's walls, forever tied to the place where her heart was broken.**

A Presence That Lingers

Julia's ghost is **not a quiet one**. Guests and employees have reported **feeling her presence**, particularly in the **second and third floors on the west side of the building**, where she is said to have stayed.

But it is **men** who most often experience her spirit.

- Many **male guests** have reported hearing **a soft, feminine voice whispering in their ear** when no one else was in the room.

- Some claim to have felt **an invisible presence brushing against them**, as if someone was trying to get their attention.

- The most unsettling reports describe **Julia herself appearing in the dim glow of the hotel's lights**, her ethereal form seen **dancing at the foot of the grand staircase**—a ghostly performance that fades before anyone can approach.

Some believe that **Julia is still searching for love**, that her spirit lingers in the hope that someone will see her, truly see her, and not turn away.

Others think that she remains as **a warning, a reminder of the loneliness that once consumed her.**

Either way, **she has not left.**

The Tragic Ghost of Julia Lowell

More Than One Haunting

Julia is not the **only** ghost who has refused to check out of the Copper Queen.

Other spirits have been reported throughout the years, each adding to the hotel's eerie reputation.

The Young Boy Who Roams the Halls

Guests have frequently spoken of **a small boy**, seen running through the hallways and peeking around corners. Sometimes, he is heard giggling—an innocent sound that turns unsettling when you realize **there are no children staying at the hotel.**

No one knows exactly who he is or where he came from, but his presence is undeniable.

The Man in the Top Hat

Another lingering spirit is that of **a tall man dressed in a black top hat and formal suit**, appearing in various parts of the hotel. His identity is unknown, but he is often seen as a shadowy figure **standing silently in doorways** or watching guests from a distance before vanishing into thin air.

Unlike Julia, he does not whisper, dance, or reach out. He simply watches.

A Hotel That Never Sleeps

The Copper Queen Hotel remains **one of Arizona's most iconic landmarks**, drawing history buffs, ghost hunters, and thrill-seekers from all over. While many come for its charm and Old West ambiance, others come **hoping for a glimpse of the spirits that still call it home.**

For those brave enough to spend the night, there is a warning:

- **If you hear soft whispers when no one is there…**
- **If you catch a glimpse of a shadow moving across the room…**
- **If you feel an unseen hand brush against your skin…**

You are not alone.

Some guests leave with nothing but a fond memory of an elegant, historic hotel.

Others leave **with a story they will never forget.**

And some, just maybe, **never leave at all.**

Brunckow's Cabin: The Bloodiest Cabin in Arizona

(Near Tombstone, AZ – Established 1858)

There are places in the American West where **violence has soaked so deeply into the land** that even time cannot erase its stain.

And then there is **Brunckow's Cabin.**

Built in **1858** by German mining engineer **Frederick Brunckow**, this small adobe structure was supposed to be **a gateway to fortune**, a mining outpost meant to unearth the riches hidden beneath the rugged Arizona soil. Instead, it became a place of **death, betrayal, and bloodshed**—earning its infamous title as **"the bloodiest cabin in Arizona history."**

It is said that **more than 21 people** met their gruesome end here between **1860 and 1890**, their bodies often left to rot in the Arizona sun, many of them buried **right where they fell**.

Even hardened prospectors and outlaws steered clear of the place, whispering that **something unnatural lurked there**. Some claimed it was simply the curse of greed, that the land itself had turned against those who sought to profit from it.

Others believed something far worse:

That the **spirits of the murdered still walk the ruins of Brunckow's Cabin**, forever **trapped in the place where they met their violent end**.

A Cabin Built for Gold, Stained with Blood

Frederick Brunckow arrived in **Arizona Territory** with dreams of striking it rich. Along with a small team of men—including a cook and several miners—he established a **remote mining operation** near what would later become **Tombstone, Arizona**.

But the promise of gold has always been a dangerous thing. It **twists men's hearts**, turning friends into enemies, fueling **jealousy, paranoia, and betrayal.**

Brunckow never lived to see his fortune.

In **1860**, he was **murdered in cold blood**, reportedly by **his own workers**, who also **killed several others** before fleeing into the desert.

When authorities arrived, they found a **scene of carnage**—bodies scattered, **Brunckow's own corpse left in the dark shaft of his unfinished mine**, his pickaxe **stained with his own blood.**

It was the first murder at Brunckow's Cabin.

But it would **not be the last.**

A Place Where Death Never Left

After Brunckow's murder, the cabin should have been abandoned.

Instead, it became **a magnet for bloodshed.**

metal sign marking the historic site of **Brunckow's Cabin**, established in **1858**

The years that followed saw the **deaths of at least 21 others**, though some claim the number could be **much higher**. Murders, gunfights, betrayals, and unexplained killings all played out within its crumbling adobe walls, each death adding to the weight of **something dark and unrelenting.**

Among the many who met their end there:

• **Miners who turned on each other, fighting over gold and supplies.**

• **Outlaws and drifters who sought shelter, only to meet their fate in the dead of night.**

• **A land surveyor who was brutally ambushed on-site.**

Each violent death seemed to **feed the legend of the cabin**, turning it from a simple outpost into something else—**a place tainted by its own history.**

By the **late 1800s**, even the most desperate of men refused to stay there.

Superstitions grew. Some miners swore they saw **shadowy figures lurking near the ruins**, moving **without sound**, appearing and disappearing **without explanation**. Others reported hearing **muffled gunshots and anguished cries** echoing through the night, as if the past was **playing itself over and over again, refusing to be silenced.**

The cabin was no longer just **a relic of the Old West**.

It had become a **graveyard where the dead did not rest.**

A Haunting Born of Violence

Even today, **Brunckow's Cabin remains one of Arizona's most feared and avoided locations**. Though it is little more than **a crumbling ruin**, its reputation as **a cursed place** has never faded.

Those brave enough to visit report chilling encounters:

• **Disembodied voices** whispering from the wind, speaking in languages long forgotten.

• **Phantom footsteps** crunching across the desert floor, though no one else is around.

• **Unseen hands** brushing against the living, as if the dead are reaching out from the past.

• The overwhelming **sense of dread** that washes over visitors as soon as they step inside the ruins.

Some believe **the spirits of the murdered are still trapped there**, their restless souls forever bound to the place of their violent ends. Others claim **the land itself is cursed**, rejecting anyone who dares disturb it.

Whatever the truth may be, one thing is certain:

Brunckow's Cabin is more than just a piece of history.

It is a **reminder of how greed, violence, and betrayal can leave behind scars that refuse to fade.**

Some places forget their past.

This one never will.

So if you ever find yourself **near the ruins of Brunckow's Cabin**, under the wide, merciless Arizona sky, be careful where you step.

You may **not be alone.**

And if you hear a voice whisper your name?

Run.

Arkansas

The Crescent Hotel: America's Most Haunted Hotel

(Eureka Springs, AR – Established 1886)

Some hotels are famous for their elegance. Others are known for their history.

And then there's **the Crescent Hotel in Eureka Springs, Arkansas**—a place that is **famous for its ghosts.**

Perched high on a hill overlooking the Ozarks, the **Crescent Hotel** was built in **1886** as a **luxurious resort** for the wealthy elite seeking relaxation and healing in the mineral waters of Eureka Springs. With its **grand Victorian architecture, stunning views, and lavish amenities**, it was meant to be **a paradise** in the mountains.

But paradise, it seems, **never truly lasted here.**

Over the years, the building transformed—**from a high-society resort to a college, and then to something much darker.**

And today, it is **known not for its luxury, but for its ghosts.**

Dubbed **"America's Most Haunted Hotel,"** the Crescent is home to **numerous spirits**, many of them trapped by a **past filled with deception, suffering, and death.**

If walls could talk, the ones at the Crescent Hotel **would scream.**

The Haunting of the Crescent Hotel – Where the Spirits of the Past Never Rest

A Hotel with a Haunted Past

In its early days, the Crescent was a glamorous getaway for the wealthy. But as the decades passed, it struggled to keep its doors open.

By the **early 20th century**, the resort **fell into decline** and was repurposed into **a college for young women**. Even during this period, whispers of **unexplained occurrences** began to circulate. Students and staff reported **strange noises, doors opening on their own, and a presence that seemed to lurk in the shadows.**

But nothing compared to what was coming next.

In **1937**, the Crescent took on **its darkest chapter** when it was purchased by **Norman G. Baker**—a **millionaire inventor, radio personality, and self-proclaimed doctor** who had **no real medical training.**

Baker **transformed the Crescent into a hospital and health resort**, promising miraculous cures for **cancer and other deadly diseases.** Desperate patients traveled from all over the country, hoping for a second chance at life.

Instead, they found **something far worse.**

Baker's so-called "cures" were nothing more than **useless elixirs, fraudulent treatments, and outright lies.** He exploited the sick, taking their money while offering them **no real hope of survival.**

Many **died within the walls of the Crescent**, their last moments spent in **false belief that they were being healed.**

Baker was eventually exposed as a fraud, arrested, and **the hospital was shut down.** But by then, **the damage had been done.**

The spirits of those who **suffered and died** under his care **never left.**

Ghosts of the Crescent Hotel

With its **grim history**, it's no surprise that the Crescent Hotel is considered **one of the most haunted locations in America**. Guests, staff, and paranormal investigators have reported **countless supernatural encounters**—some playful, some terrifying, but all unexplained.

Michael: The Stonemason Who Never Left

One of the most well-known spirits at the Crescent is **Michael**, a **red-haired Irish stonemason** who **died during the hotel's original construction**.

According to legend, Michael was **working on the roof** when he **lost his balance** and fell to his death, landing **in what is now Room 218**.

His spirit is still there.

Guests staying in **Room 218** have reported:

- **Hearing loud banging on the walls**, as if someone is still hammering away at stone.

- **Lights flickering on and off**, even when the switches are untouched.

- **The feeling of unseen hands brushing against them while they sleep.**

- **Objects moving on their own**, as if an invisible force is playing tricks on the living.

Some visitors have even claimed to **see Michael himself**—a shadowy figure standing **at the foot of the bed**, watching them before vanishing into thin air.

His fall may have been accidental, but **his presence at the Crescent is anything but.**

The Nurse and the Haunting of the Hospital Halls

Another well-known ghost is that of **a nurse**, seen **pushing a gurney through the hallways**.

She is believed to be a remnant of the Crescent's time as **Baker's fraudulent hospital**, forever trapped in a **repetitive loop** of tending to patients that were beyond saving.

Guests have reported hearing:

- **The sound of wheels squeaking down the empty corridors.**

- **Faint moaning and whispers**, as if sick patients are still calling for help.

- **Shadowy figures in hospital gowns**, seen wandering the halls before disappearing through walls.

And sometimes, those who sleep in **what used to be patient rooms** wake up to **the sensation of cold hands touching their forehead**—as if someone is checking for a fever, even though the nurse **has been dead for decades.**

The Spirits of Baker's Victims

Perhaps the **most tragic spirits** within the Crescent are those of **the patients who never left**.

Those who came seeking hope and were met with **only suffering**.

Visitors have seen **figures dressed in white hospital gowns**, staring blankly at them before **vanishing into the walls**. Some report feeling **intense sadness** upon entering certain rooms, as if the air itself is heavy with grief.

And in the basement—where Baker kept his **"secret morgue"**, storing the bodies of the dead before disposing of them—**a dark energy lingers**.

Some claim to see **mist-like figures rising from the floor**, while others hear **soft crying and murmuring** in the empty space.

It is as if the very walls of the Crescent Hotel **have absorbed the sorrow, the deception, and the fear that once filled the halls.**

A Hotel That Refuses to Rest

Today, the **Crescent Hotel is still open for business**, welcoming guests who are drawn to its haunted history as much as its charm. Paranormal investigators have captured **voices, shadows, and unexplained movements** throughout the building, cementing its reputation as **one of the most active paranormal sites in the country.**

Some guests check in for the thrill.

Others come hoping **to experience something unexplainable**.

But there are those who come for a **different reason**—not to see a ghost, but to **feel the history** that has made the Crescent what it is.

Because in a place like this, history is **not just written in books or told in whispers**.

It is **felt**.

It **lives**.

And for those who listen closely enough, it **speaks.**

If you ever find yourself walking through the halls of the **Crescent Hotel**, pay attention to the air around you.

Listen for the echoes of footsteps on the wooden floors.

Watch for the flickering of the lights, the movement in the corner of your eye.

And if you hear a whisper in your ear, soft and chilling…

You are not alone.

Some guests leave with a memory.

Others leave with **a story they will never forget.**

And some?

Some never leave at all.

The Allen House: Arkansas' Most Haunted Home

(Monticello, AR – Built 1905-1906)

Some homes are built to shelter families. Others seem destined to **trap their ghosts.**

Rising above the quiet streets of **Monticello, Arkansas**, the **Allen House** is an elegant relic of the early 20th century, its towering turrets and ornate woodwork a testament to a time of wealth and prestige. But beneath its beauty lies **a story of sorrow, mystery, and restless spirits.**

For decades, those who have lived in or even stepped inside the house have spoken of **unseen figures, strange whispers, and chilling sensations**—as if the past still lingers, unwilling to be forgotten.

The house's **most well-known spirit is that of Ladell Allen**, the daughter of the home's original owner. In **1948, she took her own life inside the house**, and ever since, **her presence has never truly left.**

Some places are haunted by **tragedy alone.**

The **Allen House** is haunted by **something more.**

(Monticello, AR – Built 1905-1906) Some homes are built to shelter families. Others seem destined to **trap their ghosts**

A House Built on Wealth… and Sorrow

The **Allen House** was built between **1905 and 1906** by **Joe Lee (J.E.) Allen**, a wealthy businessman who spared no expense in designing **one of the grandest homes in Arkansas.**

For years, it stood as a symbol of **prosperity and refinement**, hosting lavish gatherings and housing generations of the Allen family. But like so many grand estates, it was **not immune to misfortune.**

In **1948**, the home became the site of an event that would mark it forever.

Ladell Allen, J.E. Allen's daughter, took her own life inside the house.

She drank **cyanide-laced punch** in her bedroom on **Christmas night**, her reasons **shrouded in mystery**. Some say it was **heartbreak**, others believe she suffered from **depression**, but whatever her reasoning, **the walls of the**

Allen House would never forget what happened that night.

The Ghost of Ladell Allen

Soon after Ladell's death, **strange things began happening inside the Allen House.**

Those who lived there—or even visited—reported **unsettling experiences**:

• **Shadowy figures seen in the upstairs windows, even when the house was empty.**

• **Soft sobbing and whispers in the night**, as if someone was reliving their final moments.

• **Doors slamming shut on their own**, as if the house itself was protesting against unwanted guests.

• **The faint scent of perfume lingering in the air**, even when no one was there.

But the most chilling encounters?

Ladell herself.

Several visitors claim to have seen **a woman dressed in early 20th-century clothing, drifting through the hallways**, her form fading into the shadows before they could fully comprehend what they were seeing. Others report feeling **a presence standing behind them**, only to turn and find nothing there.

Some believe that **Ladell never left the Allen House**, forever bound to the place of her final, tragic decision.

And if the reports are to be believed, she's **not alone.**

The Paranormal Legacy of the Allen House

After the Allen family, the house **changed owners multiple times**, and each new occupant seemed to add to its haunted history.

Several families who lived in the house have reported **a constant presence**, eerie noises in the dead of night, and **a sensation of being watched.**

One former resident even claimed that they would wake up in the middle of the night to find **furniture moved, lights flickering, and windows opening on their own.**

In later years, **ghost hunters and paranormal investigators** began focusing their attention on the Allen House, drawn by its **reputation as one of Arkansas' most haunted locations**.

Some of the eerie findings include:

- **Unexplained EVPs (electronic voice phenomena)** capturing **whispers and voices** responding to questions.

- **Infrared cameras detecting strange shapes and cold spots** where there should be none.

- **Mysterious footsteps** echoing through the halls, long after everyone had left.

Despite its beauty, the Allen House carries **an undeniable heaviness**—a lingering sadness, as if its walls **remember every sorrowful moment** that has ever taken place within them.

A House That Refuses to Let Go

Today, the **Allen House remains one of the most infamous haunted sites in Arkansas**.

Though it has been restored and is periodically open for tours, visitors continue to report **strange sensations, unexplained activity, and the overwhelming feeling that they are never truly alone.**

Some spirits fade with time.

Others, like Ladell Allen, never stop searching—for answers, for peace, or for something no one will ever understand.

So if you ever find yourself standing outside the **Allen House**, looking up at its looming silhouette against the night sky, **watch the windows carefully.**

And if you see a shadow move where no one should be, ask yourself:

Is someone watching you?

Or is **the house itself waiting for you to step inside?**

Because **once you do, you may never forget what you feel.**

And neither will it.

California

The Whaley House: California's Most Haunted Home

(San Diego, CA – Built 1857)

Some houses are built for comfort. Others become **something else entirely—a stage where the past refuses to fade, where spirits seem unwilling to leave.**

Standing in **San Diego's historic Old Town**, the **Whaley House** is more than just a beautifully preserved **Greek Revival-style mansion**. It is **a relic of California's past, a place where life and death intertwine**, where the echoes of history whisper through its halls.

Built in **1857** by **Thomas Whaley**, the home was meant to be **a symbol of prosperity**, a grand residence that would stand as a testament to his success. But instead, it became **a place of tragedy, loss, and lingering spirits.**

It is a house where **history was written in blood and sorrow**, where death was woven into the foundation before the first brick was even laid.

And today, it stands as **one of the most haunted locations in America**—a house where the past still **walks.**

A House Built on Death

Thomas Whaley was a **successful businessman**, a man of ambition who saw **San Diego's potential** and seized it. He designed his home to be more than just a residence—it would also house **a general store, a courthouse, and even a small theater**, making it a hub of business and culture in early California.

But Whaley may not have realized that **he was building his dream home on cursed ground.**

Before the Whaley House stood, the land had been the site of **public executions**.

And one of the most infamous deaths to take place here was that of **James "Yankee Jim" Robinson**, a convicted criminal whose final moments left a stain that could never be erased.

The Ghost of Yankee Jim Robinson – Executed in 1852 for Stealing a Boat, His Spirit Still Haunts the Gallows Site Where the Whaley House Now Stands

The Ghost of "Yankee Jim"

In **1852**, five years before Whaley built his home, **James "Yankee Jim" Robinson** was sentenced to death for **stealing a boat.**

By today's standards, the punishment seems **horrific**, but in the rough and lawless world of **19th-century California**, justice was swift and merciless.

On the day of his execution, **a crowd gathered in Old Town**, watching as a makeshift gallows was prepared. Yankee Jim was led to the noose, **his wrists bound, his fate sealed.**

But the hanging did not go smoothly.

The noose was **too loose**.

Instead of a quick death, Yankee Jim **kicked and struggled**, his body **thrashing for nearly 15 minutes** before finally going still.

His death was slow, painful—and perhaps, **unfinished.**

Years later, when the Whaley family moved into their new home, **they were not alone.**

Thomas Whaley himself was the first to report **strange occurrences. Heavy footsteps** echoed through the house at night, **thudding along the halls and staircases**, as if **an unseen presence was still walking the floors**.

The Whaleys believed it was **Yankee Jim**—the man who had died on this very ground—**still lingering, still walking, still refusing to leave.**

And he was just the **first of many spirits to make their presence known.**

A House of Suffering

The Whaley family's time in their grand home was marked by **tragedy**.

- **In 1858**, just a year after moving in, **Thomas and Anna Whaley's 18-month-old son, Thomas Jr., died of scarlet fever.**

- **In 1885, their daughter, Violet Whaley, took her own life inside the house.** She had endured a **failed marriage**, public shame, and depression so deep that she saw no escape. Her final note read: **"Mad from life's history, swift to death's mystery."**

The house that was meant to be a place of **joy and prosperity** had instead become **a place of sorrow and death.**

And the spirits of those who suffered within its walls **never left.**

Paranormal Encounters: The Whaley Family Still Watches

For over a century, **visitors, staff, and ghost hunters** have reported **unexplained phenomena** within the Whaley House.

Some of the most common encounters include:

1. Yankee Jim's Heavy Footsteps

To this day, people still hear **slow, heavy footsteps** moving up and down the staircase, despite **no one being there**.

Some say the presence is **oppressive**, a lingering shadow that **watches, listens, and waits.**

2. The Ghost of Violet Whaley

- Some visitors have reported seeing **a young woman standing at the window, dressed in 19th-century clothing, her expression sad and distant.**

- Others say they **feel an overwhelming sense of sorrow in certain rooms**, as if the weight of Violet's grief **still lingers**.

3. The Phantom Scents and Voices

- The scent of **old-fashioned perfume** sometimes fills the air, even when no one is around.

- Visitors hear **disembodied whispers and laughter**, as if the past is **still playing out just beyond their reach.**

4. Apparitions of the Whaley Family

- The **figure of a man**, believed to be Thomas Whaley himself, has been seen **standing at the top of the staircase**, watching those who dare to enter.

- Others have reported seeing **Anna Whaley, dressed in period attire**, appearing and disappearing in the hallways.

America's Most Haunted House?

The **Whaley House** has been investigated by **countless paranormal experts, ghost hunters, and skeptics**, all hoping to explain—or disprove—its reputation as **America's most haunted home.**

The findings?

- **Photos capturing mysterious shapes and orbs.**
- **EVP (Electronic Voice Phenomena) recordings of ghostly voices responding to questions.**
- **Visitors reporting physical sensations—cold chills, unseen touches, and an unshakable feeling of being watched.**

Even **official tour guides**, who have worked in the house for years, admit that **something lingers here.**

A House That Refuses to Die

Today, the **Whaley House is a museum**, open to the public—

though some visitors leave with **more than just a history lesson.**

Some leave **with an encounter they cannot explain.**

Some leave **with the feeling that they were not alone.**

And some?

Some say they feel the house itself watching them.

If you ever find yourself standing in the **Whaley House**, listening to the silence, watching the shadows shift in the dim light, and hearing the unmistakable sound of **footsteps on the stairs when no one is there…**

Ask yourself:

Is it just history that lingers here?

Or is something else **waiting in the dark**?

Because in the Whaley House, the past is never truly **gone.**

It **walks.**

And it **watches.**

The Queen Mary: The Ghost Ship of Long Beach

(Long Beach, CA – Launched 1936, Retired 1967)

Some ships are built to sail the seas.

Others **never truly dock.**

The **RMS Queen Mary** was once a **majestic ocean liner**, a floating palace of luxury that carried **royalty, Hollywood** celebrities, and World War II soldiers across the Atlantic. It was **a marvel of engineering, a beacon of elegance, and a witness to history.**

But beneath its grand ballroom, its lavish staterooms, and its polished decks, **the Queen Mary hides a darker tale**—a legacy of **tragedy, death, and restless spirits.**

Since it was permanently **moored in Long Beach, California, in 1967**, the Queen Mary has transformed into **a museum, a hotel, and a hotspot for ghost hunters** who seek to uncover its chilling secrets.

Because even though the ship no longer sails, **some say it is still very much alive.**

And those who have stepped aboard have **never forgotten what they experienced.**

A Ship of Elegance and War

The **Queen Mary** was launched in **1936** by the Cunard Line, an ocean liner company known for building some of the world's most luxurious ships.

At the time, she was one of the **largest, fastest, and most glamorous vessels ever built**. With art deco interiors, sweeping staircases, and grand dining halls, she was a **floating palace for the wealthy and elite.**

Her guest list was legendary—**Winston Churchill, Clark Gable, and even Queen Elizabeth herself** walked her decks, basking in her splendor.

The Queen Mary's Eternal Voyage: Once a luxurious ocean liner, now a ghostly relic of the past. Shadowy figures drift through its haunted corridors, echoing the tragedies of wartime souls and lost passengers. Step aboard... if you dare.

But when **World War II erupted**, the Queen Mary's **elegance was stripped away**, and she was repainted in dull gray, becoming a **troop transport vessel** known as **the "Gray Ghost."**

• She **carried over 800,000 troops** across the Atlantic.

• She **set speed records for her crossings**, often evading enemy submarines.

• She **was rumored to be on Hitler's most-wanted list**, a target for destruction.

But war came at a cost.

One of the Queen Mary's most tragic moments occurred in **1942**, when she accidentally **collided with the HMS Curacoa**, a British escort ship. The **Curacoa was sliced in half, sinking almost instantly**, and **over 300 sailors lost their lives.**

The Queen Mary **never stopped to help**—wartime protocol demanded that she keep moving to avoid being attacked. Survivors **were left to fend for themselves in the freezing waters**, their final screams swallowed by the Atlantic.

To this day, **some believe their spirits remain aboard, unable to find peace.**

A Haunting on the High Seas

After the war, the **Queen Mary was restored to her former grandeur**, returning to her role as a luxury liner until **her retirement in 1967**.

But when she dropped anchor in Long Beach and became a floating hotel, **strange things began happening**.

Guests and staff began reporting **unexplained noises, ghostly figures, and eerie sensations.** Paranormal investigators flocked to the ship, and soon, the Queen Mary gained **a reputation as one of the most haunted locations in the world.**

Among the ship's most infamous hauntings are:

1. The Lady in White

Perhaps the most famous ghost aboard, the **Lady in White** has been seen **gliding down the grand staircase**, her elegant dress shimmering in the dim light.

- Some say she was **a first-class passenger from the 1930s**, forever dancing in the ballroom where she once waltzed.

- Others believe she is **a lost soul**, unable to leave the ship even in death.

She does not speak.

She only drifts **silently through the halls**, her presence **felt, but never fully understood.**

2. The Haunted Pool Deck

One of the most chilling locations aboard the Queen Mary is **the now-empty First-Class Swimming Pool.**

Though no water has filled the pool in decades, **something lingers there.**

• Visitors have reported **hearing the laughter of children**, their voices echoing through the empty space.

• Wet footprints have appeared **out of nowhere**, leading from the pool to the changing rooms.

• Some claim to have seen **a little girl with long hair**, peeking from behind a pillar before vanishing into thin air.

No official records confirm a drowning in the pool.

But if the spirits remain, **someone must have been lost.**

3. The Engine Room & Door 13

Deep within the **bowels of the ship**, the **engine room** is said to be one of the **most active paranormal hotspots.**

The most infamous location?

Door 13.

This massive watertight door was **the site of a gruesome accident**, where **a young crew member was crushed to death** during a routine drill.

Since then, visitors have reported:

• **Seeing a figure in overalls standing near the door.**

• **Feeling an icy touch on their skin as they pass through.**

- **Hearing distant, muffled screams**, as if the moment of his death replays over and over again.

Those who dare venture into the engine room **often leave with more than they bargained for.**

A Ship That Refuses to Rest

Over the years, **the Queen Mary has been featured in numerous paranormal investigations**, with experts capturing:

- **Shadowy figures caught on thermal cameras.**
- **Unexplained whispers and voices recorded in EVP (Electronic Voice Phenomena) sessions.**
- **Cold spots and sudden changes in temperature, even in the dead of summer.**

Even skeptics admit that there is **something strange about the Queen Mary.**

A Night on the Queen Mary: Will You Stay?

Today, the **Queen Mary is open to the public**, offering **ghost tours, overnight stays, and paranormal investigations** for those brave enough to step aboard.

Many guests check in hoping for a glimpse of the past.

Some get **more than they expected.**

Some wake in the night to the sound of **phantom footsteps outside their door.**

Some hear **the distant cries of lost souls, still calling for help.**

And some say they feel **a presence standing at the foot of their bed**, unseen but undeniable.

The Queen Mary may **no longer sail**, but **her spirits are still adrift**.

They **walk her decks, whisper in her halls, and wait in the dark corners where history refuses to die.**

So if you find yourself on board, listen carefully.

Watch the staircases. Watch the pools. Watch the halls.

Because if you do, you might just see them.

And they will see you, too.

Colorado

Beneath the breathtaking peaks of the Rocky Mountains, beyond the golden plains and deep canyons, **Colorado holds onto its ghosts.**

Some walk the halls of **a grand hotel**, where laughter once echoed and secrets were whispered in dimly lit corridors. Others linger in the **shadows of an old mansion**, where time seems frozen, and the past is never truly gone.

If you dare to step inside these haunted places, **be prepared for what you might find**.

Because in Colorado, **history does not rest.**

And sometimes, **it watches you.**

The Stanley Hotel: A Grand Hotel Where Ghosts Check In... But Never Check Out

(Estes Park, CO – Opened 1909)

Imagine arriving at **The Stanley Hotel** as the sun begins to dip behind the Rockies. The crisp mountain air carries the scent of pine and history. The grand white façade looms ahead, its **red roof striking against the fading blue sky**.

You step inside, and the air changes.

The chandelier-lit lobby is elegant, warm—even inviting. But there is **something else here, something unseen**. A flicker of movement in the corner of your eye. A whisper you can't quite make out. A shiver up your spine, though the air is still.

This is the **Stanley Hotel**, and if you listen closely, you might hear the past **stirring.**

A Place of Dreams... and Nightmares

Freelan Oscar Stanley built this grand retreat in 1909, envisioning **a luxurious escape for the wealthy**, a place where visitors could breathe in the mountain air and leave their worries behind. **For decades, the hotel welcomed the rich, the famous, and those seeking adventure in the wilderness.**

But when **Stephen King checked in for the night in 1974**, something else was waiting for him.

King and his wife, **Tabitha**, arrived just as the hotel was preparing to close for the winter season. The vast, empty corridors felt **eerily silent**. That night, in **Room 217**, King had a nightmare—his young son was running through the halls, screaming, as a **fire hose slithered after him like a serpent.**

King woke up, heart pounding.

By the time morning came, the plot for **The Shining** was fully formed.

But **Room 217** was haunted long before King's terrifying dream.

The Haunting of Room 217

Would you dare spend a night in **Room 217**?

Many who have tried tell the same story:

• Lights flicker **on and off**, even when no one is touching the switch.

• Luggage is **moved or unpacked by unseen hands**.

• Guests feel **a presence**—sometimes a gentle one, like a caretaker making sure they are comfortable.

Could it be **Elizabeth Wilson**, the hotel's most famous ghost?

She was a **housekeeper in 1911**, injured in a **gas explosion** while lighting lamps in the room. She survived, but to this day, **her spirit is said to linger, tending to guests just as she did in life.**

But **not all spirits here are so kind.**

The Fourth Floor: A Playground for the Dead

As you climb the grand staircase to the **fourth floor**, the air feels **heavier**. This was once **the servants' quarters**, and many of the spirits who linger here **belong to children.**

• Laughter **echoes down the halls** when no one is there.

• Tiny footsteps **run past you**, but when you turn, the hallway is empty.

• Some guests wake in the middle of the night to find **a ghostly child standing beside their bed**, watching them curiously before fading into nothingness.

And then, there is the **Grand Staircase.**

Photographs taken here sometimes capture **something that wasn't there when the shutter clicked**—a shadowy figure, a glowing orb, or, most unsettling of all, **a face watching from the balcony above.**

So if you stay the night at **The Stanley**, take a deep breath before turning off the lights.

Because you are **never alone.**

The Peabody-Whitehead Mansion: A House That Knows Your Name

(Denver, CO – Built 1889)

Now, let's take you somewhere different.

Away from the grand halls of a famous hotel, away from the luxury and laughter, to **a house that sits in silence, waiting.**

The **Peabody-Whitehead Mansion** in **Denver** is not as well-known as the Stanley Hotel.

But those who have been inside know **it should be.**

It is a house with **a pulse**, a house where people step inside and **immediately feel watched**.

Some leave in minutes.

Others never speak of what they experienced.

And those who stay? **Well... not all of them come out the same.**

The house in 2023. Built in 1889, this mansion has a reputation for hauntings, especially after being featured on the Travel Channel's *Ghost Adventures*. Visitors have reported cold spots, apparitions, and unexplained noises. (Image Wikipedia commons)

A Mansion of Secrets

Built in **1889**, the Peabody-Whitehead Mansion has housed **politicians, doctors, and businessmen**. It has seen wealth, power, and influence.

But it has also seen **something else.**

Over the years, visitors and owners alike have reported **strange occurrences** that make even the bravest ghost hunters uneasy:

- **Unseen hands brushing against them in empty rooms.**

- **Chilling whispers in the darkness, calling their names.**

- **Cold spots that appear suddenly, freezing them to the bone—even in the heat of summer.**

And then there are the **apparitions.**

Some say they have seen **men in Victorian-era clothing**, standing by the windows before **vanishing into thin air**.

Others report **a darker presence**, something that makes the hair on their necks stand up, something that feels **deeply, unnervingly aware of them.**

The Room That No One Enters

There is **one room in the house** where **no one stays for long.**

Those who have **dared to enter** report:

- A sudden, overwhelming feeling of **dread**.

- A sensation that **something is standing behind them**, breathing down their neck.

- The urge to **leave immediately**—or else.

Even paranormal investigators have struggled to stay inside for more than a few minutes.

What is waiting in that room?

Something left behind?

Or something that was always there?

Will You Visit?

The **Stanley Hotel** and the **Peabody-Whitehead Mansion** stand as testaments to **Colorado's haunted history**—two places where **spirits walk, where echoes of the past refuse to fade, where the veil between worlds seems dangerously thin.**

Would you dare to **stay the night** in Room 217?

Would you step inside the **Peabody-Whitehead Mansion**, knowing something might **already know your name?**

If you do, remember this:

Ghosts do not always appear when you want them to.

But sometimes, they are already there, waiting.

And sometimes, **they follow you home.**

Connecticut

Whispers of Curses and Witches

There are places in **Connecticut** where the past is not just remembered—it is **felt**.

Where the forests seem to **watch you**, where the land carries **an unspoken weight**, where history refuses to rest.

Some speak of a **ghost town cursed from its very beginnings**, abandoned to the wilderness as if **something unnatural had claimed it.**

Others tell the tale of a **woman accused of witchcraft**, a figure of fear and superstition whose legend refuses to fade.

Whether you believe in curses or not, one thing is certain:

In Connecticut, some stories do not stay buried.

Dudleytown: The Cursed Ghost Town of Connecticut

(Cornwall, CT – Abandoned 19th Century)

There are ghost towns scattered across America, remnants of a time when settlements rose and fell with the tides of industry and fortune.

But **Dudleytown is different.**

No gold rush left it behind. No economic downturn sent people fleeing.

Dudleytown **was abandoned for another reason.**

And those who have dared to step onto its forsaken land speak of **an overwhelming sense of dread, of shadows moving where there should be none, of whispers in the trees when the wind is still.**

A Town Born Under a Curse?

The origins of **Dudleytown's dark reputation** begin with the very family that gave it its name: the **Dudleys**.

Legend has it that the Dudleys were **descendants of Edmund Dudley**, an English nobleman who was **executed for treason in 1510**. According to folklore, before his death, **a terrible curse was placed upon his bloodline**—one that would follow his descendants wherever they went.

Where whispers of the past linger in the wind, Dudleytown stands frozen in time—forever cursed, forever forgotten

The Dudley family eventually made their way to **Connecticut in the 1740s**, settling in what would become **Dudleytown**, a small farming community tucked deep in the Litchfield Hills.

At first, all seemed normal.

But then, **the misfortunes began.**

• **People vanished into the woods, never to be seen again.**

• **Strange illnesses spread, wiping out entire families.**

• **Madness took hold of some residents, leading them to take their own lives.**

By the **mid-1800s**, Dudleytown had become **a place of silence**. Homes stood empty, **overtaken by the creeping wilderness**.

The remaining residents **packed up and left**, some claiming **they had seen things in the woods—things they could not explain.**

Dudleytown **was abandoned.**

But was it really empty?

The Paranormal Encounters

Today, Dudleytown is **off-limits**, officially closed to the public due to **vandalism, trespassing, and the eerie experiences of those who ignored the warnings.**

Yet, stories persist.

Those who have managed to step onto the land report:

- **An immediate sense of unease**, as if being watched by unseen eyes.

- **Disembodied whispers**, calling their names from the trees.

- **Dark figures moving in the distance**, vanishing when approached.

- **Cameras malfunctioning**, batteries draining mysteriously, photographs coming out blank.

Some visitors have even reported **being overcome with dizziness or nausea**, feeling as if something **was trying to drive them away.**

Local historians dismiss the **curse of Dudleytown** as mere legend.

But if that's true, why do so many people leave the area **with terror in their eyes**?

Some places lose their people.

Dudleytown lost its soul.

And whatever remains there **does not want to be disturbed.**

The Legend of Hannah Cranna: The Wicked Witch of Monroe

(Monroe, CT – 19th Century)

Not all witches are found in **Salem.**

Some, like **Hannah Cranna**, lived in the quiet, misty hills of **Connecticut**, where whispers followed her through the streets, where neighbors **lowered their voices when she passed**, where **fear shaped a legend that still lingers.**

They called her **"The Wicked Witch of Monroe."**

And even in death, **she made sure her legend would never be forgotten.**

A Woman Feared by Her Neighbors

Hannah Hovey lived in **Monroe, Connecticut**, in the **1800s**, a time when **superstition ran deep** and accusations of **witchcraft** were never far from people's lips.

Her spirit never rests... the Witch of Connecticut still watches from beyond the grave, waiting for those who dare to disturb her eternal slumber.
(Picture Wikimedia Commons)

Hannah was known for her **sharp tongue** and **strange ways**. She lived alone after the **mysterious death of her husband**, who had supposedly **walked out one night and never returned.**

Locals began to **whisper** that she had caused his death—that she had **summoned something unnatural** to take him away.

And soon, **more strange occurrences began.**

- When a farmer **refused to give Hannah a free pie**, his **livestock mysteriously died the next day.**

- When a group of men **mocked her**, their **carts overturned on the road for no reason.**

- When Hannah **cursed a neighbor's home**, it was **struck by lightning weeks later.**

Coincidence? Or **something more?**

To the people of Monroe, the answer was clear:

Hannah Cranna was a witch.

And they **feared her.**

Her Final Curse

As Hannah grew old, she knew her time was coming.

Before she died, she **made one final demand:**

She was to be carried to her grave by hand—NOT by wagon.

She warned that **if her coffin was transported any other way, there would be consequences.**

But after she passed, the townspeople **ignored her request.**

They placed her casket on a **wagon** and set off toward the cemetery.

But as the funeral procession moved through town, **the casket suddenly slid off the wagon... and the coffin burst open.**

In that moment, a **storm erupted out of nowhere**, lightning flashing across the sky.

The terrified mourners had no choice.

They **carried her casket the rest of the way—by hand—just as she had instructed.**

From that day forward, strange things happened near **Hannah Cranna's grave**.

- **Lights flickered** in homes near the cemetery, though there was no storm.

- **Mysterious figures** were seen walking near her tombstone, vanishing into thin air.

- Some **locals claimed to hear laughter in the wind**, a cackling voice carried through the trees.

Even today, her **grave is a place of unease.**

Would you dare visit at night?

Witchcraft, Curses, and the Haunted Hills of Connecticut

The stories of **Dudleytown** and **Hannah Cranna** are separated by time, but they share **one chilling truth**:

Some places refuse to let go of their past.

Dudleytown is **silent, but never truly empty.**

Hannah Cranna is **buried, but never truly at rest.**

And if you ever find yourself **wandering through Connecticut's forests or walking its old cemeteries**, listen carefully.

Feel the air.

Watch the shadows.

Because some say **the past is still watching.**

And sometimes... **it follows you home.**

Delaware

The Ghost of Samuel Chew: Delaware's Restless Judge

Dover, Delaware—a city of historic streets, colonial buildings, and whispers of the past. But **some echoes never fade**.

Among the most famous spirits to haunt these quiet roads is **Chief Justice Samuel Chew**, a man of **law, principle, and unshakable authority**. His story is not one of violent death or betrayal. Instead, it is **a haunting fueled by pride, mockery, and the refusal to be forgotten**.

For more than **250 years**, his ghost has been **seen, heard, and even felt**, lurking in the streets of Dover, beneath the **old poplar tree**, and within the **walls of the courthouse**.

And those who dare to **mock his name** often find themselves **on the receiving end of his wrath**.

The Restless Judge of Dover: Beneath the moonlit poplar tree, the ghost of Chief Justice Samuel Chew lingers, forever watching, forever waiting.

This is not just a ghost story—**this is a warning**.

The Life of Samuel Chew: A Man of Power and Respect

Before he became **a ghost**, Samuel Chew was **one of the most powerful men in Delaware**.

Born in **1693**, he came from a **wealthy and influential family**, known for their prominence in law and politics. His father, Benjamin Chew, was also a distinguished lawyer and judge, and Samuel followed in his footsteps, earning a **reputation for fairness and wisdom**.

His career was illustrious:

- He served as **Chief Justice of the Supreme Court of Delaware**, overseeing some of the colony's most important legal decisions.

- He was known for his **measured judgments and unwavering commitment to justice**.

- He **commanded respect wherever he went**—or, at least, he tried to.

Because despite his status, **not everyone took Samuel Chew seriously.**

And the reason?

His name.

Mockery and the Curse of "Chew, Chew, Chew!"

In the 1700s, **political rivalries were brutal.**

Samuel Chew had enemies—**men who opposed his rulings, disagreed with his judgments, or simply resented his influence.** And in their efforts to discredit him, they found **one weakness to exploit:**

His last name.

"Chew" was easy to ridicule, and **mocking Samuel Chew became a cruel sport** among his detractors.

At political gatherings, in taverns, and even in the streets, they would chant:

"Chew, Chew, Chew!"

Laughter would follow. **Men would smirk and jeer, calling him weak, turning his very name into a joke.**

But Samuel Chew was not **a man who took insults lightly.**

Some say **he held onto those words, seething, carrying the weight of mockery with him even into the afterlife.**

And when he died in **1743**, his story **should have ended.**

Instead, **it was only the beginning.**

A Ghost That Would Not Rest

It didn't take long for **the first sightings of Samuel Chew's ghost** to begin.

At first, people dismissed the strange occurrences—**a cold breeze where there should be none, a fleeting shadow in the corner of the eye.**

But then, the **encounters became impossible to ignore.**

The Poplar Tree Apparition

One of the first places **Samuel Chew's spirit was seen** was beneath an old **poplar tree**, standing near his former home.

Late at night, **passersby reported seeing a tall, pale figure** standing motionless in the moonlight.

He was dressed in **18th-century clothing**, a **long coat and powdered wig**, just as he had worn in life.

- Some said he simply **stood in silence, watching.**
- Others claimed he **lifted a hand, as if to call someone forward.**
- The most terrifying accounts tell of **the figure suddenly**

vanishing, only to reappear **right behind the observer, whispering their name.**

Was this **a restless spirit demanding justice?**

Or was **Chew waiting for those who had once mocked him**, ready to confront them even in death?

The Courthouse Haunting

If there was **one place Samuel Chew refused to leave**, it was the **courthouse** where he had once presided as Chief Justice.

Long after his death, strange things began happening inside:

• **Court clerks reported hearing footsteps echoing through the empty halls**, only to find no one there.

• **Judges working late at night felt a cold hand brush against their shoulders**, as if someone was standing behind them.

• **Documents would go missing, only to reappear neatly stacked on the judge's bench**—as if someone was still reviewing them from beyond the grave.

But the **most chilling** encounters involved **those who mocked his name**.

The Curse of Mocking Samuel Chew

The legend states that anyone who **dares to chant "Chew, Chew, Chew!"** in the streets of Dover **invites his spirit to follow them.**

And the results?

- **Some report sudden, unexplained illnesses**—waking up the next day with fever and chills, as if the ghost himself had drained them of warmth.

- **Others hear whispers at night**, their name called in a voice that does not belong to the living.

- A few have felt **a sudden, forceful shove**, as if an invisible hand was punishing them for their disrespect.

- The most terrifying stories tell of people **seeing a tall, dark figure standing at the foot of their bed**, watching them in silence.

These hauntings do not stop until the person **apologizes—out loud—for mocking his name.**

Even skeptics have learned not to **speak ill of Samuel Chew in jest.**

Because **his ghost is still listening.**

A Legacy That Will Not Die

More than **two and a half centuries** have passed since Samuel Chew's death, yet his presence **remains woven into the fabric of Dover.**

Some believe **his spirit lingers because he was never granted the respect he deserved in life.**

Others claim **he is simply watching over the law**, ensuring that justice is still carried out in the city he once ruled.

But those who have encountered **his ghost**—the cold hand, the unseen whisper, the pale figure in the dark—know one thing for certain:

He has not left.

So if you ever find yourself walking through **Dover on a quiet evening**, remember this:

- If the wind suddenly turns cold,
- If you feel a tug at your coat,
- If you see a shadow watching you from beneath the poplar tree…

Do not laugh.

Do not say his name in jest.

And whatever you do, **do not chant "Chew, Chew, Chew."**

Because some ghosts **never stop demanding respect.**

And **Samuel Chew is still waiting.**

Final Warning

If you ever visit **Dover's old courthouse** or walk beneath the poplar trees at dusk, **be mindful of the air around you.**

If the shadows feel too long, if the air feels too still, if the chill reaches your bones even in the height of summer…

You may not be alone.

And the Judge may be watching.

Florida

Beneath the swaying palms and sunlit shores of **Florida**, a darker history lingers.

Some places are soaked in **tragedy**, their past seeping into the present, refusing to be forgotten. Others carry **a curse so deep** that even the pavement itself seems haunted.

Here, in the oldest city in America, **a lighthouse stands as a beacon—not just for ships, but for lost souls.**

And on a desolate stretch of highway, **drivers vanish, radios go silent, and unseen forces twist fate in terrifying ways.**

This is **Florida's haunted legacy**.

This is where **the past refuses to die.**

The St. Augustine Lighthouse: A Beacon for the Dead

(St. Augustine, FL – Built 1874)

The **St. Augustine Lighthouse** has stood watch over the Atlantic for nearly **150 years**, guiding sailors through storms and treacherous waters.

But if you listen carefully, beyond the crash of the waves, beyond the cry of the gulls, you may hear **something else.**

A whisper.

A child's giggle.

Footsteps echoing when no one is there.

Because this lighthouse is **not just home to the living.**

It is **one of the most haunted places in Florida.**

And those who have stepped inside **have never forgotten what they saw.**

A Lighthouse Built on Sorrow

In **1874**, construction of the **St. Augustine Lighthouse** was nearing completion. It was meant to be **a guardian of the coast, a symbol of safety and guidance**.

But instead, it became **a place of tragedy.**

The construction crew had **families**, and among them were **two young sisters**, the daughters of a lighthouse worker.

As children do, they **found adventure** in the unfinished site, exploring, playing, **laughing**. But one summer day, **their game became their last.**

The Drowning of the Lighthouse Sisters

A large **supply cart** sat on the site, used to transport materials down to the water.

Guiding the Lost Souls: The St. Augustine Lighthouse, where light meets darkness and the past lingers in the winds.

To the **two young girls**, it seemed like the perfect ride.

They climbed in, giggling, pushing off, **riding the cart down toward the shore.**

But something went wrong.

The cart **gained too much speed, veering off course**, and instead of stopping safely—

It plunged into the water.

Workers rushed to help, but **it was too late.**

The two sisters **drowned beneath the waves**, their laughter **replaced by silence**.

Their father, devastated, continued his work on the lighthouse, **finishing what had taken everything from him.**

And when the lighthouse was finally completed, **it stood in mourning.**

Because **the girls never left.**

The Ghostly Encounters: Echoes of the Past

To this day, visitors and staff **report eerie encounters inside the lighthouse**:

• **Children's laughter drifts through the air, even when no one is there.**

• **Shadowy figures move up the spiral staircase, vanishing before they reach the top.**

• **Tiny footprints appear in the dust, then disappear just as quickly.**

Some say the girls still **play in the lighthouse**, forever trapped in a childhood that ended too soon.

But **they are not the only ones who remain.**

The Keeper Who Never Left

Another spirit haunts the lighthouse—a former **lighthouse keeper**, still watching over his domain.

Visitors often **smell the scent of cigar smoke**, though no one is smoking.

Late at night, **footsteps echo from the keeper's quarters**, as if someone is **pacing, waiting, watching.**

Some believe it is **the father of the drowned girls**, still **grieving, still protecting, still trapped.**

And if you dare climb **to the very top**, be prepared:

Some have felt a hand on their back—guiding them, warning them.

Or perhaps, **trying to push them over the edge.**

The "Dead Zone" of Interstate 4: A Highway to Nowhere

(Lake Monroe, FL – The Haunted Stretch of I-4)

Most roads take you **somewhere.**

But **one stretch of highway in Florida** takes you somewhere **you may never return from.**

A place where engines **stall for no reason**, where GPS devices **glitch**, where accidents happen **too often to be coincidence.**

Some call it **a cursed road.**

Some call it **a portal to the dead.**

Most just call it **the "Dead Zone" of I-4.**

And if you drive through it, **you might not be alone.**

A Road Built Over the Dead

To understand **why this stretch of I-4 is haunted**, you have to go back **to the 1800s**, when Florida was still wild, untamed land.

In **the 1880s**, a small group of **German immigrants** settled near **Lake Monroe**, searching for **a new life, a fresh start**.

They built **homes, farms, a small community**—but their dreams were **short-lived**.

A devastating **yellow fever epidemic** swept through the settlement.

One by one, **they died.**

Fathers, mothers, **children**—wiped out by the disease.

Those who survived **buried the dead** in a small, unmarked **graveyard**, then **left the land forever.**

For decades, **the graves remained untouched**, swallowed by time and the thick Florida wilderness.

Until **the 1960s**, when engineers broke ground on **Interstate 4.**

And they did **not stop for the dead.**

The Consequences of Disturbing the Graves

When construction workers **discovered the old burial site**, they had a choice:

Respect the dead? Or pave over them?

They chose **the latter**.

The graves were **never moved, never properly honored**. Instead, asphalt was laid **directly over the bodies**, turning **a final resting place into a highway**.

And then?

The accidents began.

The Curse of the Dead Zone

Since the construction of I-4, this **small, four-mile stretch near Lake Monroe** has been plagued by:

• **A staggering number of accidents**, far higher than other parts of the highway.

• **Drivers reporting sudden radio interference**, their music replaced by **static or ghostly whispers**.

• **Mysterious figures appearing on the roadside**, only to vanish when cars get closer.

• **Engines stalling for no reason**, refusing to start until they are **towed away from the area.**

Some say it is **just coincidence**.

Others believe the **spirits of the German settlers** are **still there, still restless, still angry** at the disrespect shown to their graves.

And if you ever find yourself driving through the **Dead Zone** late at night, remember this:

- If your radio suddenly **goes silent**...
- If you feel a **chill in the air**, despite the Florida heat...
- If you see **something standing on the roadside, watching**...

Do not stop.

Do not **speak their names.**

And whatever you do, **do not look in your rearview mirror.**

Because some roads **are not meant to be traveled.**

And **some spirits never forgive.**

Florida's Ghostly Legacy

From the **haunted beacon of the St. Augustine Lighthouse** to the **cursed pavement of Interstate 4**, Florida holds **more than just history**.

It holds **spirits, echoes, and unfinished business.**

Some places are haunted by **memories**.

Others are haunted by **those who never left.**

And if you ever visit, **be careful where you step, where you drive, and what you say.**

Because in Florida, **some ghosts still walk among the living.**

And some roads **do not lead where you think they do.**

Georgia

Beneath the moss-covered oaks and along the winding rivers of **Georgia**, history lingers like a whisper on the wind.

Some places hold onto **their past so tightly** that the past refuses to stay buried.

In the murky waters of **Lake Lanier**, beneath the elegant balconies of **The Marshall House**, and among the weathered gravestones of **Oakland Cemetery**, **ghosts still walk**—some seeking justice, some longing for peace, and some, perhaps, simply waiting for you to listen.

These are the **haunted places of Georgia**.

And if you step too close, **you might not walk away alone.**

Lake Lanier: The Drowned Town That Still Haunts the Living

(Northern Georgia – Created in the 1950s)

If you stand on the shores of **Lake Lanier** at dusk, the water looks calm, reflecting the golden sunset.

But beneath the surface, the past is **never truly at rest**.

For decades, **swimmers have drowned in unexplained accidents**, boats have capsized with no warning, and eerie apparitions have appeared along the shore.

Locals say it is **cursed**.

Because **Lake Lanier is not just a lake.**

It is **a graveyard.**

A Lake Built on the Dead

In the **1950s**, the U.S. Army Corps of Engineers **flooded entire communities** to create Lake Lanier, displacing families, submerging homes, and covering **graveyards** with water.

Churches, schools, houses—entire towns disappeared beneath the waves.

The government claimed they had relocated **all the graves**, but **locals knew the truth:**

Not all the dead had been moved.

And soon, **strange things began happening.**

- Swimmers would suddenly **feel hands pulling them down**, though no one was there.

- Fishermen saw **ghostly figures walking across the surface of the water**, vanishing into the mist.

- Drivers crossing the lake's bridges at night reported **seeing a woman in a flowing blue dress standing on the roadside—only for her to disappear when they stopped.**

This is the spirit of **Delia Parker Young**, and her legend is one of the most chilling in Georgia.

The Lady in Blue: The Ghost of Delia Parker Young

In **1958**, two friends—**Delia Parker Young and Susie Roberts**—were driving across the **Lanier Bridge** when their car **skidded off the road and plunged into the lake**.

For months, no one found the wreckage.

Then, a fisherman made a grisly discovery.

A **body, floating facedown in the water**—its arms missing, the dress **a tattered shade of blue**.

It was **Delia Parker Young**, but **Susie's body was never found.**

To this day, **Delia's ghost roams the shore**, searching for something lost.

- **She appears to drivers late at night**, staring blankly before disappearing into the darkness.

- **Boaters hear splashing and cries for help**, but when they search, no one is there.

- **Swimmers report icy hands brushing against their ankles**, as if something unseen **is trying to pull them under.**

Is it Delia?

Or is it **the hundreds of other souls** still buried beneath the waves?

Because in Lake Lanier, **the dead do not rest.**

And sometimes, **they reach for the living.**

The Marshall House: The Ghosts of War and Disease

(Savannah, GA – Built 1851)

Savannah is known for its **grace and beauty**, but beneath its charm lies **a dark and haunted history**.

And nowhere is this more evident than **The Marshall House**.

This grand hotel, with its **elegant balconies and timeless architecture**, hides a gruesome past:

During the Civil War and deadly yellow fever epidemics, it was not a hotel—it was a hospital.

A place of **pain, suffering, and death**.

And those who perished **never truly left.**

The Haunting of The Marshall House

Guests who check into The Marshall House **often check out with a ghost story.**

- **The spirit of a soldier** has been seen walking the halls, **his boots echoing on the hardwood floors**, only to vanish before reaching the end of the corridor.

The walls of The Marshall House whisper with the echoes of the past—soldiers' agony, fevered cries, and the lingering shadows of those who never left (Picture Wikimedia Commons)

- Some visitors wake up **feeling their blankets being pulled off them**, as if an unseen nurse was checking on them.

- Others have reported **hearing children's laughter**, but when they look—**there are no children in sight.**

One of the most terrifying encounters happens on the **fourth floor**.

During renovations, **workers uncovered human remains beneath the floorboards—amputated limbs, discarded and forgotten** from the days when the hotel was a Civil War hospital.

Since then, guests have reported waking up to **the sensation of invisible hands touching their legs**—as if a long-dead doctor **is still performing surgery.**

If you ever stay at The Marshall House, be careful where you step.

Because some patients **never left the hospital.**

And **they may be watching you sleep.**

Oakland Cemetery: Atlanta's City of the Dead

(Atlanta, GA – Established 1850)

Some cemeteries are quiet, solemn places.

Oakland Cemetery is not.

As the **oldest and most famous burial ground in Atlanta**, it is the final resting place of **Confederate soldiers, politicians, and lost souls whose names have long been forgotten.**

And some of them **are still walking among the graves.**

The Ghosts of Oakland Cemetery

Visitors have reported chilling encounters within the cemetery walls:

- **Shadowy figures drifting between the tombstones** at dusk.

- **Disembodied voices calling out names**, though no one else is around.

- The sound of **a little girl laughing**, followed by the sight of a small, ghostly figure **bouncing a ball.**

Whispers of the Forgotten: In the misty shadows of Oakland Cemetery, lost souls drift between the tombstones—watching, waiting... and never truly at rest

This **young girl** is one of Oakland's most well-known spirits.

Some say she was **a victim of a yellow fever outbreak** in the 1800s, her life cut short before she could truly experience childhood.

Others claim she **was left behind when her family fled Atlanta during the Civil War,** her spirit forever **waiting for someone to take her home.**

She has been seen **playing near her own grave**, tossing a ball against a headstone, then giggling before vanishing into the mist.

And if you hear her laughter?

Do not follow.

Because some spirits **do not want to be found.**

The Haunted Heart of Georgia

From the **drowned ghosts of Lake Lanier** to **the phantom soldiers of The Marshall House** to **the wandering dead of Oakland Cemetery**, Georgia is a land where **history does not sleep.**

Some souls are lost.

Some seek justice.

And some, **perhaps, are waiting for you.**

So if you ever find yourself **standing by the water's edge, walking through a haunted hallway, or stepping over an old grave**, ask yourself:

Who is watching?

Because in Georgia, **the past never lets go.**

And sometimes, **it reaches for the living.**

Hawaii

'Iolani Palace: The Restless Spirits of Hawaii's Last Monarchs

(Honolulu, Oʻahu – Built in 1882)

At the heart of **Honolulu**, behind grand gates and towering palm trees, stands **'Iolani Palace**, a place of **royalty, sorrow, and spirits.**

It is the only **official royal palace in the United States**, once home to Hawaii's last ruling monarchs—**King Kalākaua** and his sister, **Queen Liliʻuokalani**, whose reign ended in heartbreak.

And now?

Many believe the **royal spirits still remain.**

Where royalty once reigned, now only restless spirits linger. 'Iolani Palace stands as a silent witness to a kingdom lost, its walls echoing with the sorrow of Hawaii's last monarchs, forever trapped in the shadows of their own legacy

A Palace of Power and Betrayal

Built in **1882**, 'Iolani Palace was meant to be a **symbol of strength, sovereignty, and the enduring power of the Hawaiian Kingdom.**

But by **1893**, the palace was no longer a home to royalty—it had become **a prison.**

Queen **Lili'uokalani**, Hawaii's last ruling monarch, was **forcibly overthrown** by American and European businessmen, backed by U.S. military forces.

For eight months, she was **imprisoned in her own palace**, locked away **on the upper floor**.

Her crime?

Trying to protect her people.

The Queen was made to sit in silence **as her kingdom was stolen from beneath her feet**.

She spent her days sewing a **beautiful quilt**, each stitch a memory, a prayer, a piece of her sorrow.

She never ruled again.

And some say **she never left**.

The Ghost of Queen Liliʻuokalani

Many visitors and palace staff **have felt her presence.**

- **Unexplained footsteps echo through the upper floors**, as if someone is pacing—just as she did during her imprisonment.

- **Soft Hawaiian chanting** has been heard, though no one is there.

- **The scent of fresh flowers drifts through the halls**, despite no lei or blossoms being present.

But the most unsettling encounters happen **in her former bedroom.**

- Some have **seen a shadowy figure standing by the window**, gazing out toward the land she lost.

- Others say **the air grows heavy** when they enter, as if the walls themselves remember the sorrow she endured.

And on **quiet nights**, when the moon bathes the palace in silver light, guards patrolling the grounds have reported **the faint, ghostly sound of a woman crying.**

Is it the Queen, mourning her stolen kingdom?

Or is it something deeper—a **reminder that history cannot be undone, and justice was never served?**

Other Spirits of 'Iolani Palace

Queen Lili'uokalani is not the **only presence that lingers here.**

- Staff members **often hear whispers** in empty hallways, **as if the voices of the past are still carrying out royal business.**

- Heavy doors **open and close on their own**, sometimes with **enough force to shake the room.**

- **Orbs of light appear in photographs**, hovering near the grand staircase where dignitaries once arrived.

Some believe the spirits are **protecting the palace**, still watching over what was once theirs.

Others say they are simply **waiting—for a time when their kingdom is restored.**

And if you visit, **be respectful.**

Because in 'Iolani Palace, **the past is still very much alive.**

Morgan's Corner: The Hanging Tree and the Spirit of Revenge

(Nuʻuanu Pali Drive, Oʻahu – The Most Infamous Haunted Road in Hawaii)

If you drive down **Nuʻuanu Pali Drive** late at night, beneath the thick canopy of trees, the air grows heavy, the shadows deepen, and the silence feels **unnatural.**

There, at **a sharp curve in the road**, sits a place known as **Morgan's Corner.**

It is not a place where people linger.

Because **something is watching.**

A Road Stained with Death

Morgan's Corner has a **long and dark history**—a place whispered about for decades, where tragedy has taken root.

The most **infamous story** happened in the **1940s**, when a brutal murder sent shockwaves through the island.

A **widowed woman** lived alone in a small house near Morgan's Corner.

One night, **two escaped prisoners broke in, looking for valuables**.

But when they found **nothing to steal**, they **killed the woman instead**, leaving her body behind.

Her spirit?

Locals say **she never left.**

And she **wants revenge.**

The Ghost of the Hanging Woman

The legend says that **on certain nights, if you stand beneath the twisted old tree at Morgan's Corner, you will see her.**

- A **pale figure, swinging slowly from the branches**, her eyes dark, her face twisted in sorrow.

- Some hear **a faint choking sound**, as if she is still gasping for air.

- Others report feeling **fingers brush against their necks**, leaving an icy chill in their wake.

But the **most terrifying** encounters come from those who **mock the legend.**

Many have **challenged the ghost**—daring her to appear, **calling out insults** in the dead of night.

They always regret it.

- **Some claim their cars refuse to start**, no matter how many times they turn the key.

- Others **drive away, only to see a shadowy figure in their rearview mirror**, sitting in the backseat.

- And a few have been **pushed or scratched by unseen hands**, as if the spirit is making sure they never return.

Morgan's Corner is not just a haunted road.

It is **a warning.**

Hawaii's Haunted Legacy

Hawaii is a place of beauty and legend, but **its history is written in sorrow, betrayal, and spirits that refuse to fade.**

At '**Iolani Palace**, the Queen still walks, mourning her lost kingdom.

At **Morgan's Corner**, a restless soul waits in the darkness, watching for those who dare to disrespect her story.

Some say the spirits of Hawaii **are guardians**.

Others say they are **warnings**.

But if you visit these places, **do not take them lightly.**

Because in Hawaii, **the past is not forgotten.**

And **some ghosts never let go.**

Idaho

The Old Idaho State Penitentiary: A Prison That Refuses to Forget

(Boise, ID – Operated from 1872 to 1973)

The iron gates loom ahead, rusted with age but still **holding the memories of the men who once passed through them.** The sun bakes the stone walls, and the air feels strangely still, as if the land itself is **holding its breath.**

This is **the Old Idaho State Penitentiary**, a place where **criminals, murderers, and the damned** spent their final days.

The echoes of **chains rattling, boots pounding against stone, and the muttered curses of forgotten men** still seem to hang in the air, **a prison that never truly emptied.**

The bars may be rusted, the cells long empty —but the walls still remember the tortured souls who never escaped. (Picture Wikimedia Commons)

A Place of Misery and Violence

When the prison first opened in **1872**, it was meant to be a place of **justice**. But over the decades, it became **something much darker**—a place of **cruelty, suffering, and death.**

• Cells were **tiny, damp, and overcrowded**, offering little protection from the scorching summers and brutal winters.

• Prisoners lived in **filth and despair**, where violence was as common as the air they breathed.

• Some men went **mad** within these walls, clawing at the stone, whispering to unseen figures in the corners of their cells.

The worst of them were sent to **Cell House 5**, home to **the death row inmates**, where men **spent their last nights** staring at the ceiling, waiting for the moment when the rope would tighten around their necks.

Some of them still wait.

The Hauntings of Cell House 5

As you walk through the prison today, it is **silent**—at least, at first. But those who visit Cell House 5 often leave with **stories they cannot explain**.

- **Footsteps echo along the hallway**, even when no one else is there.

- **Heavy cell doors slam shut by themselves**, as if someone is still inside.

- Visitors feel **a weight pressing down on them**, a suffocating presence that makes their skin crawl.

Some say it is **the spirits of the executed**, still reliving their final moments.

Others claim **it is something else entirely**, something born from the sheer misery that soaked into these walls for over a century.

But the most terrifying stories?

They come from those who have seen **the shadows.**

The Shadow Figures of the Penitentiary

There are whispers of **shadowy figures** that move through the cellblocks, **darker than the darkness itself.**

- **Guards have reported seeing shapes dart between cells**, vanishing before they can take a second look.

- **Tourists have captured strange figures in photographs**, standing in the very places where men took their final breaths.

- Some **feel a cold breath on their necks**, only to turn around and find... **nothing.**

One visitor, a skeptic, laughed at the ghost stories before **stepping into an empty cell alone**.

When he came out, his face was pale.

His hands were shaking.

He refused to say what he had seen.

And he never returned.

The Hartman House: The Shadow That Walks the Halls

(Caldwell, ID – Built in the early 1900s)

Unlike the prison, **the Hartman House does not look like a place of horror**.

From the outside, it is **a charming early 20th-century home**, with **gabled windows and a welcoming front porch**.

But the moment you step inside, **something feels off**.

The air is **too still**.

The silence is **too heavy**.

And if you listen closely, you might hear **a soft creak of the floorboards upstairs**—as if someone is walking just out of sight.

A Man Who Never Left

The Hartman House was once the pride and joy of **a wealthy businessman**, a man who poured his heart into every inch of its design.

- He lived there for **decades**, tending to the home with meticulous care.

- He planned to **pass it down through generations**, never wanting to leave.

- And then, **he died.**

Some say he was **not ready to go**.

And some believe he **never did.**

The Ghost in the Upstairs Window

Visitors and former residents of **the Hartman House** have reported **strange encounters** that defy explanation:

- **A shadowy figure stands at the upstairs window**, watching the street below.

- **Unexplained cold drafts** move through rooms, even when the air is still.

- Objects **shift on their own**, moving inches at a time, as if an unseen hand is rearranging things.

But the most terrifying stories?

They come from those who have been **followed.**

Staring from the shadows, the ghost waits... watching, waiting—its presence lingering in the still air, as if following those who dare to look away

The Feeling of Being Watched

There is a hallway in **the Hartman House** where many have felt **an overwhelming sense of being watched.**

Some **walk through it and feel a sudden chill**, as if stepping into a place where they are **not welcome.**

Others claim that if you stand too long in the hallway, **you will feel someone step up behind you.**

One visitor, brave enough to linger, **heard breathing right beside his ear.**

He turned, expecting to see another guest.

There was no one there.

He ran from the house and refused to return.

Idaho's Ghostly Secrets

From the **cold, haunted corridors of the Old Idaho State Penitentiary** to the **unseen figure that lingers in Hartman House**, Idaho is a place where **the past refuses to fade.**

Some spirits are trapped by **guilt, rage, or suffering.**

Others simply **do not want to leave** the places they once called home.

And some?

Some are **waiting**—for someone to notice them, to acknowledge them, to remember that they were once **alive.**

If you ever visit these places, **be respectful.**

Because in Idaho, **some ghosts are watching.**

And some of them **want you to know they are still here.**

Illinois

The McPike Mansion: The House That Watches

(Alton, IL – Built in 1869)

High on a hill overlooking the town of **Alton, Illinois**, stands **the McPike Mansion**—a once-grand estate that has become **one of the most haunted locations in the Midwest.**

With its boarded-up windows, **peeling paint, and collapsing staircases**, the house seems to **watch those who pass by**, as if waiting for someone brave enough to step inside.

But be warned:

The McPike Mansion does not welcome visitors.

Because **its former residents may still be there.**

The McPike Mansion never sleeps... its empty windows watch, its halls whisper, and its unseen residents are never truly alone.
(Picture Wikimedia Commons)

The Mansion's Dark History

Built in **1869**, McPike Mansion was once **the grand home of Henry Guest McPike**, a wealthy businessman, land developer, and former mayor of Alton.

- The house was **lavish**, filled with fine furniture, elegant chandeliers, and **the latest Victorian luxuries.**

- It hosted **high society gatherings**, where the elite of Illinois dined and danced in its halls.

- But after **McPike's death**, the mansion slowly **fell into decay**, eventually becoming **abandoned.**

And that's when **the hauntings began.**

The Ghosts of McPike Mansion

Visitors and paranormal investigators have reported **terrifying encounters** inside the mansion:

- **Doors creak open on their own**, as if unseen hands are still welcoming guests.

- **Shadowy figures drift through the hallways**, their faces hidden in darkness.

- **Unexplained whispers** echo from empty rooms, **soft voices murmuring in the dead of night.**

But the most chilling encounters involve **two spirits**—those of **the mansion's original owner, Henry McPike, and a former servant named Sarah.**

The Spirit of Henry McPike

Some say that **Henry McPike himself still roams the house, watching over his former home.**

- His ghost has been seen **standing near the grand staircase**, where he once greeted guests.

- Visitors have reported **cold spots** in rooms where he spent most of his time.

- And some claim to have heard **his footsteps pacing back and forth**, as if he is **unsettled, waiting for something—or someone.**

But **not all spirits in McPike Mansion are friendly.**

The Ghost of Sarah, the Servant

One of the most **terrifying spirits** is that of **Sarah**, a former domestic servant who is believed to have **died in the house.**

- Visitors have reported feeling **a hand brushing against their arm**, only to turn and find **no one there.**

- Some have seen **a misty apparition in the basement**, where Sarah is said to **still linger.**

- Others have heard **her soft, breathy voice calling their names**—a whisper from **beyond the grave.**

The McPike Mansion is **not just a house.**

It is **a memory frozen in time, a place where the past refuses to let go.**

And if you enter, **the spirits may not let you leave.**

Bachelor's Grove Cemetery: The Graveyard of the Unrested

(Midlothian, IL – Established in the 1800s)

Deep in the woods outside **Midlothian, Illinois**, hidden beyond an overgrown path, lies **Bachelor's Grove Cemetery**—a place known for **its ghostly apparitions, flickering lights, and strange, unexplainable events.**

Once a simple, rural burial ground, it has become **one of the most haunted cemeteries in America**—a place where the dead **walk, whisper, and watch.**

Do you dare step inside?

A Cemetery with a Dark Reputation

Established in the **early 1800s**, Bachelor's Grove was **meant to be a peaceful resting place** for early settlers.

But over time, it became a **place of tragedy and fear.**

- **Gravestones were vandalized**, some even stolen, angering the spirits within.

- **Bodies were dumped in the pond beside the cemetery**, victims of Chicago's infamous crime underworld.

- Locals reported **phantom cars, flickering lights, and eerie voices** calling their names.

And then came **the Lady in White.**

The Ghostly Lady on the Tombstone

One of the most **famous spirits** in Bachelor's Grove Cemetery is the **White Lady**, also known as the **Madonna of Bachelor's Grove.**

She is seen **sitting on a tombstone**, dressed in a flowing white gown, **cradling an invisible baby in her arms.**

- Some say she **lost her child in life**, and now she **wanders the graveyard, looking for it in death.**

- Others believe she is **a guardian spirit**, protecting the cemetery from further destruction.

- But those who **see her** report an overwhelming **sense of sadness**, as if they can **feel her sorrow.**

And when you blink?

She vanishes.

Amidst the forgotten tombstones, she waits — a sorrowful mother, forever searching for the child she lost, vanishing with the blink of an eye, leaving only an eerie chill in the air

Phantom Vehicles and Vanishing Lights

Bachelor's Grove isn't haunted by just ghosts—**strange, spectral vehicles have also been reported.**

- Some drivers have seen **an old-fashioned black car** on the dirt road near the cemetery, only for it to **disappear without a trace.**

- Others have spotted **floating orbs of light**, weaving between the tombstones as if searching for something.

- Paranormal investigators have recorded **strange energy**

readings, as if the spirits are **trying to make themselves known.**

But the most terrifying experiences happen to those who **come alone.**

Many visitors report the **feeling of being watched**, even when there is **no one else around.**

Some have **felt a cold hand on their shoulder**, only to turn and find **nothing but shadows.**

And a few have left the cemetery with **scratches on their skin**, as if something **didn't want them there.**

Illinois' Haunted Past Still Walks Among Us

From the **ghostly halls of McPike Mansion** to the **shadowy pathways of Bachelor's Grove Cemetery**, Illinois is home to **spirits that refuse to rest.**

Some are **lost souls**, searching for the past.

Some are **watchful guardians**, protecting what was once theirs.

And some?

Some do not want you here.

So if you ever find yourself wandering through **an abandoned house, an old graveyard, or a forgotten road**, listen carefully.

Watch the shadows.

And if you feel a **chill in the air**, know this:

You are not alone.

Because in Illinois, **the past is still waiting.**

And **sometimes, it reaches for the living.**

Indiana

Bridges are meant to connect, to guide travelers safely from one side to another.

But in **Indiana**, some bridges do more than just carry you across.

Some hold onto **tragedy**, to **lives lost and souls left behind**.

In **Avon**, a towering railroad bridge echoes with the **screams of a doomed worker, forever trapped in stone**.

And in **Clinton Falls**, a covered bridge whispers with **the giggles of a little girl whose life was stolen by the waters below**.

Step carefully when you cross.

Because in Indiana, **some bridges do not forget.**

The Haunted Avon Bridge: Screams from the Stone

(Avon, IN – Built in the 1850s)

The **Avon Haunted Bridge** rises from the land like a solemn giant, its **weathered stone arches** stretching over the train tracks below.

During the day, it is just **an old railroad bridge**, a relic of Indiana's past.

But at night?

It is **something else entirely.**

Those who have walked near it after dark **swear they have heard something**—something **coming from inside the stone itself**.

A **low, hollow knocking**.

A **muffled scream**.

A voice, distant yet **desperate**, as if calling from beneath the very ground.

Because **someone is still trapped inside.**

Trapped in Stone: Beneath the towering Avon Haunted Bridge, echoes of a lost soul still knock from within—forever waiting to be set free.

A Fatal Mistake: The Man Buried in the Bridge

Legend tells that when the bridge was being constructed in the **1850s**, a **worker lost his footing** and tumbled into **a vat of wet cement**.

- His coworkers **could not save him**.

- They could only watch as he **sank into the thick, gray mixture**, his screams fading into silence.

- And in the rush to complete the bridge, **his body was never removed.**

The cement hardened around him, **sealing him inside the very structure of the bridge.**

But he was **not at rest.**

The Hauntings of the Avon Bridge

For over **150 years**, locals have claimed to **hear the man's ghost still trying to escape.**

• **A rhythmic knocking** echoes from the bridge's massive stone supports—**as if someone is pounding from the inside, begging to be let out.**

• Some claim to hear **a voice moaning**, carried by the wind, saying **"Help me... let me out..."**

• Train conductors **report hearing screams** as they pass over the bridge late at night.

Some say that **if you stand beneath the bridge and knock three times,** you will hear **a knock back**—a message from **the man buried alive.**

Others believe the bridge is cursed.

• **Accidents have happened on the tracks**, as if some unseen force is **pulling people toward their doom.**

• **A few have reported seeing shadowy figures standing on top of the bridge**, only to **vanish into thin air.**

The Avon Bridge is **not just haunted**.

It is **a tomb.**

And if you listen closely, you may hear **the echoes of a soul still trying to escape.**

Edna Collins Bridge: The Little Girl Who Waits for a Ride

(Clinton Falls, IN – Early 1900s)

Nestled deep within the **Indiana countryside**, the **Edna Collins Bridge** looks like any other **quaint, covered bridge**.

But **don't let its peaceful appearance fool you**.

For over a century, travelers have whispered of **a presence that lingers here**—a small, shadowy figure, waiting, always waiting.

And if you drive through the bridge at night, **she might just ask you for a ride**.

The Story of Edna Collins

The legend of **Edna Collins** is one of **innocence lost, of childhood stolen by the water below**.

- In the early **1900s**, Edna was **a little girl who lived nearby**, often playing in the creek beneath the bridge.

- She loved to **splash in the water**, and her parents would let her swim **while they waited in the car nearby**.

- But one day, **Edna never came back**.

When her parents went to check on her, **they found only silence**.

The water rippled.

The trees swayed.

And then, **they saw her lifeless body floating in the current.**

Edna had drowned.

And her parents, **devastated**, never forgave themselves for not watching closer.

But some say **Edna never really left.**

The Ritual to Summon Edna

For decades, travelers passing through **Edna Collins Bridge** have spoken of **a chilling tradition**—a ritual said to **bring Edna's spirit forward.**

The instructions are simple:

1 Drive onto the bridge at night and come to a complete stop.

2 Turn off your headlights.

3 Honk your horn three times.

And then... **wait.**

Some say **you will hear soft footsteps outside your car**, circling, stopping just beside your window.

Others have **seen small handprints appear on their car doors**, as if Edna **is reaching out, hoping for someone to take her home.**

And the most terrifying stories?

They come from those who have seen her **standing in the middle of the road**, her figure barely visible in the darkness.

A little girl in an old-fashioned dress.

Her face pale, her eyes filled with longing.

If you see her?

Do not get out of your car.

Because some say if you **open your door**, Edna will **climb inside**—and you may never be able to get her out.

Indiana's Haunted Bridges: Where the Dead Still Walk

Bridges are meant to **carry people across**, to **guide travelers safely from one side to another**.

But **some bridges in Indiana do more than that.**

- **The Avon Haunted Bridge** holds a man **buried alive**, his spirit still knocking, still screaming for release.

- **Edna Collins Bridge** is home to a little girl **who drowned too soon**, forever waiting for a ride home that will never come.

These bridges are not just **structures of wood and stone**.

They are **memorials of unfinished stories, of souls trapped between worlds, of echoes from the past refusing to fade.**

And if you ever find yourself **crossing one of these bridges**, remember this: **Listen carefully.** Watch the road.

And if you hear a knock from below… **don't knock back.**

Because in Indiana, **some ghosts are just waiting for you to answer.**

Iowa

Beneath the endless fields of **Iowa**, where corn stretches toward the sky and small towns seem frozen in time, **the past refuses to rest**.

Some houses are filled with **memories of love and laughter**.

Others? **They hold something darker.**

In **Villisca**, a simple white house became the setting for **one of the most brutal unsolved murders in American history** —a crime so horrific that **the walls still whisper with echoes of that bloody night.**

And in **Scotch Grove**, an abandoned asylum known as **Edinburgh Manor** hides **shadows that watch, whispers that call, and spirits that refuse to be forgotten.**

These are not just ghost stories.

These are places where history lingers, where the past still reaches out... sometimes for you.

The Villisca Axe Murder House: The Home That Screams in the Night

(Villisca, IA – June 10, 1912)

Villisca is a quiet town—**a place where neighbors know each other, where the world seems safe and predictable.**

But in **1912**, something happened that **changed everything.**

A crime so shocking, so **unthinkably brutal**, that the very name **Villisca** would forever be tied to one of **the most horrifying unsolved murders in American history.**

And now, over a century later?

The house where it happened still stands.

Still waiting.

Still haunted.

The Night of Terror

On the night of **June 9, 1912**, the Moore family—**Josiah and Sarah, along with their four children—returned home from church.**

They were **happy, safe, unaware** that **someone was already inside the house, waiting.**

That night, as they slept, **someone took an axe and murdered every person inside.**

- Josiah **was struck so many times his face was unrecognizable**.

- Sarah **met the same gruesome fate**.

- Their children—**Herman, Katherine, Boyd, and Paul**—were **slaughtered in their beds**.

- Even their two young guests, **Lena and Ina Stillinger**, were **brutally killed**, their blood staining the wooden floors.

An article in *The Day Book*, Chicago, June 14, 1912, depicting five of the victims and the house

No one heard the screams.

No one saw the killer come or go.

And **no one was ever caught.**

The town of Villisca **never forgot.**

And neither did the house.

The Haunting of Villisca Axe Murder House

Today, the **Villisca Axe Murder House** is open for tours—**but those who step inside often leave with more than just a ghost story.**

Visitors report **chilling encounters**:

- **Children's voices** echo through the empty rooms, their laughter **turning to cries**.

- **Objects move on their own**—chairs slide, doors creak open, lamps crash to the floor.

- **Dark shadows** slink through the halls, appearing in the corners of visitors' eyes before vanishing.

- **EVP recordings** have captured voices saying **"Get out"** and **"It happened here."**

Some brave souls **spend the night**, hoping to witness the paranormal.

Many **leave before dawn.**

And those who stay?

Some wake to find **small handprints on their skin, as if something unseen touched them in the night.**

The Villisca Axe Murder House is **not just haunted**.

It is waiting.

Waiting for someone to **solve the mystery.**

Or perhaps... **to claim another victim.**

Edinburgh Manor: The Asylum That Watches

(Scotch Grove, IA – Built 1910, Abandoned 2010)

Some places are built with **good intentions**.

And yet, **somehow, they become something else.**

For over **a century**, **Edinburgh Manor** stood as a home for those who had **nowhere else to go**—the mentally ill, the abandoned, the lost.

But if its walls could talk? **They would scream.**

The walls of Edinburgh Manor have seen the unspeakable... the lost souls still linger, watching—waiting—for their next visitor.
(Image Wikipedia Commons)

A Place for the Forgotten

The land where **Edinburgh Manor** now stands has a **long, chilling history**.

Before the manor, there was **the Poor Farm**—a facility where those deemed **unfit for society** were sent to live out their days.

- **The mentally ill.**
- **The disabled.**
- **The elderly who had no family.**
- **The homeless, the criminals, the unwanted.**

Some died of **natural causes**.

Others?

Their deaths were **never explained**.

When the Poor Farm was torn down, **Edinburgh Manor was built in 1910**, meant to **offer better care**.

But those who lived there **tell a different story.**

- **Patients were locked away**—sometimes for **decades**, forgotten by the outside world.
- **Torturous treatments** were common—primitive methods of dealing with **mental illness.**
- Some **patients vanished**, their records erased, their fates unknown.

By the time **Edinburgh Manor shut its doors in 2010**, it had housed **over 150 deaths**.

And **not all of them left.**

The Haunting of Edinburgh Manor

After its closure, **Edinburgh Manor became a hotspot for paranormal investigators**—and the things they found **were deeply disturbing.**

• **Disembodied voices whisper in the halls**, calling out names, crying, sometimes even laughing.

• **Doors slam shut on their own**, locking people inside rooms they cannot explain.

• **Dark figures move through the corridors**, lurking in doorways, watching from the shadows.

• **Visitors report feeling a presence standing behind them**, breathing against their necks.

Some believe the spirits of **former patients** are still trapped inside, confused, **searching for a way out.**

Others think something **darker** lurks in the basement, something that **feeds on fear.**

One investigator spent the night alone.

By morning, he was **found outside, shaking, unable to explain what had happened.**

He would never return.

Iowa's Haunted Past Refuses to Fade

Some stories are written in history books.

Others?

They are written in blood.

• In **Villisca**, the house where **an entire family was slaughtered** still stands, filled with **unanswered questions and restless souls.**

• In **Edinburgh Manor**, the shadows of **lost patients and broken minds** still creep through the empty halls, whispering to those who dare to listen.

These places are not just haunted.

They are **trapped in time**, their tragedies playing out **over and over again**, waiting for someone to notice.

So if you ever visit?

Be careful where you step.

Because in Iowa, **the past is not done with the living.**

And sometimes, **it reaches for you.**

Kansas

Stull Cemetery: The Gateway to Hell

(Stull, KS – A Cemetery of Shadows and Secrets)

There are haunted cemeteries.

And then there is **Stull.**

A place where the air grows still, where the trees whisper **secrets in a language long forgotten.**

A place so feared that even locals **refuse to speak its name after dark.**

Because Stull Cemetery is said to be one of the seven gateways to Hell.

The Legend of Stull Cemetery

Stull, Kansas, is a tiny, almost-forgotten town—**just a few roads, a church, and a graveyard on a hill.**

But the legends surrounding **that graveyard** have made it one of **the most infamous paranormal locations in the United States.**

Where shadows linger and forgotten whispers echo—Stull Cemetery, the gateway to the unknown

- Some say **Satan himself** visits Stull **twice a year**, emerging from a hidden portal in the cemetery to walk among the living.

- Others whisper that **witches and occultists once gathered here**, performing dark rituals beneath the full moon.

- And the most chilling rumor?

That somewhere in the cemetery, **there is a stairway leading directly to Hell.**

A place where **those who enter never return.**

The Disappearances and Disturbances

For decades, those who have dared to enter **Stull Cemetery** have reported strange and terrifying encounters:

- **Visitors have vanished**, only to be found hours later—disoriented, confused, with no memory of what happened.

- **Unseen forces push people to the ground**, as if trying to drag them beneath the earth.

- **The wind stops entirely**, leaving the cemetery in an unnatural silence, even when the trees outside are swaying.

- **Crosses have been found turned upside-down**, despite no evidence of human disturbance.

And then there's the church—**or what's left of it.**

The Church That Wouldn't Fall

For years, an abandoned **stone church stood at the edge of the cemetery**—a place said to be used for **rituals, sacrifices, and demonic summoning.**

Locals claimed the building was cursed.

- **It had no roof, yet rain never touched the inside.**

- **No matter how hard the wind blew, the structure would not collapse.**

- **Those who tried to tear it down suffered mysterious accidents.**

Eventually, the church **was demolished**, but **the legends did not die with it.**

Because **the Devil's Gate is still there.**

And those who step too close **may never step back.**

The Sallie House: The Haunting That Hurts

(Atchison, KS – The Most Dangerous House in Kansas)

Most haunted houses **whisper with ghostly echoes**, flickering lights, and cold chills.

The **Sallie House** does more than that.

It **attacks.**

The Story of Sallie: A Little Girl's Revenge?

In the late **1800s**, the house at **508 N. 2nd Street in Atchison, Kansas**, was home to a local doctor.

One day, **a desperate mother rushed to his door, carrying her young daughter—Sallie.**

Sallie was suffering **from severe stomach pain**, later believed to be **appendicitis.**

The doctor **acted fast**, but in his haste, he made a fatal mistake:

- **He began surgery before the anesthesia fully took effect.**

- Sallie awoke mid-operation, screaming in agony.

- And then... she died on the table.

Some believe her **spirit never left the house.**

Others believe **something far darker took her place.**

The Haunting Begins

For years, the house sat quietly—until **the 1990s**, when a young couple, **Tony and Debra Pickman**, moved in.

And that's when **the nightmare began.**

- **Objects moved on their own**, sometimes thrown violently across the room.

- **Dark figures appeared in hallways**, watching from the shadows.

- **Unseen hands scratched, burned, and attacked Tony Pickman**, leaving deep marks on his skin.

What started as **mild disturbances** quickly escalated into **something terrifying.**

The Physical Attacks

Unlike many haunted houses, **Sallie House is aggressive.**

- Visitors report **feeling intense pressure on their chests**, as if something is **trying to suffocate them.**

- **Doors slam shut violently**, trapping people inside rooms.

- The most terrifying encounters involve **direct physical harm**:

  - **Deep scratches** appearing on people's backs, arms, and legs.

  - **Burning sensations** on the skin, as if someone is holding a flame against them.

○ Some report waking up **covered in bruises**, unable to remember what happened.

And yet, **despite all this**, some believe **Sallie is not to blame.**

That **something else is in the house.**

Something **far more sinister.**

A Demon in Disguise?

Some paranormal investigators **do not believe that Sallie is the true spirit haunting the house.**

• **They believe something darker is using her image to lure people in.**

• **It pretends to be a small, harmless girl—then attacks when people let their guard down.**

• **It feeds off fear, growing stronger with every visit.**

The house has been **investigated by ghost hunters, psychics, and skeptics**, all of whom have left with **one terrifying truth**:

Something is inside the Sallie House.

And it **wants to hurt you.**

Kansas' Most Terrifying Legends Live On

Some haunted places are filled with **restless spirits searching for peace**.

But **Stull Cemetery and the Sallie House** are different.

- **Stull is a place of darkness**, a rumored **gate to Hell**, where even the Devil himself is said to walk.

- **The Sallie House is a trap**, where a spirit—**or something far worse—lashes out at those who dare to enter.**

These are not places for the faint of heart.

They are places where **the past is dangerous, where legends live, where something unseen is always watching.**

And if you visit, **be careful.**

Because in Kansas, **some ghosts don't just haunt...**

They hunt.

Kentucky

Kentucky is known for **rolling bluegrass fields, bourbon distilleries, and legendary horse races**. But beneath its charm lies a **darker history**—one of disease, death, and the occult.

In **Louisville**, an abandoned hospital still echoes with the cries of the dying, where **thousands of tuberculosis patients took their last breath**. Those who enter **Waverly Hills Sanatorium** speak of **shadowy figures lurking in the halls, voices whispering in the dark, and something unnatural watching from Room 502.**

And in **Wilder**, a lively bar called **Bobby Mackey's Music World** hides a chilling secret. Before it was a honky-tonk, it was **a slaughterhouse, then the site of demonic rituals, and even a murder scene.** Visitors report **phantom footsteps, objects moving on their own, and ghostly hands scratching at their skin.**

These are not just haunted places.

These are places where something waits.

And **if you go looking for ghosts, you might find something far worse.**

Waverly Hills Sanatorium: Where Death Never Left

(Louisville, KY – Built in 1910, Abandoned in 1982)

On a lonely hilltop in **Louisville**, a **massive, decaying building** looms against the sky.

Its windows are shattered.

Its walls are stained with age.

And if you listen closely, the wind carries **the soft sound of coughing, footsteps echoing through empty corridors… and whispers that should not be there.**

This is **Waverly Hills Sanatorium**—one of the most haunted locations in America.

A place where **tens of thousands died**, and where **some of them never left.**

The Plague of Death: Tuberculosis Takes Hold

In the **early 1900s, tuberculosis was a death sentence**.

- The disease spread rapidly, infecting thousands with **no cure in sight**.

- Patients suffered **horrific symptoms**—bloody coughs, weight loss, fever, and **eventual suffocation as their lungs filled with liquid.**

- Entire families were wiped out, and hospitals were **overrun with the dying.**

To control the outbreak, **Waverly Hills Sanatorium** was built —**a massive hospital meant to isolate the sick.**

At its peak, **over 400 patients lived inside at one time.**

But **most never left.**

And **Waverly became more than just a hospital.**

It became a **waiting room for death.**

The halls of Waverly Hills still echo with the whispers of the forgotten... shadows move, doors creak, and death lingers, never truly leaving. (Image in Public Domain)

The Death Tunnel: The Secret of Waverly Hills

With so many dying every day, the hospital faced a **terrible problem**:

How do you remove **hundreds of dead bodies without terrifying the living patients?**

The answer was **the Death Tunnel**.

- A **500-foot underground tunnel** was built beneath the sanatorium.

- Each night, **workers would silently wheel out the corpses, dumping them into carts that rolled down the dark tunnel.**

- The sick never saw the dead leave, **but they knew**—and **they waited for their turn.**

By the time **Waverly Hills closed in 1961**, it had seen **over 63,000 deaths**.

And some say **many of those spirits still linger.**

The Hauntings of Waverly Hills

Paranormal investigators call Waverly Hills **one of the most active haunted locations in the world.**

- **Shadow figures move through the halls**, darting from room to room.

- **Disembodied voices whisper names**, calling out to visitors.

- **Cold spots appear suddenly**, chilling people to the bone—even in the summer heat.

- **Objects move on their own**, doors slam, and the feeling of **being watched is overwhelming.**

But the **most terrifying presence** lurks in **Room 502**.

Room 502: The Nurse Who Never Left

The **fifth floor of Waverly Hills** was reserved for **mentally unstable tuberculosis patients**.

But the **most infamous ghost** belongs to **a nurse who worked there**.

- In the **1930s**, a young nurse discovered she was **pregnant by a doctor who refused to marry her.**
- Alone and ashamed, she **hanged herself in Room 502.**
- **Her body swayed for hours before anyone found her.**

Visitors today report:

- **Seeing her shadow standing in the doorway of Room 502.**
- **Hearing sobbing echoing through the halls.**
- **Feeling an overwhelming sense of despair when stepping inside the room.**

Some believe she **wasn't alone when she died.**

That **something in the hospital drove her to do it.**

And that **whatever it was… is still there.**

Bobby Mackey's Music World: The Bar That Hides the Devil

(Wilder, KY – Built in the 1800s, Still Open Today)

During the day, **Bobby Mackey's Music World** is a honky-tonk bar—a place of **live music, dancing, and laughter**.

But when the lights go down, it becomes **something else**.

A place where **the shadows move on their own**.

Where **phantom footsteps echo on the dance floor**.

And where some believe **the Devil himself still lingers**.

A History Drenched in Blood

Before it was a bar, **Bobby Mackey's had a much darker past.**

- In the **1800s**, it was a **slaughterhouse**. The basement contained **a deep well where animal blood drained away**.

- Rumors say **occult groups later used this well for Satanic rituals**, sacrificing animals—and possibly humans—**to summon dark forces**.

- In the 1890s, a young woman named **Pearl Bryan** was found **decapitated nearby**—her head **never recovered**. Some say **her murderers tossed it into the well as an offering to the Devil.**

The place became known as **"Hell's Gate."**

And some believe **it is still open.**

The Hauntings of Bobby Mackey's

Those who visit Bobby Mackey's report **terrifying experiences**:

• **Unseen hands push or scratch them**, leaving marks that appear out of nowhere.

• **Phantom voices whisper in their ears**, calling them by name.

• **Shadow figures move through the bar**, watching from the corners.

Even Bobby Mackey himself—**a skeptic**—has admitted **that something is inside his bar.**

And one man?

He almost didn't make it out alive.

Welcome to Bobby Mackey's... where the ghosts don't just watch—they reach out.

The Possession of Carl Lawson

Carl Lawson was a **longtime employee** at Bobby Mackey's.

But over time, **he began acting strangely**.

- He spoke of **hearing voices calling to him**.

- He saw **dark figures in the basement, whispering in a language he didn't understand.**

- And then, **one night, something took over.**

Carl's **body convulsed**, and his voice changed.

A **priest was called in** to perform an exorcism.

Carl screamed, **his voice turning guttural, inhuman.**

The priest commanded, **"What is your name?"**

And the voice inside Carl answered:

"I am the Devil."

After the exorcism, Carl returned to normal.

But he refused to go back to the basement.

And **Bobby Mackey's Music World** remains one of **the only places in America with an official warning that it may cause "spiritual harm."**

Kentucky's Darkest Secrets Are Still Alive

- In **Waverly Hills**, the spirits of **thousands of tuberculosis patients still walk the halls**, their whispers floating through the empty rooms.

- In **Bobby Mackey's Music World**, the past is soaked in **blood, possession, and a doorway that may lead somewhere far worse than Hell.**

Some ghosts haunt out of **sorrow.**

Others haunt out of **anger.**

And some?

They never left at all.

So if you visit, **step carefully.**

Because in Kentucky, **some places never let go.**

Louisiana

Myrtles Plantation: A House of Restless Spirits

(St. Francisville, LA – Built in 1796)

Standing beneath the twisted branches of **centuries-old oak trees**, **Myrtles Plantation looks like a postcard from the past**.

Its grand columns, sweeping verandas, and elegant charm hide **a sinister truth**—one that has earned it a reputation as **one of the most haunted plantations in America.**

And if you walk its halls, **you may not be alone.**

The Legend of Chloe: The Vengeful Spirit

The most **famous ghost** of Myrtles Plantation is **Chloe**, an enslaved woman whose tragic story **still lingers within the walls of the house.**

As the legend goes:

- **Chloe was owned by Judge Clark Woodruff, the plantation master.**

- When she **fell out of favor**, she was punished—**some say her ear was cut off** as a warning.

- **Desperate to regain her place**, she **baked poison into a birthday cake**, intending to make the family sick so she could "nurse them back to health."

- Instead, **the judge's wife and two daughters died.**

Her punishment?

Death.

The other enslaved workers **dragged Chloe outside, hanged her from a tree, and threw her body into the Mississippi River.**

But Chloe never truly left.

Standing beneath the twisted branches of **centuries-old oak trees, Myrtles Plantation looks like a postcard from the past.** (Picture Wikimedia Commons)

The Haunting of Myrtles Plantation

Today, visitors claim that **Chloe's ghost still walks the grounds:**

- **A woman in a green turban appears in mirrors and photographs**, watching guests from the shadows.

- **Unseen hands pull on people's clothing**, as if someone is trying to get their attention.

- **Candles flicker and go out on their own**, as if something is moving through the house.

- Some say that at **night, whispers drift through the halls**, carrying words no one can understand.

But Chloe is **not the only ghost** at Myrtles Plantation.

The Other Ghosts of Myrtles Plantation

- **The Ghost of a Young Girl:** A barefoot child has been seen **playing near the staircase**, only to vanish when approached.

- **The Haunted Mirror:** An antique mirror inside the plantation **reflects more than just the living—the faces of spirits appear in its glass, staring back at visitors.**

- **The Murdered Man:** One former owner, **William Winter, was shot on the porch** and **staggered inside, collapsing on the 17th step of the staircase.**

  ○ Some claim to hear **his dying footsteps**, endlessly repeating his final moments.

Myrtles Plantation **is not just a historic home.**

It is a house of the dead.

And **they do not rest.**

LaLaurie Mansion: The House of Unspeakable Evil

(New Orleans, LA – Built in 1832)

If there is a place where **horror itself has taken root**, it is **the LaLaurie Mansion.**

Its elegant balconies and grand architecture **hide a secret so dark that even in a city filled with ghost stories, this one stands apart.**

Because here, inside these walls, **human screams once filled the air.**

And some say they **never truly stopped.**

The Monster of Royal Street: Madame Delphine LaLaurie

In the **early 1800s, Madame Delphine LaLaurie** was known as a **wealthy socialite—a woman of refinement, beauty, and power.**

She was **admired by New Orleans high society.**

But **behind the doors of her mansion, something horrifying was happening.**

- **Enslaved people in her home began to vanish.**

- **Neighbors heard screams in the night, but LaLaurie always had an excuse.**

- Then, in 1834, a fire broke out in the mansion.

And what rescuers **found inside the house shook them to their core.**

The Torture Chamber Discovered

Firefighters **forced their way into a locked upstairs room—** and **what they saw was straight out of a nightmare:**

• **Enslaved men and women were chained to the walls,** their bodies mutilated.

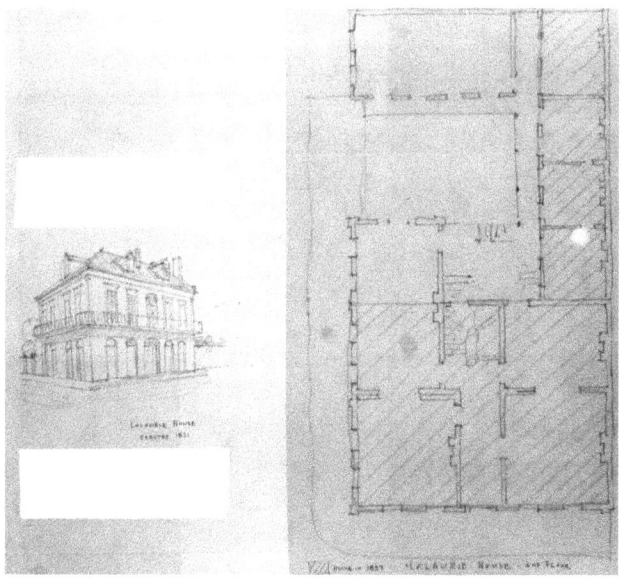

Behind these walls lurked unimaginable horrors—step inside the infamous LaLaurie Mansion, where elegance masked unspeakable evil. Please note that the current structure has undergone various modifications over the years, so contemporary floor plans may differ from the original 1832 design.

- Some were **barely alive, their wounds festering**, their eyes filled with **unspeakable horror**.

- One woman had **her mouth sewn shut**, another had **her limbs broken and reset in twisted positions**.

The people of New Orleans **were horrified**.

An **angry mob stormed the mansion**, but **LaLaurie escaped**, disappearing forever.

Her victims, however, **never left**.

The Haunting of LaLaurie Mansion

Since that day, the LaLaurie Mansion has been **one of the most haunted places in New Orleans**.

- **Phantom screams echo from the upper floors**, as if the tortured souls are still crying for help.

- **Chains rattle in the dead of night**, dragging across the floor.

- **Visitors report feeling choked or scratched**, as if unseen hands are trying to pull them into the darkness.

- Some have seen **figures standing at the windows**, staring down into the streets below.

Even those who **don't believe in ghosts** admit that the mansion **feels wrong**—as if **the very walls are soaked in pain**.

Some say the house is **cursed**.

That **evil never left it**.

And that **Madame LaLaurie's victims are still inside, screaming for justice.**

Louisiana's Haunted Legacy: Ghosts That Refuse to Rest

• At **Myrtles Plantation**, the spirit of **Chloe** still lingers, watching, waiting, and **whispering in the night**.

• At **LaLaurie Mansion**, the victims of **unspeakable cruelty still haunt the house**, forever trapped where they suffered.

These places are more than just haunted.

They are **scarred by history**, forever marked by **tragedy, horror, and the souls who can never move on.**

So if you visit?

Listen closely.

Because in Louisiana, **some ghosts still scream.**

And **some shadows do more than watch.**

Maine

Maine is a land of **rugged coastlines, whispering pine forests, and roads that stretch into the misty unknown.** But beneath its natural beauty lies **a darker side**, where **ghostly figures still walk the roads they died on and where eerie melodies drift through the cold Atlantic winds long after the players have turned to dust.**

Some ghosts **wait for redemption**.

Others **warn the living to stay away**.

And some?

Some are **trapped in an endless loop of sorrow and madness**—a song that plays over and over, echoing through time itself.

In **Hancock County**, a **headless bride appears on a lonely stretch of road, searching for the ride she never completed.**

And on **Seguin Island**, an abandoned lighthouse still hums with the sounds of **a piano that no longer exists**, a tune played by a woman whose tragic fate is burned into the walls of the house where she died.

If you find yourself in either of these places, **listen carefully**.

Because some ghosts never stopped searching… and some never stopped screaming.

The Ghostly Bride of Catherine's Hill

(Route 182, Hancock County – A Journey That Never Ends)

The road winds **through the darkened forest**, twisting like a serpent beneath the glow of your headlights.

Route 182 is quiet—too quiet.

No other cars.

No houses in sight.

Just the **endless, pressing weight of the trees**, their branches arching overhead like skeletal fingers.

You've heard the stories, of course.

Everyone in **Hancock and Cherryfield** has.

Some say she's **just a legend**—something to tell outsiders to **make the hair on their necks stand up**.

But others…

Others say she is **very, very real**.

A Wedding That Never Came

The legend begins **on a night just like this one**.

A young woman—**Catherine**—was traveling down this very road **on the night before her wedding**.

The story goes that she was in a **horse-drawn carriage**, the kind you might see in a fairy tale.

Her **veil was long and flowing**, her **white dress as pristine as freshly fallen snow**.

She was **happy, excited, ready for a future filled with love and laughter**.

But then—

Something **went terribly wrong**.

- Perhaps the **horse was spooked** by something lurking in the woods.

- Perhaps the **driver lost control**, his hands slipping on the reins.

- Or perhaps, **fate itself had decided that Catherine was never meant to reach her wedding day**.

The **carriage overturned**, the wheels catching on jagged rocks.

Wood splintered.

Metal twisted.

And **Catherine was thrown violently from the carriage**, her head **striking the sharp edge of a boulder**.

By the time they found her body...

She was no longer whole.

Her **head had been severed from her body**, her beautiful wedding gown now stained with the deep red of **a love story cut short**.

She waits in the mist, forever searching for a ride that will never come... Will you stop for the Ghostly Bride of Catherine's Hill

A Ride That Never Arrives

Since that night, **Catherine has never left Route 182**.

Drivers passing through the **fog-covered stretch of road** often report **seeing a woman standing by the roadside**, her long **white dress billowing in the wind**.

- If you slow down, she will **raise a hand, signaling for a ride**.

- If you stop, she will **wordlessly climb into the car**, her veil pulled over her face.

But whatever you do—

Do not look at her.

Because those who **glance into the rearview mirror** often find themselves **staring into a dark void where her head should be.**

And then—

She vanishes.

The seatbelt still fastened.

The car door never opening.

And the only thing left behind?

The faint scent of damp earth... and something much older.

If you refuse to stop?

You might **not make it down the road at all.**

Some drivers report feeling **a sudden grip on their shoulder**, as if **icy fingers are trying to pull them off the road.**

Others see a **figure in white suddenly standing in the middle of the highway**, forcing them to swerve into the darkness.

But the worst fate is reserved for **those who drive past without acknowledging her at all.**

Because **if Catherine doesn't get her ride… she just might follow you home.**

The Murderous Melody of Seguin Island Lighthouse

(Off the Coast of Phippsburg – A Song That Never Ends)

The **lighthouse stands alone.**

A **gray stone tower**, battered by **centuries of wind, salt, and time**.

Few people come to **Seguin Island** anymore.

Not since the lighthouse was **automated in the 1980s**.

Not since the last **human keepers fled**.

Not since the music **started playing again.**

The Lighthouse Keeper's Descent into Madness

The story begins in the **mid-1800s**, when a young lighthouse keeper **arrived on Seguin Island with his new wife**.

At first, they were **happy**, despite the **loneliness**.

The sea stretched out endlessly before them, the world **nothing but crashing waves and the distant glow of passing ships**.

But the days were **long**.

And the nights were **even longer**.

In an attempt to **comfort herself**, the young wife **played the piano**.

At first, the sound was **beautiful**, filling the house with warmth.

But there was a problem.

She only knew one song.

And so, **day after day, night after night, the same melody echoed through the small lighthouse, over and over, never stopping.**

It became **a slow, creeping madness**.

The **same notes, the same tune, the same refrain**, until the sound itself felt like it was **crawling inside the keeper's skull, burrowing deep.**

Until, one day—

He **snapped.**

- He grabbed **an axe**.
- He **destroyed the piano**, its wood splintering into jagged shards.
- And then, **he turned the blade on his wife**.

By the time the townspeople **found him**, it was too late.

She was **dead**, her **blood staining the very floorboards where she had once played**.

And the keeper?

He had **turned the axe on himself**, leaving the lighthouse to **fall silent forever.**

Or so they thought.

The Music That Never Stopped

To this day, **visitors to Seguin Island report hearing something… impossible.**

- A **faint piano melody**, floating on the wind.

- **The same song, over and over**, even though **there is no piano on the island anymore**.

- Some sailors claim to have seen **a shadow standing at the lighthouse window**, watching them as they pass.

And the **most terrifying stories**?

They come from **those who dare to stay overnight**.

- Some wake up to find **deep scratches on their arms**, as if **someone was trying to wake them.**

- Others feel an **icy breath against their neck**, though **no one is there.**

- A few have even heard **a woman crying in the night**, sobbing softly **as the piano plays on.**

Some say the **keeper and his wife are trapped on the island forever.** That **he still stalks the lighthouse, searching for his next victim.**

And that **she still plays… hoping someone will finally listen.**

Maine's Haunting Warnings: Stop and Listen, or Pay the Price

Some ghosts **wait for a ride**. Some ghosts **play the same song forever**.

But one thing is certain—

If you see Catherine standing on Route 182, you had better stop.

And if you ever visit Seguin Island, and hear a piano playing from inside the lighthouse?

Run.

Because **some music should never be heard.**

And **some ghosts never stop waiting.**

The waves crash, the wind howls... but beneath it all, the eerie notes of a phantom piano still play—a melody of madness, isolation, and a spirit that refuses to fade.
(Image Public Domain)

Maryland

Maryland is a place where **history and legend intertwine**, where **the past lingers** in the salty air of the Chesapeake Bay and the **shadows beneath the towering oaks**. It is a land of **old battlefields, forgotten prison camps, and roads where something unnatural waits in the darkness.**

Some ghosts **mourn their fate.**

Some **warn travelers not to venture too far.**

And some?

Some **are still searching for something… or someone.**

At **Point Lookout Lighthouse**, where **the spirits of war still whisper in the halls**, visitors have felt **unseen hands brush against them** and heard **the distant cries of soldiers who never found their way home.**

Along **Fletchertown Road**, something lurks in the trees—**half-man, half-goat, all rage**—a creature that **hunts those who dare to stray too far into the darkness.**

And in **Waldorf**, at the **Dr. Samuel A. Mudd House**, the spirit of **a man branded a traitor** still paces the floor, **forever haunted by a decision that changed history**.

If you visit these places, **listen carefully**.

Because in Maryland, **the dead still speak... and something else listens.**

Point Lookout Lighthouse: A Prison for the Dead

(Scotland, MD – Where the Civil War Never Ended)

The lighthouse at **Point Lookout** was meant to be a **beacon of hope**, guiding ships safely through the **fog and treacherous waters** of the Chesapeake Bay.

Instead, it became a **beacon for the dead.**

The white-washed walls and **fading red roof** may look ordinary, but **the air here feels heavy, as if the very land remembers the horrors that took place on these shores.**

And if you stand too long in the dark corridors of the lighthouse, **you might hear the voices of those who never left.**

The Civil War's Forgotten Dead

During the **Civil War**, Point Lookout was transformed into something far worse than a lighthouse.

- It became **a hospital, a military fort, and a prison camp.**

- Over **50,000 Confederate soldiers** were **crammed into disease-ridden tents**, surrounded by **high wooden fences and armed guards.**

- The conditions were **brutal**—men **froze in the winter, starved in the summer, and died from disease faster than the doctors could bury them.**

- The dead were stacked **like firewood**, buried in **unmarked graves**, their names **lost to history.**

And **some of them never left.**

The Hauntings of Point Lookout

Those who visit **Point Lookout Lighthouse** report **unsettling encounters:**

- **Disembodied voices call out in the dead of night**, whispering names that **no one remembers.**

- **Doors slam shut without warning**, as if **something unseen is still trying to keep the prisoners in.**

- **Cold spots appear suddenly**, so icy that they leave visitors **shaking, even in the heat of summer.**

The lighthouse **has been investigated by paranormal experts**, and **EVPs (electronic voice phenomena) have captured ghostly whispers.**

And the **most chilling encounters**?

Those belong to **the spirits of soldiers still standing watch.**

Ghostly Figures and Phantom Marches

- **A Confederate soldier has been seen standing in the doorway**, staring out to sea. His **uniform is tattered**, his **face gaunt with hunger**—but his eyes? **They burn with something that still lingers.**

- **Visitors have heard boots marching in the lighthouse halls**, heavy footsteps **echoing against the wooden floors**, even when no one else is inside.

- **Some have felt a ghostly hand on their shoulder,** gripping them as if to **warn them of something unseen.**

But the most **terrifying presence** in the lighthouse?

She is **not a soldier**.

She is **something else.**

The Woman in White

One of the most famous **spirits of Point Lookout** is the **woman in white**, a spectral figure seen in the upstairs hallway.

- **She appears suddenly,** her **dress flowing like mist**, her **face hidden by her long hair.**

- Visitors report feeling an **overwhelming sadness in her presence,** as if she is **searching for someone she lost.**

- Some believe she was a **nurse who cared for dying soldiers,** or **a grieving widow waiting for a husband who never returned from war.**

A former lighthouse keeper once woke in the night to the **sound of weeping**.

When he opened his eyes, he saw her.

Standing at the foot of his bed.

Watching him.

When he turned on the light—**she was gone**.

But the room remained **ice-cold**, and the air **smelled of damp earth and something long buried**.

Point Lookout **is not just haunted**.

It is **a prison for the dead.**

And **if you visit, be careful where you step.**

Because **some spirits are still searching for a way out.**

The Goatman of Fletchertown Road: The Beast in the Trees

(Bowie, MD – Half Man, Half Beast, All Terror)

The road is narrow, winding, **swallowed in darkness**.

The trees along **Fletchertown Road grow too close together**, their branches twisting like **grasping fingers**.

Locals **warn against driving here after sunset**.

Because in the woods, **something is waiting**.

Something **not quite human**.

The Origin of the Goatman

The legend of the **Goatman** has haunted Maryland for **generations**.

Some say he was **a scientist**, working at the **Beltsville Agricultural Research Center**, experimenting with **human and goat DNA**.

Something **went wrong**.

Something **terrible**.

- **The experiment turned against its creators**, escaping into the woods.
- Now, it hunts—filled with rage, hunger, and an urge to kill.

Others say the Goatman **has always been here**.

That he is **a demon from the depths**, a creature summoned by **occult rituals long forgotten**.

But whatever he is—

He is real.

Encounters with the Goatman

The stories are **always the same**:

- A car **breaks down along Fletchertown Road**.
- The driver **steps out to check the engine**.
- The trees **rustle**—something is **moving in the dark**.
- A **low, guttural growl**—half animal, half **human**.

And then?

They run.

Because those who **don't**—never come back.

Locals have found **abandoned cars**, their doors **hanging open, the occupants missing**.

All that remains? **Deep, hoof-like footprints leading into the woods.** Some who have **escaped the Goatman** say they saw **his face**.

A **twisted mockery of a man**, with **slit-pupil eyes and horns that curl like a ram's**.

Others **only heard the sound**—

The scraping of hooves on pavement.

And then—

The smell of blood.

Born from science, cursed by darkness—he watches from the shadows, waiting.

The Ghost of Dr. Samuel Mudd: The Doctor Who Couldn't Escape His Fate

(Waldorf, Maryland – A House Frozen in Time and Haunted by History)

The **Dr. Samuel A. Mudd House** stands like a relic from another era, its **white clapboard walls and dark shutters unchanged by time**. Nestled in the quiet countryside of **Waldorf, Maryland**, it looks like any other preserved historic home—**but those who step inside know better.**

The air is **thick with the weight of the past**, and the silence is **unnatural**, as if the house itself is waiting—**watching**.

Some who visit say they feel **a presence, a heavy energy that clings to the walls like a shadow that refuses to fade**.

Others say they have **heard the echo of footsteps on the wooden floorboards**, moving slowly, methodically—**as if someone is still pacing in deep contemplation**.

And some?

Some claim to have **seen the doctor himself**, standing in the dim candlelight, **his face lined with sorrow, his eyes filled with something far heavier than time—regret**.

A House Marked by History

To understand why **Dr. Samuel Mudd's house is haunted**, you must first understand the **man himself—and the moment in history that changed his life forever**.

On the night of **April 14, 1865**, the world shifted.

President **Abraham Lincoln was shot** in Ford's Theatre by **John Wilkes Booth**, a well-known actor turned Confederate sympathizer.

The nation stood in shock, the streets of Washington D.C. filled with **whispers of conspiracy** and **rumors of who might have helped Booth escape**.

And in the early hours of **April 15**, in the quiet countryside of Maryland, **Dr. Samuel A. Mudd's fate was sealed**.

The past lingers within these walls... shadowy figures roam, unseen footsteps echo, and Dr. Mudd's spirit still waits—for redemption or something far darker. (Image Wikimedia Commons)

The Night John Wilkes Booth Arrived

It was still dark when **a rider approached Dr. Mudd's house**, knocking at the door with urgency.

Booth, along with **his accomplice David Herold**, had **fled Washington under the cover of night**, riding hard into Maryland's back roads.

By the time they reached **Mudd's home**, Booth was **in agony**—his leg was **badly broken**, possibly from **his dramatic leap from Lincoln's theatre box after firing the fatal shot**.

Dr. Mudd, known for **his skill as a physician**, led the injured man inside, unaware that he had just **offered sanctuary to one of the most wanted men in American history**.

Or did he know?

This question **would haunt Mudd for the rest of his life**.

Some believe he was simply **a doctor doing his duty**, providing medical aid to a wounded traveler.

Others insist that **he was part of Booth's escape plan all along**, a willing conspirator who knew exactly whom he was treating.

What we do know is this—

By **the time the authorities arrived**, Booth was gone.

And Dr. Samuel Mudd was **about to be arrested for treason**.

Imprisoned for Conspiracy

In the aftermath of **Lincoln's assassination**, chaos gripped the nation.

Anyone suspected of aiding Booth **was hunted down without mercy**.

Mudd was arrested, **tried as a conspirator, and sentenced to life in prison** at **Fort Jefferson, a remote island prison in the Gulf of Mexico**.

He barely survived.

- **Conditions were brutal**, with prisoners suffering from **disease, starvation, and violent guards**.

- The air was **thick with salt**, the walls **covered in mold**, and the cries of **dying men filled the night**.

- Dr. Mudd himself **contracted yellow fever**, coming close to death.

But fate had one final twist—

In 1867, a **deadly yellow fever outbreak** swept through the prison. **With no doctors left alive**, Mudd used his medical training **to save the guards and inmates alike**.

His efforts **won him a pardon**, and in **1869, he was freed**.

He returned to Maryland, back to his family, back to the house where it all began.

But **something had changed**.

Some say **he was never the same man after prison**.

And some believe **his spirit has never truly left**.

The Haunting of the Dr. Samuel Mudd House

The Mudd House is **a perfectly preserved time capsule**, with **original furniture, old family portraits, and the very room where Booth was treated that fateful night**.

And yet, something about the house **feels... wrong**.

The energy inside is **heavy**, as if the house itself is burdened by the **guilt, sorrow, and controversy** that still lingers.

Visitors and paranormal investigators have reported **unsettling encounters**:

• **Ghostly footsteps echo through the hallways**, as if someone is **still pacing in thought, deciding his fate over and over again.**

• **Cold spots appear suddenly**, especially in **Booth's sickroom**, where Mudd tended to the assassin's shattered leg.

• **Strange knocking sounds** have been heard **on doors at night**, just like the knock that woke Mudd on the night Booth arrived.

And the most **unsettling** encounters?

They involve **the ghost of Dr. Samuel Mudd himself.**

The Doctor Who Never Left

• **A shadowy figure has been seen in the upstairs hallway**, moving from room to room.

• Some visitors have looked into the **mirror in Mudd's bedroom**, only to see **a second figure standing behind them**—a **man in 19th-century clothing, staring with sorrowful eyes.**

• **Tour guides have felt a cold hand grip their arm**, as if someone is trying to **get their attention, trying to explain something.**

And those who **ask questions about the conspiracy**—those who **wonder aloud whether Mudd was truly innocent**?

They report feeling a **sudden chill**, as if **the house itself is warning them to be careful what they say.**

Because **Dr. Mudd is still here.**

And maybe, after all this time, he's still trying to **clear his name.**

A House Trapped in Time

The **Dr. Samuel A. Mudd House is more than just a museum**.

It is **a place where history breathes**, where **the past lingers just beneath the surface, refusing to fade.**

- Was Dr. Mudd **an innocent physician caught in the wrong place at the wrong time**?

- Or was he **a willing accomplice to one of the greatest crimes in American history**?

The truth **may never be fully known**.

But one thing is certain—

Dr. Mudd never truly left his house.

And if you stand in the doorway at night, you might hear it—

The sound of **soft footsteps on the old wooden floors**.

A **cold breath against your neck**.

And if you turn around, maybe—just maybe—

You'll see a man standing in the dim light, staring back at you.

Still **waiting to be heard.**

Maryland's Haunted Past Refuses to Fade

Some ghosts are **trapped by tragedy**.

Some are **bound to the places where they suffered**.

And some, like Dr. Samuel Mudd, are **forever caught in the moment that changed everything.**

His house is **more than a historic landmark—**

It is **a place where history is still very much alive.**

So if you visit, **be respectful.**

Because in this house, **the past is never truly past.**

Massachusetts

The Haunted Legacy of The Omni Parker House

(Boston, MA – Where the Founder Never Left)

Standing **in the heart of Boston, The Omni Parker House** has been **a symbol of luxury and grandeur since 1855**.

It has hosted **literary giants like Charles Dickens, famous politicians like John F. Kennedy, and even revolutionaries plotting in the candlelight of its tavern**.

But not everyone who entered the Omni Parker House **left it behind**.

Some guests?

They're still here.

The Man Who Refused to Check Out

The most **famous ghost of The Omni Parker House** is none other than **its founder, Harvey Parker**.

- Parker was **obsessed with running a perfect hotel**, personally **overseeing every detail**, ensuring guests were **comfortable, well-fed, and attended to with care**.

- Even after **his death in 1884**, many believe that **his spirit never stopped managing the hotel**.

And if you stay here, you might just see him yourself.

Encounters with Harvey Parker

Guests staying in **rooms on the 10th floor** have reported seeing **a tall man with a dark beard and a Victorian-era coat** standing **at the foot of their bed**.

- Some say he **leans in slightly, as if checking to see if they are enjoying their stay**.

- Others describe **a sudden, eerie coldness in the room**, followed by **a faint whisper that sounds like Parker himself, still ensuring his guests are well cared for**.

Hotel staff have also reported strange occurrences:

- **Bellhops hear footsteps in empty hallways**, only to turn and find **no one there**.

- **Elevators arrive on their own, stopping at floors that no one has requested**—as if someone is still **making his rounds**.

One guest, after asking the front desk about **strange noises in his room**, was shown **a photograph of Harvey Parker**.

His face **turned pale**.

"That's him," he whispered.

"That's the man I saw last night."

The elevator arrives… but no one called it.
The man in the photo? He was here last
night. But he's been dead for years

The 3rd Floor and the Mysterious Laughing Woman

While Parker's spirit is perhaps **the most well-known**, he is **not the only ghost** roaming The Omni Parker House.

- The **third floor** is said to be **the most active**.

- Guests have heard **the laughter of an unseen woman** in the hallway late at night, even when the floor is completely empty.

- Some have felt a **soft touch on their shoulder**, only to turn and find… **nothing**.

Even Charles Dickens, who once **stayed at the hotel while touring America**, is said to **still roam the halls in spectral form**.

The Omni Parker House is **not just a hotel**.

It is **a place where history refuses to fade—and where some guests simply never check out**.

The Red Lion Inn: The Spirits of Stockbridge's Grand Hotel

(Stockbridge, MA – A Place of Unseen Guests and Midnight Visitors)

The **Red Lion Inn** is one of **New England's oldest operating inns**, standing **since the 1700s**.

Its walls have seen **colonial travelers, revolutionaries, and generations of families passing through**.

But some of its guests **have never left**.

The Hauntings of the Fourth Floor

If you ever find yourself **checking into a room on the fourth floor**, be prepared.

Because **this is where the spirits roam most freely**.

Guests and staff alike have reported chilling encounters:

• A **young girl in a Victorian dress** has been seen **wandering the hallways**, carrying **a bouquet of flowers**.

• She does not speak.

- She does not make a sound.

- She simply **walks... then disappears into thin air.**

Some guests have reported waking up in the middle of the night to find **her standing in the corner of their room, watching them silently before fading away into the darkness.**

But the girl **is not alone.**

Because **the man in the top hat is still waiting, too.**

The Shadowy Man in the Top Hat

Another frequently spotted spirit at The Red Lion Inn is **a man dressed in formal 19th-century attire, complete with a top hat.**

- Guests report waking up to see **his shadowy figure standing at the foot of their bed.**

- Others have glimpsed him **in the reflection of mirrors**, only to turn and find **the room empty.**

- Some **hear soft footsteps in their room**, pacing back and forth, though the floorboards remain still.

Who is he?

No one knows for sure.

But his presence is **felt by many**, and those who have encountered him say **his energy is impossible to ignore.**

At The Red Lion Inn, some guests check in—but they are never truly alone. Shadowy figures linger, whispers drift through the halls, and unseen eyes watch from the foot of your bed. (Picture Wikimedia Commons)

A Heavy Presence in the Night

While the **specters of The Red Lion Inn** are not known to be violent, **they do not shy away from making their presence known.**

Some guests have reported the unsettling sensation of **someone standing over them while they sleep.**

- They wake up **unable to move**, feeling **an invisible weight pressing down on their chest**.

- Others have described the sensation of **a hand brushing against their cheek**, only to find **nothing but air.**

And then there are those who hear **whispers in the empty hallways**—soft voices speaking in **languages long forgotten.**

It's as if the inn itself **exists between two worlds**, where history and the present are **blurred together**, and the guests of yesterday **still walk among us.**

Massachusetts' Haunted Hotels: Where the Past Never Checks Out

• At **The Omni Parker House, Harvey Parker himself still roams the hallways**, ensuring his guests are comfortable—even in death.

• At **The Red Lion Inn, a young girl carrying flowers and a shadowy man in a top hat still make their nightly rounds**, forever tied to the inn where they once stayed.

These places are **more than just historic hotels**.

They are **portals to the past, where the dead still move among the living**.

So if you find yourself staying in **one of Massachusetts' haunted hotels**, remember:

• If you hear **a soft knock on your door at night**, but no one is there...

• If you wake to find **a figure standing in your room, watching you silently**...

• If you feel a sudden chill and hear **a whisper in the darkness**...

You are not alone.

Because in these hotels, **the past never checks out.**

Michigan

The Holly Hotel: A Ghostly Gathering That Never Ends

(Holly, MI – Built in 1891, Haunted Ever Since)

Tucked away in the small town of **Holly, Michigan**, the **Holly Hotel** is a place of **elegance, fine dining, and something just beyond the veil of the living**.

Built in **1891**, it has welcomed **travelers, celebrities, and high-society guests** for over a century.

But it has also **survived fires, witnessed tragedy, and collected more than a few lingering spirits along the way**.

Today, the Holly Hotel is **famous for its hauntings as much as its hospitality**.

And those who work here **have long since accepted that they share the space with those who refuse to move on**.

Check in if you dare... but beware—some guests never leave

The Phantom Cigar Smoker: The Ghost of Mr. Hirst

If you ever smell **cigar smoke drifting through the air**, even though **smoking is banned inside the hotel**, you might be standing in the presence of **Mr. Norris Hirst**, the former owner of the Holly Hotel.

- **Hirst ran the hotel with pride** in the early 1900s and was known for **his high standards and commanding presence.**

- Even in death, it seems **he never truly gave up his role as host**.

- Guests and staff report **smelling his cigar smoke in the hallways**, even when **no one is smoking**.

- Some have even seen **a well-dressed man in period clothing**, walking through the dining room **before vanishing into thin air.**

One former employee recalls staying late to **close up the restaurant** when she heard a **man's deep voice** behind her say, **"Everything in order?"**

She turned around.

No one was there.

But the unmistakable scent of cigar smoke filled the air.

The Little Girl Who Laughs in the Shadows

Not all the ghosts at the Holly Hotel are **former owners**.

Some are **much younger**.

Guests have reported **hearing the giggles of a little girl**, even when no children are present.

- Her **shadow has been seen running up the stairs**, only to disappear before reaching the top.

- Some guests have felt **a tug at their clothing**, as if a small hand is trying to get their attention.

- One guest awoke to find **a little girl standing at the foot of their bed**, watching them with **wide, curious eyes**.

When they blinked—

She was gone.

Strange Occurrences at the Holly Hotel

The paranormal activity **at the Holly Hotel is constant**:

• **Disembodied voices** are heard in empty rooms.

• **Dishes rattle on their own**, even when no one is in the kitchen.

• **Guests wake up to find their furniture slightly moved**, as if someone **was rearranging the space while they slept**.

One thing is clear—

The Holly Hotel is still very much alive.

Even if **some of its residents are not.**

The Landmark Inn: The Heartbroken Spirit of Room 502

(Marquette, MI – A Love Lost to the Great Lakes)

Overlooking the cold waters of **Lake Superior**, **The Landmark Inn** is a place where **romance and tragedy intertwine**.

It has hosted **presidents, celebrities, and weary travelers** since the early 20th century.

But its most **famous guest never checked out**.

Because she is **still waiting.**

The Librarian Who Loved a Sailor

Decades ago, before the Landmark Inn was known for its **ghostly legend**, a young woman worked as a librarian in Marquette.

- She **fell in love with a sailor,** a man who promised he would **return to her after one last voyage across Lake Superior.**

- He never did.

- His ship was caught in a storm, **swallowed by the icy waves,** and **never seen again.**

Heartbroken, the librarian **checked into Room 502 at the Landmark Inn.**

And there, she **waited.**

And **waited.**

Until **she could wait no more.**

She died in that room—some say **of a broken heart,** others **by her own hand.**

And ever since, she has been **searching for her lost love.**

The Hauntings of Room 502

The librarian's spirit is said to **haunt Room 502,** where guests have experienced:

- **The sound of soft weeping** in the middle of the night.

- **A cold, unseen presence sitting on the edge of the bed.**

- **The feeling of being watched,** as if someone **is waiting for you to speak.**

Some guests **wake to find their blankets slowly being pulled off them,** as if someone **is climbing into bed beside them.**

One man reported waking up to see **a woman in period clothing standing by the window**, staring out at Lake Superior.

She turned toward him.

And as he sat up, **she disappeared.**

The Echoes of Lost Love

Even outside Room 502, the librarian's presence is felt.

• **Guests walking past the room late at night have heard whispers through the door**, though no one was inside.

• Staff members have found **the door locked from the inside**, even when the room was vacant.

• Some have seen **a shadowy figure in the hall**, moving toward Room 502—**then vanishing just before reaching it**.

She is still there.

Still waiting.

Watching the horizon.

Hoping that one day, her sailor will return.

Michigan's Haunted Hotels: Where Spirits Linger and Love Never Dies

• At **The Holly Hotel**, the **former owner still roams the halls, his cigar smoke lingering in the air**, while **a little girl giggles in the darkness**.

• At **The Landmark Inn**, a **heartbroken librarian stands at** the window, searching the waves for a ship that will never return.

These hotels are more than just **historical landmarks**.

They are **haunted by love, loss, and spirits that refuse to move on**.

So if you ever check in and **hear a knock on your door when no one is there**—

Or **wake up to find a shadowy figure standing by your bed**—

Don't be afraid.

They've just been waiting **a very long time…**

And maybe, just maybe, **they're hoping you'll listen to their story.**

Minnesota

Minnesota is a land of **endless lakes, towering pines, and a deep history woven through its streets and buildings.** Some places are **filled with music and laughter**, others **stand as silent monuments to the past**. But some?

Some hold onto the echoes of tragedy.

At **First Avenue in Minneapolis**, the music never truly stops —even for the ghost of a woman who allegedly took her own life there during **World War II. She still lingers, caught in the rhythm of a place that was supposed to bring her joy.**

And high above **Duluth**, on the lonely heights of **Enger Tower**, ghostly figures appear in the mist, **watching from the shadows of a place meant to honor the past.**

Some spirits **dance in the darkness.**

Others **stand in silence, waiting for something only they can see.**

And if you visit?

They might be watching you, too.

First Avenue: The Ghost That Dances in the Dark

(Minneapolis, MN – Where Music and Mystery Collide)

The heart of **Minneapolis' music scene beats inside a dark, windowless building known as First Avenue**.

Legends like **Prince, The Replacements, and Hüsker Dü** have performed here, their sounds echoing through its cavernous walls.

The air is **thick with history**, the walls lined with stars bearing the names of artists who **left their mark on the stage**.

But First Avenue has more than just music legends.

It has a ghost.

The Woman in the Coat Room

The most **famous ghost of First Avenue** is a woman known only by her **tragic ending.**

- The story goes that during **World War II**, a young woman, devastated by heartbreak or despair, **hanged herself inside the venue's coatroom.**

- No one knows exactly **why she did it**, but her presence has **never left**.

- Ever since, her **shadowy figure has been seen near the**

coat check area, appearing suddenly before **fading into the darkness**.

Strange Encounters at First Avenue

Staff and visitors **have experienced chilling encounters** with the spirit of First Avenue:

• **Apparitions of a woman in an old-fashioned dress** appear near the coatroom, her figure flickering **like a shadow caught in the stage lights**.

• Employees cleaning up after concerts have heard **soft crying**, only to find **the room empty**.

• Some **feel a sudden drop in temperature**, their skin prickling **as if someone unseen has just passed by**.

But the most **disturbing stories** come from those who have **seen her face-to-face**.

One security guard, closing up late at night, **felt a presence behind him**.

He turned—

And there she was.

A **pale woman, standing motionless in the darkness, watching him with hollow eyes**.

Before he could react—

She was gone.

More Than One Ghost?

Some believe **she is not alone**.

Other staff members have reported **strange occurrences in the main ballroom:**

• **Lights flicker** at random, even when the electrical system is working perfectly.

• **Shadows move across the stage**, as if unseen performers are **rehearsing for a show that will never come.**

• Some **feel something brush against them in the crowd**, turning to find **no one there.**

First Avenue **is alive with music, energy, and history.**

But **when the last song ends, and the lights go down, the ghosts of its past remain.**

So if you find yourself **alone near the coatroom, feeling a sudden chill creep up your spine**—

You're not alone at all.

Enger Tower: The Spirits Watching from the Heights

(Duluth, MN – A Beacon Overlooking the City... and Something Else Entirely)

Perched high above **Duluth**, Enger Tower **rises like a stone sentinel**, offering sweeping views of **Lake Superior, the harbor, and the city below.**

Built in **1939** as a tribute to **Bert Enger**, a Norwegian immigrant who **donated much of his fortune to Duluth**, the tower was meant to be **a place of peace and remembrance.**

But some who visit **say it is anything but peaceful.**

High above Duluth, something watches from the shadows... and it's been waiting for you

The Haunting of Enger Tower

Visitors who climb the **five stories to the top of the tower** sometimes report **something strange—something they can't explain.**

• Some say they feel **eyes watching them**, though no one is there.

• Others describe **a shadowy figure moving along the edges of their vision**, disappearing before they can look directly at it.

• A few claim to have seen **a misty apparition standing at the top, gazing out over the lake**.

And the most terrifying encounters?

They happen **at night.**

The Man in the Mist

One local legend tells of a **mysterious figure that appears in the fog** surrounding Enger Tower.

- He is described as **tall and thin**, wearing what looks like **a long coat or cloak.**

- He **stands completely still**, his back to visitors, **staring out at Lake Superior.**

- Some who try to approach **find that he vanishes before they can get too close.**

One hiker, climbing the hill to the tower at sunset, reported seeing **a man standing near the stone walls, his hands resting on the railing as if deep in thought.**

As the hiker called out a greeting—

The man disappeared.

Not **walked away**.

Not **faded into the trees**.

Simply vanished.

Leaving behind **only silence and the cold whisper of the wind.**

Other Strange Phenomena

Enger Tower is **not just home to shadowy figures.**

- **Disembodied voices echo from the stairwell**, as if someone unseen is **climbing the tower alongside visitors.**

- **Faint whispers drift through the air**, even when the tower is empty.

- Some visitors describe **feeling a sudden cold presence**, even on warm summer days.

One family, taking a photo at the top, later discovered **an extra figure in their picture**—a **blurred, ghostly face peeking out from behind the stone wall.**

They were the only ones there.

Or so they thought.

The music never stops, but neither does she... a shadow in the rafters, a whisper in the dark, and the lingering presence of a soul that never left. (Image Public domain)

Minnesota's Haunted Landmarks: Where the Past Still Waits

• At **First Avenue**, the ghost of **a woman lost in despair** still lingers, caught in the rhythm of a place where **she once danced but never left**.

• At **Enger Tower**, **a shadowy figure stands watch over Duluth**, waiting for something only he knows.

Some spirits **cry out in sorrow**.

Some **stand in silence, staring out at a world that has long since moved on.**

And some?

Some **are waiting for you to see them.**

So if you visit—

If you hear **footsteps behind you in the tower stairwell**...

If you feel **a hand brush your shoulder at First Avenue**...

If you see **a shadow standing just out of reach in the mist**...

Don't turn away.

Because in Minnesota, **the ghosts are always watching.**

Mississippi

Mississippi is a state where the **past is never far behind**, where **stories of betrayal, murder, and revenge still echo through the woods**. In some places, **the living are not alone**, and the dead continue to walk, waiting for something—perhaps justice, perhaps peace, or simply **someone to witness their final moments**.

At **Stuckey's Bridge** in Meridian, the **ghost of a notorious innkeeper who once robbed and killed travelers still carries his lantern**, walking the riverbank where his own violent end awaits.

And at the **Amos Deason House in Ellisville**, the **ghosts of the Civil War** still walk the halls, with the **screams of a man murdered in cold blood** forever embedded in its walls.

These are not just ghost stories—they are **the lingering shadows of history**, refusing to fade into the past.

Stuckey's Bridge: The Haunting of a Killer Innkeeper

(Meridian, MS – A Bridge That Has Seen Death and Vengeance)

There's a place in **Meridian**, Mississippi, where **the past comes alive in the most chilling way**.

Stuckey's Bridge—a humble crossing over the **Chickasawhay River**—is not known for its beauty or its engineering. Rather, it is infamous for the dark history it holds.

The Legend of Stuckey

The story begins with a man named **Stuckey**, a notorious figure in the **Mid-19th century**. Stuckey was believed to have been **connected with the infamous Dalton Gang**, a group of outlaws who roamed the American West, robbing banks and trains.

But Stuckey didn't just rob banks. He ran an **inn** near the bridge, where **travelers and weary souls would stop for rest**. Unfortunately for them, this was the last stop they would ever make.

• Legend says that Stuckey **lured guests to his inn**, offering them food and shelter before robbing them blind.

• Some say he **murdered those who resisted**, burying their bodies **along the riverbank**.

Eventually, Stuckey's **bloodthirsty deeds caught up with him**, and he was **captured, tried, and hanged from the very bridge he once used to rob his victims**.

But death, it seems, was not enough to stop him.

The river whispers of blood and betrayal... a lantern glows in the darkness, footsteps echo on the bridge, and Stuckey's ghost still walks —forever bound to the crimes of his past. (Image Wikimedia Commons)

The Haunting at Stuckey's Bridge

Since his hanging, **Stuckey's ghost** has been seen **near the bridge**, continuing to **wander the banks of the river where he once committed his grisly acts**.

Witnesses—some of whom claim to have visited the area in search of the legend—report seeing a **shadowy figure** of an **old man carrying a lantern**, his face **hidden in darkness**.

- **The lantern** swings in his hand, casting an eerie light on the water's edge, as he **walks slowly back and forth**, as if still searching for someone.

- Others hear **the sound of loud splashes** coming from the river, followed by the **screams of a man**—as though

Stuckey's ghost is reenacting his own hanging, struggling against the rope that once strangled him.

One visitor, walking near the bridge late at night, claimed to have heard **heavy footsteps behind him**, only to turn and find **nothing**. Moments later, the air became **ice-cold**, and the faint **smell of rotting flesh filled the air**, as though the past **refused to stay buried**.

A Dark Energy That Lingers

The legends surrounding Stuckey's Bridge continue to be told, and some locals claim to feel an **unnerving presence** in the area.

• People walking across the bridge at night often report the sensation of being **watched**, as though **someone is following them**, just out of sight.

• Some have described feeling **a cold hand brush against their skin**, and others have found **their lanterns and flashlights flickering inexplicably**, as if **Stuckey is still in control of the light**.

If you ever visit Stuckey's Bridge, remember: **You're not just walking across a bridge.**

You're walking across **a place of death and vengeance**, where the **ghost of a killer still roams**.

The Amos Deason House: A Mansion Steeped in Blood and Betrayal

(Ellisville, MS – A Home Where Ghosts Never Rest)

In the quiet town of **Ellisville**, Mississippi, there stands a house that seems ordinary on the surface. But **beneath its stately walls** and **broad porches lies a history steeped in betrayal, bloodshed, and ghosts that refuse to fade**.

The **Amos Deason House**, built between **1855 and 1860**, was once home to **Amos Deason**—a Confederate sympathizer and prominent local figure.

The Assassination of Major Amos McLemore

In **1863**, during the height of the Civil War, a local drama unfolded that would forever mark this house with the stains of blood.

Amos McLemore, a Confederate major, had been sent to **punish deserters and Confederate sympathizers**. Among his targets was **Newt Knight**, a farmer and **Union sympathizer** who was **leading a resistance movement** in the area.

The tension reached its peak when Knight confronted McLemore and, in an act of **cold-blooded revenge, shot and killed** him at the doorstep of the Deason House.

Knight was later **captured**, but the house remained forever marked by the brutal death of the Confederate major.

The Haunting of the Amos Deason House

Since the tragic death of McLemore, the **Amos Deason House** has been **plagued by paranormal activity**. Guests and visitors have reported:

- **Unexplained noises—footsteps, muffled voices, and the sound of doors creaking**—coming from empty rooms.

- **Cold spots**, particularly in the room where McLemore was **gunned down**—visitors report an **overwhelming sense of dread** that accompanies them when they approach.

- **Shadows and apparitions**, often seen out of the corner of one's eye, **standing in doorways or watching from upstairs windows**.

But the most disturbing of these phenomena is the **presence of a man**—most likely the spirit of **Amos McLemore himself, forever tied to the place of his murder**.

The Ghost of Amos McLemore

Those who have spent time in the house at night often report the **sight of a tall, dark figure**, wearing what appears to be **Confederate military attire**.

- Some claim to have **seen him standing near the staircase**, his **eyes dark and cold, watching the room as if searching for something**.

- Others have heard **the faint sound of a man's voice**, whispering **softly, as though trying to say something to those who pass by**.

Visitors to the house who have wandered into the rooms late at night have described feeling **watched**, with a **sudden drop in temperature** and **the sensation of something—or someone—standing just behind them.**

And **then there are the voices**.

Guests have often reported hearing **a voice in the house**, faint but distinct, **murmuring commands** or **whispering their names**.

Lost in the echoes of time, he watches...
searching for justice that never came

A House Cursed by the Past

It is believed that the **Amos Deason House is haunted not just by McLemore's spirit**, but by the energy of **the Civil War itself**—a war filled with **betrayal, violence, and the deaths of countless soldiers and civilians.**

Some have described feeling **an overwhelming sadness** when stepping into the house, as though the **grief of all who died here has been trapped** within its walls.

For the people who have entered, the house has never been just a **witness to history**—it has become **a participant in the tragedy**, forever marked by the lives and deaths that shaped it.

Mississippi's Haunted History: Death, Betrayal, and the Ghosts That Remain

• At **Stuckey's Bridge**, the ghost of a **murderous innkeeper still roams,** his lantern flickering along the riverbanks where his victims met their end.

• In the **Amos Deason House**, the **ghost of a murdered Confederate major** watches over the house that bears his blood, his spirit forever tied to the violent act of betrayal.

These places are more than just **sites of murder and violence**—they are **markers of the past**, where the dead refuse to fade and **the ghosts of Mississippi's history** continue to haunt the present.

So if you ever visit these haunted locations, be prepared.

Because in Mississippi, **some spirits are waiting for you to listen.**

Missouri

Epperson House: The Haunting of a Campus Landmark

(Kansas City, MO – A Home Filled with Ghosts and Whispers)

At the heart of the **University of Missouri-Kansas City (UMKC)** campus, amidst the hustle of students and the rush of modern college life, stands a **grand old house** that seems almost out of place among the contemporary buildings and modern lecture halls. It's a house that, despite the bustling energy around it, carries with it the **weight of time**—and some believe, the **spirits of those who never truly left**.

Epperson House, built in the early **20th century**, was once the home of a wealthy businessman and philanthropist, **William Epperson**. A man of high stature, Epperson built the house with great pride, hosting **dignitaries, politicians**, and guests from all walks of life within its walls. The house was, at one point, the center of social and political circles, a place where the **elite** gathered, and history was made.

However, like many grand estates, **Epperson House carries with it more than just stories of wealth and prestige**. It holds **secrets**, some of which have **never been fully understood**—and some of which are said to still walk its hallways.

The Tragic End of William Epperson

Though Epperson was known for his philanthropy and success, the final chapter of his life was far from peaceful. According to local accounts, **William Epperson passed away under mysterious circumstances**. Some say it was the result of natural causes, while others whisper that his death was **less than accidental**—perhaps even the result of foul play. However he died, one thing is clear: Epperson's passing was **unexpected**, and it was **soon after his death that the strange occurrences began.**

The house, once a place of joy and bustling activity, began to feel **different**. Those who lived and worked near the estate reported **unexplained noises—footsteps in the hallways when no one was around** and the unmistakable sound of **doors creaking** when the house had been locked up tight. But it wasn't just the physical sounds that disturbed those in the house—it was something deeper, something far harder to explain.

The Haunting Begins: Whispers in the Walls

Shortly after the property changed hands, the first **whispers of a haunting** began. Students living in the nearby dorms or working in the vicinity started hearing strange **footsteps echoing through the halls late at night**, long after the house had emptied for the day. Staff members working in nearby buildings felt an eerie **presence** in the area, especially around the house's **grand front steps**—as if someone invisible was always just behind them. But no one was there. Or was there?

The echoes of the past still linger... whispers in the dark, footsteps with no owner, and doors that creak open—inviting you into the unknown

Over the years, reports began to accumulate, building a clear picture of **Epperson House's haunted reputation**. More than just sounds, **figures in period clothing began to appear**—often **standing motionless in doorways**, their faces **shrouded in mystery**. These apparitions were not of the modern world; they were **dressed in clothing from the turn of the century**, with **hats, coats, and long flowing skirts**.

Sometimes they would simply **stand still** as if **waiting for something, or someone, to arrive**. At other times, the figures would **move silently across the rooms**, disappearing as quickly as they had appeared.

The Eerie Sounds That Echo Through Time

Perhaps the most chilling of all the phenomena are the **sounds**—especially the soft sounds of **laughter**, **whispers**, and **faint piano music**. On several occasions, witnesses have claimed to hear the unmistakable sound of a **piano being played** in one of the upstairs rooms, even though the house was completely **empty**. The melody was haunting, soft, and forlorn, as if someone—perhaps Epperson himself—was **still lingering in the home he once cherished**.

Other times, it was the sound of **laughter**—light and airy, though **it always seemed to come from nowhere**. Staff members cleaning the building late at night would find themselves alone in the quiet rooms, but the **laughter** would echo around them, like the remnants of an old conversation that had long since ended. Some visitors say that they've felt an **unnerving chill in the air**, as if they had walked into a place caught between two worlds—**the world of the living, and the world of the dead.**

A Watchful Figure at the Window

One of the most persistent and unsettling ghostly reports concerns a **figure standing by the window** of Epperson House. On several occasions, students and passersby have seen the **silhouette of a man** standing by the large, **arched windows** that face the street. The figure is always **dressed in formal, early-20th-century clothing**, and he is always **looking out over the yard**, as though waiting for someone—or perhaps just **waiting for time to pass.**

Some reports claim that the figure is **never clearly visible**, always a **shadow against the light**. But the feeling of **being watched** is unmistakable. Those who have seen the figure often describe a sense of being drawn in, as if the figure is beckoning them to come closer—but only when they take a step forward does it **vanish without a trace**.

The House That Still Waits

Why does **Epperson House** still haunt those who enter it? Why does **Epperson's ghost** refuse to leave? Some believe that **Epperson House was more than just a home for its owner**—it was a **place he loved deeply**, perhaps the only place he truly felt at peace. For years, the house hosted the **elite** and the **famous**, but it also stood as a silent witness to the many **conversations, celebrations**, and **heartbreaks** of those who crossed its threshold. Epperson's **spirit may simply not be ready to let go of that connection**, still walking the hallways, ensuring that the home he built remains as it once was—a **place of grandeur, history, and memories.**

Others believe the house may be haunted by more than just **Epperson's spirit**. Could the **other apparitions** be remnants of the **lives that once filled the rooms**, those who **came and went over the years**, leaving their own indelible marks on the walls?

Still Waiting for an Answer

As the sun sets over the campus and the lights of UMKC flicker on, Epperson House remains a place where **the past refuses to fade**. Visitors, students, and faculty all seem to know the same thing—that **there is something beyond the physical walls of Epperson House**, something that lingers long after the building has emptied.

Epperson's ghost, and the others that haunt the house, don't seem to be malicious. But they are **restless**, caught between the world of the living and the world of the dead. They wait for something—perhaps for **Epperson's house to finally be understood**, or for their stories to be heard.

Next time you pass by Epperson House, you may find yourself **looking up**—and if you do, you might just see a figure in the window, **waiting for someone to come home**.

Vaile Mansion: A House Marked by Tragedy and Spirits

(Independence, MO – A Mansion That Hides More Than Luxury)

Nestled in the quiet, historical town of **Independence**, Missouri, **Vaile Mansion** stands as a stunning testament to wealth, ambition, and the relentless passage of time. Built in the **1880s** by **industrialist Harvey Vaile**, the mansion was once a **symbol of prosperity and high society**—its elegant high ceilings, polished chandeliers, and grand verandas made it the epitome of **luxury and refinement**. Yet beneath the surface of this magnificent estate, there are **whispers of a history steeped in grief, tragedy, and spirits** that still linger in the rooms where time stands still.

A Mansion Shrouded in Tragedy

Harvey Vaile's life, like his mansion, was one of **remarkable success**—he made his fortune in the **railroad industry** and was a man of ambition. The mansion he built was more than just a house; it was a **dream realized**, a monument to his success, and the symbol of the life he envisioned with his beloved wife.

But as so often happens in stories of great mansions and wealth, **the good times didn't last**.

In **1890**, shortly after they moved into the house, Harvey's world came crashing down. His wife, who was the heart of their home, **passed away unexpectedly**, leaving Harvey to confront a **grief so deep that it seemed to cast a shadow over the entire estate**. The vibrant mansion, once alive with laughter and love, became a place of **heavy silence**.

Some believe that **this immense loss**, this **unexpected tragedy**, was the **beginning of the mansion's hauntings**. As if the **house itself, which had once been filled with life and love, could not escape the sorrow it held within its walls**. The weight of grief, it seems, **sank into the very foundation of the house**, lingering like an unspoken memory.

The Hauntings of Vaile Mansion: A History That Won't Let Go

As the years passed, the mansion changed hands, but the **ghosts of Vaile Mansion never left**. Visitors to the mansion today report a variety of **eerie and unsettling experiences**, as if the spirits of the past are still trapped within the grand walls.

Many who venture into the mansion speak of an eerie chill that seems to linger without explanation. **Cold spots** appear suddenly, especially in the **main hallway**—a place that feels especially **haunted**. The temperature plummets as if something, or someone, is **drawing near**.

Some of the **most frequent sightings** are those of a **woman in a long dress**—a woman who, it is believed, is Harvey's late wife.

- **She moves silently through the rooms**, her footsteps light and ethereal, as though the weight of the world no longer presses on her shoulders.

- **Her form appears most often near the grand staircase**, a place that was likely once the site of many happy memories. Visitors have described seeing her **standing motionless**, her face **turned towards the balcony**, as if waiting for someone. But when they approach, she **disappears**—fading into the **thin air** as if she had never been there at all.

The grand halls of Vaile Mansion hold more than just history... shadows shift, whispers linger, and the past refuses to stay buried.
(Image Wikimedia Commons)

The Weight of Unfinished Business

It is said that sometimes, when night falls and the mansion is quiet, the **staff and guests alike report feeling a heavy, unmistakable presence**.

- Many have described the feeling as if **someone is standing just behind them**, watching them, but when they turn around —**the room is empty.**

- **An oppressive silence** falls over certain rooms, and some claim to hear **soft, mournful voices calling from the empty rooms**—whispers of a woman still longing for her husband.

Some believe these voices are the **echoes of Harvey's wife**, searching the halls for the man she lost long ago. The sound is almost **imperceptible**, a faint **cry that lingers in the background**, like a secret that the house is trying to keep.

An Unearthly Connection

Despite these sightings and unsettling experiences, the spirits of **Vaile Mansion** do not seem to be malevolent. There is no **wrath in their presence**—only a **quiet sadness** and the **unanswered longing** that seems to fill the house like smoke. The ghosts that remain are simply **tied to the place**, perhaps drawn by the **unfinished business of love lost** and a **grief that time couldn't heal**.

Some speculate that **Harvey himself**—though never seen—may still be **present in the house**, forever bound to the woman he loved and lost. Visitors have reported **strange sensations** near the **portrait of Harvey Vaile**—a feeling of **eyes watching them**, of being **pulled back to another time**, as if he, too, is stuck in the mansion's labyrinth of memories, unable to leave.

A Mansion That Won't Let Go

The **Vaile Mansion** remains a place where history, tragedy, and the supernatural come together, creating an experience that is more than just a visit to a beautiful home.

For those brave enough to step inside, it's as if the **mansion itself becomes a living thing**, holding its **secrets close**, refusing to let the memories of its past fade away.

Many who have stayed overnight or toured the mansion have **left with the sensation that they were not alone**, as though the very **walls held the souls of those who once lived and loved within them**.

Some visitors leave **in awe**, claiming that they felt an **unearthly connection** to the house—a feeling that they were, in some strange way, being watched over by the spirits that inhabit it.

But others?

They leave with a **sense of unease**, as though the mansion's walls carry **a sorrow that is too heavy to bear**—a sorrow that **no one can truly escape**.

A Legacy of Love, Loss, and the Spirits That Endure

Vaile Mansion is **not just a piece of history**—it is a **place where the dead walk alongside the living**, and where the **past never truly fades**.

The ghosts of **Harvey Vaile's wife** and the **echoes of their lost love** still haunt the mansion, carrying with them the **grief of a bygone era**.

So, if you find yourself in **Independence, Missouri**, wandering the stately halls of Vaile Mansion, know this:

You are walking through a house that has never forgotten its past.

And neither have its ghosts.

Montana

Old Montana Prison: A Legacy of Violence and Death

(Deer Lodge, MT – The Walls That Hold More Than History)

The **Old Montana Prison** stands in **Deer Lodge** like a relic of a brutal past—a place where time seems to stand still. The **imposing stone walls**, the dark **iron bars**, and the **cold, musty air** that fills the cells all contribute to the prison's eerie atmosphere. Built in **1871**, it was originally designed to house the **most dangerous criminals** in Montana, and it quickly gained a reputation as one of the most **inhumane prisons** in the country.

Over the decades, the prison became notorious for its **violent history**—the **riots**, the **executions**, the **grueling conditions** that drove many to madness. Men who were once sentenced to spend their days inside the prison's walls **never truly left**, as the prison would become their tomb, their resting place, and in some cases, the place where they would **live forever** in the form of restless spirits.

The Ghosts of the Old Montana Prison

Those who have dared to visit the **Old Montana Prison** today have been met with the unmistakable sense that the prison is **alive with the past**, filled with the remnants of those who were never able to find peace.

Echoes of the damned still whisper through these stone walls... Do you dare step inside?
(Picture Wikimedia Commons

- In the **early mornings or late nights**, visitors have heard the unmistakable **sound of footsteps**, light but persistent, as though someone is walking down the narrow hallways of the prison. Some believe that the footsteps belong to **the ghosts of prisoners**, still pacing their cells, forever trapped in the prison they called home.

- **Cold spots** often appear in places where the temperature **shouldn't drop**. On a warm day, visitors have reported sudden, **bone-chilling coldness** near the old **execution chamber** or in the **solitary confinement cells**—places where men once fought to retain their sanity before meeting their untimely ends.

• Those who spend the night within the prison walls often report hearing **whispers in the dark**, voices that seem to **murmur unintelligible words**, like the faint echoes of men who have been forgotten by history but **are not ready to be forgotten by the living**. Some claim to have seen **figures standing in the distance**, their faces **hidden in shadow**, only to disappear the moment someone tries to get closer.

The Apparition of the Warden

The prison is also said to be haunted by a more **authoritative spirit**: that of a former **warden** who spent his life maintaining strict order within the prison's walls. His ghost, some say, still **patrols the prison**, ensuring that the **rules are upheld**, even in death. Visitors have reported seeing **a tall figure in uniform**, walking through the halls or **standing by the gates**, as though still keeping an eye on the prisoners, even from the beyond.

The Restless Spirits of Old Montana Prison

The prison's most notorious haunting, however, comes from the **spirits of those who died violently** within its walls. The **execution chamber**, where countless men met their end, is said to be particularly **haunted**.

• Some visitors have described **feeling a cold hand on their shoulder** while standing near the gallows, as though someone is **standing right behind them**.

- Others have reported the **sound of a rope creaking**, only to turn around and find **no one** standing near the gallows.

The violent, oppressive energy of Old Montana Prison has left **its mark on those who died there**, and **their restless spirits refuse to leave**.

Little Bighorn Battlefield: The Spirits of a Brutal Clash

(Crow Agency, MT – Where Soldiers and Warriors Still Fight)

The winds of **Crow Agency**, Montana, blow over the sacred grounds of **Little Bighorn Battlefield**, where one of the **most infamous battles** in American history unfolded. It was here, on June 25, 1876, that **Lieutenant Colonel George Armstrong Custer** and his **7th Cavalry** made their **last stand** against a vastly superior force of **Lakota Sioux** and **Cheyenne warriors**. The battle, which would become known as **"Custer's Last Stand,"** ended in a **decisive defeat** for the U.S. Army, with **Custer and most of his men** killed.

But the battlefield isn't just a **place of history**—it is a **sacred site**, a place where the **spirits of the fallen soldiers**, both **Native American warriors** and **U.S. cavalrymen**, are said to **still walk the earth**. The ground here is **scarred** by the violence and bloodshed of that day, and some believe the **spirits of the dead continue to fight** in a war that **never truly ended**.

The Echoes of War

Visitors to Little Bighorn Battlefield often report hearing **strange sounds** that seem to come from nowhere.

- The **sound of battle cries**, faint but unmistakable, rises in the wind. Some say it's the **warriors of the Lakota and Cheyenne**—still calling to each other in the heat of the fight.

The echoes of war never fade... Do you hear the whispers of the fallen?

- The sound of **gunshots** can sometimes be heard, echoing across the hills as if the battle **is still raging** in the spirits' minds. Some visitors claim they've seen **clouds of dust** where **phantom cavalrymen** seem to appear and vanish, moving quickly across the battlefield, **still charging the hills as they did on that fateful day**.

The Apparitions of Warriors and Soldiers

Perhaps the most unsettling aspect of Little Bighorn Battlefield is the **vision of soldiers and warriors**, seen by those who stand at the markers and **look out over the land**.

- Witnesses have reported **seeing figures in the distance**, **riding horseback**, clothed in traditional warrior attire or military uniforms, **moving silently across the battlefield**, as though still engaged in the same fight they fought over a century ago.

- Some have even described seeing **the ghostly figures of Custer's men**, still wearing their uniforms, **marching across the hilltops**, as if they are **forever trapped in their final moments**.

There are also **numerous reports of "ghost lights"** that appear on the battlefield at night—**flickering orbs of light** that some believe are the **spirits of the fallen soldiers**, still looking for their comrades, still waiting for a battle that never truly ended.

A Land of Echoes and Spirits

The battlefield is **sacred ground**, and the spirits here are not just **bound to the land**, they are **a part of it**. Some say that the spirits of **Custer's soldiers** and **the Lakota and Cheyenne warriors** are caught in an eternal struggle, forever reliving the brutal battle that claimed their lives.

Visitors to Little Bighorn often feel a **chill in the air**, even on the hottest days, and a sense of **being watched** by invisible eyes. The land itself seems to **hold the souls of those who died**, and some believe that the **spirits of the battlefield are restless**, still fighting the war they never left.

Nebraska

Hummel Park: A Place Shrouded in Darkness

(Omaha, NE – The Park Where the Past Comes Alive)

Nestled just outside the bustling city of **Omaha**, **Hummel Park** seems, on the surface, like a peaceful retreat—a place for families to picnic, for joggers to run along the trails, and for children to play among the trees. But if you ask the locals, especially those who have been around long enough, you'll hear whispers about something **darker** that lingers in the park's **shadows**.

Hummel Park has a **history steeped in unsettling urban legends**—tales of **lynchings**, mysterious **disappearances**, and a rumored **colony of albino people** who supposedly once lived in the area. But the real question is: how much of this is **truth**, and how much is the product of local fear?

The trees remember what the earth won't speak... step carefully, or you might hear the whispers too. (Picture Wikimedia Commons)

The Legends of the Park

One of the most well-known tales surrounding Hummel Park involves the **alleged lynchings** that took place there. According to some local legends, a group of men, angry with a particular individual or group, carried out a series of **brutal public executions** in the park, and their **spirits** remain there to this day. People who visit the park in the evening often describe an overwhelming **sense of unease**, particularly near the wooded areas where the hangings supposedly took place.

Another spine-chilling story is the one about the **albino people**. Some say that a colony of **albino individuals** lived in the park in the early 20th century, shunned by society and forced to live in isolation. It's said that they were **targeted by the townsfolk**, and many **believe their spirits never left**—that they still haunt the park, angry and vengeful.

The Haunting Experiences

Visitors to Hummel Park report a range of strange occurrences that suggest something **unnatural is at work**:

• **Disembodied whispers** are often heard in the silence of the woods, as if unseen voices are carrying secrets from the past.

• **The air is thick with an oppressive atmosphere**, especially after the sun sets. Some claim to feel **watched** or followed, as though something or someone unseen is lurking just beyond their vision.

• The most unnerving accounts are from those who have ventured too far into the woods, only to find themselves **unable to escape** the dense trees, as though the park's **very layout changes** to trap them.

One particularly chilling story comes from a **nighttime visitor** who was walking along the park's paths when they suddenly heard **what sounded like footsteps behind them**, despite being completely alone. When they turned around to confront whatever—or whoever—it was, they saw nothing but the eerie stillness of the park. But the footsteps didn't stop—they kept following them, until the visitor quickly fled back to their car, too frightened to turn around again.

Seven Sisters Road: The Road of Blood and Ghosts

(Otoe County, NE – The Road That Should Never Be Traveled Alone)

Seven Sisters Road, located in the **rural hills of Otoe County**, is not just an isolated stretch of road—it's a place where **legend and reality blur**, where those who travel through it after dark often encounter things **no one should see**.

The story behind the road is simple, yet horrifying. According to legend, a **man once hanged his seven sisters** along the hillsides of this winding road. Whether out of madness, revenge, or some other dark motive, the **seven sisters' spirits** are said to still haunt the hills where they met their gruesome end.

The Legend and the Unexplained

The legend of **Seven Sisters Road** is one of the **most terrifying urban legends** in Nebraska. It is said that the man who committed such an act was **driven to madness by the spirits of the sisters**, and that their **restless spirits are still tied to the land**, haunting the road where they perished.

- **Unexplained screams** have been heard late at night, coming from the hills where the sisters were hanged. The sounds seem to **carry through the trees**, and witnesses have said they can almost feel the **anguish** in those cries.

- **Eerie lights** have been reported by travelers, who claim to see **glowing orbs** or **flickering headlights** in the distance, only for the lights to disappear **once they approach**. Many believe this is the work of the sisters, trying to **lure drivers off the road** into the woods, where they are never seen again.

• **Malfunctioning vehicles** are also a common report, with car engines **cutting off unexpectedly**, headlights flickering, and radios going haywire when crossing the haunted stretch of road. Some claim their **cars won't start** once they reach the darkest point of the road.

One group of college students, brave enough to drive down Seven Sisters Road one cold October night, reported hearing **a loud bang on the roof of their car**. When they stopped to investigate, they found no trace of damage—only an eerie **silence** in the air. But as they continued their journey down the road, **a shadowy figure** appeared in front of them, **blocking the path**. As the driver slammed on the brakes, the figure **disappeared**, leaving the group too terrified to move any further.

Alliance Theater: The Ghost of "Mary"

(Alliance, NE – Where the Stage Is Set for Something Otherworldly)

The **Alliance Theater**, built in **1903**, has seen its fair share of history. From silent films to vaudeville performances, it has long been a cultural landmark in **Alliance**, Nebraska. But, like many theaters with a rich history, **it has a darker side**—one that reveals itself when the **lights go out** and the doors close for the night.

Among the ghosts who are said to haunt the Alliance Theater, the most prominent is a woman known simply as **"Mary"**. No one knows who she was in life, but her presence in the theater has been felt for decades.

The Ghost of Mary

The tale of **Mary's haunting** begins like many others—she is believed to be the **spirit of a former theater patron** or even a performer who died under mysterious circumstances. Since the theater's early days, **strange occurrences** have been reported, all centered around her ghost:

- **Footsteps** are often heard in the dark, echoing down empty hallways or across the empty stage. Some staff members say they can hear **someone walking in heels**, but when they investigate, no one is ever there.

- **Disembodied voices** have been reported, particularly late at night when the theater is completely silent. Visitors have reported **faint laughter**, **whispers**, and even the sound of **someone calling their name**—always just on the edge of hearing, but never fully discernible.

- The most unsettling of all are the **sightings of Mary herself**. Patrons and staff alike have seen a **shadowy female figure** standing in the audience section or near the side of the stage, often **dressed in period clothing**. Some say they've seen her watching performances, seemingly **enjoying the show**, while others claim she simply **stares vacantly into the distance**.

Some say 'Mary' still watches from the shadows... footsteps echo when no one is there

The Theater's Eerie Atmosphere

Even for those who haven't seen Mary, there's an undeniable **atmosphere** in the Alliance Theater. It's as though the walls themselves are **charged with the energy of the past**, and as the **curtains rise**, so too do the **memories** of those who once filled the seats. Some believe that Mary's presence is not the only one—the theater, with its long history, could be home to countless other spirits, all tied to the performances, the music, and the stories told there over the years.

Nevada

Nestled amidst the vast deserts and rugged mountains of Nevada, where the **dust of the past still lingers in the air**, there are places that **carry more than just history**. These **haunted hotels**—the **Mizpah Hotel** in **Tonopah** and the **Goldfield Hotel** in **Goldfield**—are not only historic landmarks, but they are also **gateways to the supernatural**, where the **spirits of the past still walk among the living**.

In the **Mizpah Hotel**, the ghost of a **Lady in Red** is said to **haunt the fifth floor**, forever trapped by the tragic events of her life and death. **Pearls mysteriously appear on guests' pillows**, and **chilly whispers** are heard in the dead of night. Meanwhile, at the **Goldfield Hotel**, **Elizabeth's spirit**, believed to have been murdered by the owner, still roams the halls, her **crying voice** echoing through the dark corridors.

These are not just stories—they are **real accounts**, told by those brave enough to stay and **experience the paranormal first-hand**. So, if you dare to visit, you're not just stepping into a historic hotel; you're stepping into **the echoes of the past**, where **the dead still refuse to rest**.

Mizpah Hotel: A Ghost in Red

(Tonopah, NV – A Hotel Haunted by Tragedy and Beauty)

Nestled in the heart of **Tonopah**, Nevada, the **Mizpah Hotel** opened its doors in **1907**, and quickly became one of the most luxurious buildings in the small mining town. With its **rich history**, **elegant design**, and **prime location**, the Mizpah was a beacon of prosperity in the early 20th century. But like many grand hotels, the **beauty of the building hides a tragic secret**—a secret that lingers in the form of a ghostly presence.

The **Lady in Red** is the most famous resident ghost of the Mizpah Hotel. According to legend, she was a **prostitute who met a brutal end** on the fifth floor of the hotel. Some believe she was **murdered by a jealous lover or a client**, though the details of her death remain unclear. What is clear, however, is that her **spirit never left**.

The Lady in Red

The Lady in Red is said to be **dressed in a striking red gown**, with **dark hair** and a **pale face**, as she walks the fifth floor of the Mizpah Hotel. She's **not just a figure in a dress**; she is a **symbol of tragic beauty**, forever caught in the haunting sorrow of her life and death.

- **Guests who stay in the hotel**, particularly those who sleep on the fifth floor, have reported seeing her **appear suddenly**

in their rooms, standing by the bed or **staring out of the window** as if lost in her thoughts.

• Some visitors claim to have **felt a sudden chill**, as if a cold breeze has rushed through the room, only to turn around and find the room **completely empty**, except for the lingering **scent of perfume**.

• Others have heard **whispers**, soft and eerie, in the middle of the night. **Guests often awake to find pearls**, mysteriously placed on their pillows, though no one knows where they came from. These strange occurrences are often seen as gifts from the Lady in Red, **a token from a ghost still longing to be remembered**.

She still waits on the fifth floor... her whispers echo through the halls, but no one is there

Strange Happenings at the Mizpah

While the Lady in Red is the most famous ghost, she's not the only one. Guests and staff alike have reported a variety of eerie phenomena:

• **Footsteps** can be heard in the hallways at night, though no one is around.

• **Objects** like chairs or vases occasionally **move on their own**, shifting position in rooms that are locked and secure.

• The most disturbing reports come from those who have stayed in **Room 504**, the **Lady in Red's haunt**. Some guests claim to have woken up in the middle of the night to find **her figure standing in the corner of the room**, staring at them with empty eyes before vanishing into the darkness.

The Mizpah Hotel is a place where the **line between history and the supernatural** is blurred, and where the spirits of the past are still alive in the present.

Goldfield Hotel: The Spirits of the Forgotten

(Goldfield, NV – A Hotel Built on Blood and Greed)

The **Goldfield Hotel**, built in **1908**, was once considered the **grandest hotel in Nevada**, towering above the surrounding desert landscape. Located in the now-ghost town of **Goldfield**, the hotel was a **symbol of the area's wealth** during the Gold Rush, drawing in miners, investors, and travelers from all over the country.

But, like many places built on greed and ambition, the Goldfield Hotel carries with it a **dark history** that continues to haunt it to this day. Among the most infamous figures in the hotel's history is **Elizabeth**, a woman who is believed to have been **murdered by the hotel's owner** in a crime that shocked the town.

The Tragic Story of Elizabeth

Elizabeth's story is one of **betrayal and tragedy**. Some say she was a **young woman** who worked at the hotel, possibly as a **bartender or a maid**, who became involved with the hotel's owner. The details are murky, but it's believed that **the owner became obsessed with her** and, when she tried to leave him, **he murdered her in cold blood.**

Her body was never found, but her **spirit remains trapped** within the walls of the hotel, forever reliving her brutal death.

Elizabeth never checked out... some say you can still hear her cries echoing through the empty halls. (Picture Wikimedia Commons)

The Hauntings of the Goldfield Hotel

The Goldfield Hotel has a reputation as one of **the most haunted hotels in Nevada,** and the stories of Elizabeth's ghost are among the most chilling. Guests and staff have reported a wide range of supernatural phenomena:

- **Unexplained noises**—the sound of **footsteps, doors creaking,** or **scraping sounds** from empty rooms—can be heard throughout the hotel, especially in the **upper floors** where Elizabeth is said to have spent much of her time.

- Some visitors have seen **a ghostly figure of a woman**, dressed in **period clothing, wandering the hallways,** her face **pale and cold**, as she searches for something—or someone.

- The most disturbing sightings happen in the hotel's **elevator**, where guests have reported **seeing a woman in white** standing silently inside, only for the elevator to **suddenly drop or malfunction** before coming to a stop on an empty floor.

Many of the hotel's ghost stories center around **Elizabeth's vengeful spirit**, which is believed to **haunt the halls, searching for justice and closure**. Some claim to have felt a **cold presence**, especially in the rooms where Elizabeth was said to have been murdered.

Unexplained Phenomena and Unsettling Experiences

The Goldfield Hotel is not just haunted by one spirit—there are **multiple entities** that roam the halls, many of them tied to the dark history of the hotel:

- Some claim to have seen **shadowy figures** moving across the walls, just out of the corner of their eyes.

- **Cold spots** appear unexpectedly, making some guests feel as though they are being **watched by unseen eyes**.

- Visitors have reported hearing **screams** or **cries for help** late at night, as though the hotel itself is haunted by the **tragic memories of all who died there**.

New Hampshire

Mount Washington Hotel: A Grand Hotel with a Haunted Legacy

(Bretton Woods, NH – The Ghost of a Forgotten Heiress)

The **Mount Washington Hotel** is one of New Hampshire's grandest and most historic hotels. Located in the heart of the White Mountains at **Bretton Woods**, this hotel opened its doors in **1902** with a lavish design meant to attract the wealthiest families and travelers. It quickly became known as a **high-society retreat**, hosting dignitaries, celebrities, and even **President Franklin D. Roosevelt**. But behind its magnificent architecture and opulent history lies a darker tale—the **spirit of Carolyn Stickney**, the wife of the hotel's founder.

The ghost of the Princess still lingers... guests wake to find her watching from the foot of their bed. (Image Public Domain)

Carolyn Stickney was known to be a **devoted wife** to the hotel's founder, and she frequently stayed at the hotel even after its completion. Tragically, **Carolyn passed away unexpectedly** at a young age in **1936**, and soon after, strange things began to happen in the hotel. Guests began reporting strange occurrences, particularly in the room where Carolyn once stayed.

The Ghost of Carolyn Stickney

The room where Carolyn Stickney stayed is now known as the **"Princess Room"**, and it is believed to be haunted by her spirit. Guests who stay in this room often report seeing **her apparition**—a **beautiful woman in a flowing gown**, standing near the window, gazing out at the mountain vistas she once adored. Some describe her as appearing **distant and melancholic**, as though she's still waiting for something—or someone.

- **Cold spots** are frequently felt in the Princess Room, even in the middle of summer. Guests often describe a **sharp chill** that settles in the air, almost as though **Carolyn's spirit is still present, longing to be noticed**.

- **Flickering lights** have also been a recurring phenomenon. **Guests report lights dimming** and **flickering on their own**, even when the room has been unoccupied for hours. Many believe this is a sign that Carolyn is trying to communicate.

- **One guest**, spending the night in the Princess Room, awoke to find the **faint smell of perfume in the air**, a scent she didn't recognize. Later, when she explored the room, she found that the perfume was not hers—it was **the scent of roses**. This eerie encounter left her feeling like **someone else was sharing the space with her**.

Guests often report an overwhelming sense of **peace**, but also an unmistakable feeling that **they are not truly alone**. Many believe that Carolyn Stickney's spirit continues to haunt the hotel, keeping a watchful eye over the **grand place she once loved**.

Pine Hill Cemetery: A Place Where the Past Won't Stay Buried

(Hollis, NH – The Haunted "Blood Cemetery")

Tucked away in the quiet town of **Hollis**, New Hampshire, lies a cemetery that has earned the ominous nickname of **"Blood Cemetery"**—a name that stems from the tragic story of **Abel Blood** and his family. The cemetery is the final resting place of **Abel Blood**, a man who lived during the 18th century. Over the years, **his descendants** continued to live in the area, and as time went on, the name "Blood" became both **legendary and unsettling** in the local lore. But it wasn't just the name that made the cemetery notorious—it was the **strange occurrences** that began to happen around the gravesites.

The Unsettling History of Pine Hill Cemetery

The cemetery is home to the grave of **Abel Blood**, who was a well-known figure in the area. But over time, the cemetery became associated with **mysterious occurrences** that drew the attention of paranormal investigators and curious visitors. Some claim that the cemetery was a place of **strange rituals**, while others believe the **spirits of the Blood family** never left, bound to the place where they were buried.

Abel Blood's grave is said to glow at night... but no one knows why

The Haunting Phenomena of Pine Hill Cemetery

Pine Hill Cemetery, despite its serene appearance, has become known for its **eerie atmosphere**, especially at night. The most famous phenomena reported by visitors include:

- **Glowing gravestones**: Some claim that **certain gravestones**, particularly those of the **Blood family**, appear to **glow softly at night**. This phenomenon has been described as an **otherworldly light**, though no one has been able to explain the cause.

- **Ghostly figures**: Visitors and local residents often report seeing **figures moving among the gravestones, wandering the cemetery grounds** in the dead of night. These apparitions are often seen as **silhouettes in white**, drifting silently between the markers.

- **Unexplained sounds**: Some visitors have heard **footsteps, whispers**, or even the **sound of someone crying** coming from the gravesites. The sound of **soft wailing** is particularly unnerving, and some claim to have heard **someone calling their name** from the darkness, only to turn around and see nothing.

- **A chilling sensation**: Perhaps one of the most consistent reports is the **feeling of being watched**. Those who walk through Pine Hill Cemetery at night often describe an overwhelming sense of unease, as though **the spirits are following them**—their eyes invisible but **always on them**.

One particularly eerie incident involved a **local resident** who, while walking through the cemetery at dusk, **felt a sudden drop in temperature**. As they walked deeper into the grounds, they noticed a **shadowy figure near the Blood family gravesite**. The figure was **still and unmoving**, but when the resident tried to approach, the figure **vanished into thin air**, leaving only an eerie silence behind.

New Jersey

New Jersey, with its diverse landscapes, has always been home to deep-rooted folklore and spine-chilling legends. Behind its bustling cities, **quiet forests**, and **desolate roads**, **spirits** and **monsters** lurk in the shadows, waiting to be uncovered by those daring enough to investigate. The **Jersey Devil**, **The Devil's Tree**, and **Clinton Road** are among New Jersey's most well-known haunted locations—each with its own unique and chilling history. So let's dive deeper into each of these eerie legends and the experiences that continue to haunt visitors to this day.

The Jersey Devil: The Creature That Haunts the Pine Barrens

(Pine Barrens, NJ – A Dark and Mysterious Monster)

The **Jersey Devil** is New Jersey's most infamous cryptid, its legend stretching back more than 250 years. The creature is described as a **winged monster with the head of a goat**,

bat-like wings, and **hooves** for feet. It's said to haunt the **Pine Barrens**, a vast, dense forest that spans across several counties in southern New Jersey. While the Jersey Devil is often regarded as a **local urban legend**, many believe there is more to this story, especially given the number of **sightings** and **strange occurrences** that have been reported over the years.

For over 250 years, eerie screams have echoed through the Pine Barrens... Some say the Jersey Devil still lurks, watching from the shadows. (Image Public Domain)

The Origin of the Jersey Devil:

The most popular story about the origin of the Jersey Devil comes from the **Leeds family**, specifically **Mother Leeds**, a woman from the **1700s**. According to legend, she had 12 children and, upon discovering she was pregnant for the 13th time, **cursed the child**, saying, "Let this one be the devil." When the child was born, it immediately transformed into a **monstrous creature** and **flew up the chimney**, disappearing into the Pine Barrens.

Some believe the Jersey Devil was **born from the spirit of the Leeds family's curse**, while others say it is a **misidentified creature** that has lived in the Pine Barrens for centuries. Despite the different versions of the story, one thing remains constant: the **Jersey Devil** is a **creature of myth and terror** whose legend has grown stronger over time.

Sightings and Encounters:

Over the years, there have been countless reports of **sightings** and **encounters** with the Jersey Devil. People claim to have seen a **large, winged creature** flying through the night sky or **moving through the thick woods of the Pine Barrens**. These are just a few chilling accounts:

- **In 1909**, a series of **sightings** were reported across the state. Residents from **Philadelphia** to **Trenton** described seeing a **bat-like creature** with glowing red eyes, **flying at great speed**.

- **Footprints** have been found in the Pine Barrens, often with **cloven hooves** and **clawed toes**. These footprints have been documented by local researchers and have remained a central piece of the mystery surrounding the creature.

• Some reports suggest that the Jersey Devil isn't just a **flying creature**; people have claimed to hear **loud screams**, described as **human-like howls** emanating from deep in the forest. These terrifying sounds, which some believe are the cries of the creature, have been said to send shivers down the spine of even the bravest souls.

Visitors to the Pine Barrens, especially those who venture into the forests after dark, often describe a feeling of being **watched** or **followed**. The experience leaves many feeling uneasy, with some claiming to have witnessed the **shadow of a large winged figure** disappearing into the trees.

The Devil's Tree: A Cursed Oak of Death

(Bernards Township, NJ – A Tree with a Bloody Past)

The **Devil's Tree** in **Bernards Township** is one of New Jersey's most well-known and **ominous locations**. This solitary oak tree is the center of numerous legends, including tales of **suicides**, **lynchings**, and **mysterious deaths**. Its **haunted reputation** stretches back for decades, and it has become the subject of local lore and cautionary tales. Many believe that the tree is **cursed**—and those who disrespect it suffer misfortune or **tragic events** shortly after their encounter.

They say the tree is cursed... those who dare to touch it often regret it

The Dark History of the Devil's Tree:

The origin of the Devil's Tree's curse is tied to the tragic and brutal history of the **early 20th century**. One of the most popular legends suggests that a **man was hanged** from the tree by a **vigilante mob**. Some versions of the story claim the man was accused of **murder**, while others say he was simply a **victim of mob justice**. Regardless of the specifics, it is widely believed that the **tree absorbed the pain and violence of this event**, and ever since, the spirits of those wronged by the tree have **remained trapped**.

Other tales speak of **suicides** near the tree, with individuals said to have **ended their lives** beneath its twisted branches. Some believe the tree became a **site for dark rituals**, with

local gangs or cults using the space to conduct secret and **sinister ceremonies**.

The Haunting of the Devil's Tree:

Visitors who approach the Devil's Tree often report a sense of unease or dread:

• **Strange sounds**—like **whispers, cries, or screams**—can be heard around the tree, especially at night when the area is quiet and still.

• Some claim to have seen **shadowy figures** or **dark silhouettes** near the tree, often disappearing when approached.

• Many who have tried to take pictures of the tree report that their **cameras malfunction** or **photos come out distorted**, with **dark shadows or orbs** visible in the shots.

• **Accidents** and **misfortunes** have been attributed to the tree, from car crashes to inexplicable injuries. Locals who have **disrespected the tree**, whether by carving into it or disturbing its grounds, claim that they've suffered **bad luck** afterward—some with tragic results.

Perhaps the most disturbing phenomenon surrounding the Devil's Tree is the sensation of **being watched**. Visitors to the tree often describe a feeling of **malicious presence**, as though something is watching them from the shadows, just out of sight.

Clinton Road: The Road of Ghosts and Urban Legends

(West Milford, NJ – A Haunted Highway of Mystery)

Clinton Road is a stretch of **desolate highway** located in **West Milford**, New Jersey, that has been **infamous** for decades. Winding through **dense forests**, and **isolated** from the busy roads of the rest of the state, Clinton Road is **shrouded in mystery** and **urban legends**. This haunted road is often considered one of the **most paranormal places** in New Jersey, drawing thrill-seekers, ghost hunters, and skeptics alike.

Clinton Road is known for its eerie, **desolate atmosphere**, where nightfall brings a **sense of dread** that seems to seep into the very ground beneath your feet. It's a road where people have encountered **ghosts, strange creatures, and phantom vehicles**, and the tales of its haunting occurrences are **varied** but equally terrifying.

The Ghost Boy and Other Legends:

One of the most famous legends surrounding Clinton Road is the tale of the **ghost boy** who allegedly **returns coins** thrown into the river near a particular bridge. According to the legend, if you throw a coin into the water and wait, a **small, ghostly hand** will rise from the depths to **return the coin** to you.

Other urban legends associated with Clinton Road include:

• **Phantom vehicles**: Travelers on Clinton Road have reported seeing **headlights in the distance**, only to have them disappear when approached. Some even claim that they've been **chased** by a **phantom car**, only for the vehicle to vanish once the driver stops.

- **Witch gatherings**: Some say Clinton Road was once a gathering place for **witches**, with dark rituals taking place under the cover of night.

- **KKK meetings**: Another chilling legend suggests that the road was also used by the **Ku Klux Klan**, adding an extra layer of horror to its already sinister reputation.

A Road That Never Forgets:

Clinton Road is more than just an isolated highway—it is a place where **urban legends** come to life. Visitors report feelings of being **watched** and describe **strange noises**—like the sound of **footsteps** or **creaking vehicles**—when there is no one else around. Some claim that the **shadows of past gatherings** still linger, leaving behind a sense of oppression.

In New Jersey, **the past is never far behind**. It **haunts the forests, lurks on dark roads**, and **lives in the very earth** beneath the feet of those who dare to venture too close. If you choose to walk through these haunted places, be prepared:

You may not walk alone.

New Mexico

New Mexico is a land of contrasts—**a place where ancient traditions** mix with the **ghosts of the Wild West**, where the **sun sets over deserts filled with history**, and where the **spirits of the past** linger, leaving their mark on the present. From the **legendary St. James Hotel** in **Cimarron**, with its violent past and haunted halls, to the **elegant La Posada de Santa Fe**, home to the restless ghost of **Julia Staab**, and the **KiMo Theater** in **Albuquerque**, where the playful spirit of a **young boy named Bobby** is said to haunt the stage—New Mexico is home to some of the **most intriguing and chilling haunted locations** in America.

Each of these places has a rich history tied to real events—**killings, hauntings, and untold stories**—which have left their **spirits forever bound** to the land, continuing to tell their tales to anyone brave enough to listen.

St. James Hotel: A Place of Blood and Ghosts

(Cimarron, NM – The Wild West Haunt)

The **St. James Hotel** in **Cimarron**, New Mexico, was built in **1872**, at a time when the West was still untamed, filled with **outlaws**, **gunfighters**, and a lawless culture that led to numerous **violent deaths**. The hotel, initially intended to serve as a luxurious stop for travelers and cattlemen, quickly became a **site of many violent encounters**. Over the years, at least **26 men are said to have died** within the hotel's walls, most of them through **gunfights** or **ambushes**, as the region was notorious for lawlessness.

The St. James became a **highly frequented establishment**, drawing in notorious figures like **Wyatt Earp**, **Buffalo Bill Cody**, and **Jesse James**—but it was also a magnet for bloodshed. The **Wild West** atmosphere of danger and violence soaked into the very floors of the hotel, and it's no surprise that the **spirits of the dead** seem to have never left.

The Hauntings of the St. James Hotel:

Today, **the St. James Hotel is renowned for its paranormal activity**. Guests and staff alike have reported chilling experiences that hint at the **spirits still haunting the premises**:

- **Cold spots** are often felt in various rooms, particularly in areas where **violent deaths** occurred. Guests have been startled by sudden drops in temperature, despite the hotel being warm and inviting.

- **The smell of cigar smoke** is a common phenomenon—strange for a modern hotel, considering the building has **long since ceased to allow smoking**. Some believe the **cigar smoke** is tied to the spirit of a **former guest or outlaw**, perhaps someone who met a violent end in one of the hotel's rooms.

- **The sound of footsteps** has been reported in the hotel's **hallways**, especially at night when no one else is around. Some believe these footsteps belong to the **spirits of those killed within the hotel**, walking the halls in their final moments.

Over 20 people were killed in this hotel... some say their spirits never left. (Pictured Wikimedia Commons)

Perhaps the most famous ghost associated with the St. James is **the spirit of a man named Thomas**—who, after being shot and killed in the hotel during a gambling dispute, reportedly continues to make his presence known. One guest claimed to have **felt a cold hand on their shoulder** in the **lobby**, only to turn around and find no one there.

La Posada de Santa Fe: The Spirit of Julia Staab

(Santa Fe, NM – A Haunted Hotel with a Tragic Love Story)

In the historic city of **Santa Fe**, **La Posada de Santa Fe** is known for its charming adobe architecture and inviting atmosphere. But this once-grand **mansion**, which was later converted into a hotel, has a **tragic and haunting past**. La Posada is built upon the foundations of the **Staab House**, a once-stately home that belonged to **Abraham Staab**, a wealthy businessman who moved to Santa Fe in the **19th century**. The house was built for his wife, **Julia Staab**, and the two lived there happily for many years.

However, Julia's life was not without hardship. She suffered the **loss of several children** and spent much of her later years in mourning. Her death, in **1896**, was sudden, and some believe she died of a broken heart. Soon after her passing, **strange things started happening in the house**—and it wasn't long before Julia's **spirit became an enduring presence**.

The Hauntings of La Posada de Santa Fe:

La Posada de Santa Fe is now a popular hotel, but many guests have **reported eerie occurrences** that seem tied to the lingering presence of Julia Staab:

- **Julia's apparition** is said to wander the hotel's halls, particularly near her former bedroom. Guests have described seeing a **beautiful woman in Victorian clothing**, standing near the window or walking through the halls as though lost in thought.

- Some guests have reported feeling **a cold breath** or **a sudden chill** when passing by certain rooms or hallways. Julia's ghost is often described as being a **sad, melancholy figure**, still mourning the loss of her children and her beloved home.

- There have also been reports of **unexplained sounds**, such as **soft whispers** or the **sound of footsteps**, as though Julia is still moving through the rooms, **watching over her former home**.

Interestingly, guests have found **coins or small objects** in the room where Julia passed away, leading many to believe she may still be reaching out, seeking **remembrance** or **closure**.

The KiMo Theater: A Haunted Stage

(Albuquerque, NM – The Ghost of Bobby)

The KiMo Theater in **Albuquerque** is not only a beloved **historic theater** but also a **haunted one**, steeped in both cultural significance and ghostly legends. Built in **1927**, the KiMo is an architectural gem, designed in the **Pueblo Deco style**, blending **Southwestern motifs** with the grandeur of the early 20th century. However, beneath its grand exterior lies a **haunting history** that involves the ghost of a young boy named **Bobby**.

The story of Bobby's death is tragic—he was a **young boy** who was **accidentally killed in the theater** when the building was still in its early years. Some believe that Bobby's **spirit became tied to the theater**, and he has since been roaming the stage and the audience areas, occasionally getting up to his mischievous antics.

The Hauntings of KiMo Theater:

Today, the KiMo Theater is known not only for its rich history and stunning performances but also for its **paranormal activity**, much of which is attributed to Bobby's playful spirit:

• Performers and staff members often report **odd occurrences** before or during shows—such as **objects being moved** or **lights flickering unexpectedly**. Some believe Bobby is responsible for these mischievous events, his spirit enjoying the attention from the living.

• One of the most famous aspects of the KiMo Theater's haunting is the **ghost boy**, Bobby, who is said to **appear in the shadows of the theater**, sometimes sitting in the audience during performances or walking through the stage.

• **Offering rituals** have developed around Bobby's spirit. Performers and crew members have been known to leave **small toys or treats** backstage, hoping to **appease Bobby** and keep him from causing any disruptions during the shows.

Bobby's spirit is said to be a **friendly ghost**, though mischievous, and his presence has become a **charming part of the KiMo Theater's atmosphere**. Visitors often claim that after a performance, they feel as though **Bobby has watched over them**, ensuring a successful and enjoyable show.

In New Mexico, the **past is never gone**, and the **spirits of the dead** continue to walk the land, **haunting the places** where they once lived, loved, and died. If you ever visit these places, remember that you are not simply visiting **historic landmarks**—you are stepping into **the realm of the supernatural**, where the **dead still live**.

New York

Amityville Horror House: America's Most Infamous Haunting

(Amityville, NY – A House Stained with Blood and Fear)

Located in the quiet suburban neighborhood of **Amityville, Long Island**, stands a house so notorious that it became the inspiration for **books, films, and endless nightmares**. In **November of 1974**, Ronald DeFeo Jr. brutally murdered his parents and four siblings as they slept peacefully in their beds, a horrific crime that would forever change the legacy of the seemingly ordinary home.

Shortly after this tragedy, the **Lutz family** moved in, unaware that their lives were about to be consumed by **terror and dread**. The family lasted just **28 days** before fleeing in fear, claiming they had been driven from their home by **violent supernatural forces**.

Six were murdered in their sleep... the ones who came after heard whispers in the walls. (Picture Public Domain)

A Haunting Legacy

Visitors, neighbors, and paranormal investigators have reported numerous eerie experiences since the infamous murders:

• **Strange voices and whispers** are often heard, particularly at night, echoing through the halls as if the walls themselves speak.

• **Shadowy figures** have been reported, moving swiftly across rooms or standing menacingly at windows, watching anyone who dares approach.

• **Sudden temperature drops**, inexplicable feelings of dread, and the sound of footsteps coming from empty rooms have left visitors shaken and frightened.

• Most chilling of all are the persistent claims of **phantom gunshots** and the feeling of **being watched by unseen eyes**, believed by some to be the spirits of the murdered **DeFeo family** still reliving their last, tragic night.

The Amityville House's gruesome past has permanently stained its reputation, transforming it into a haunting monument to tragedy and fear.

Rolling Hills Asylum: Home to Lost Souls

(East Bethany, NY – Where Spirits of the Forgotten Still Linger)

In the rural quiet of **East Bethany**, New York, sits an imposing building known as **Rolling Hills Asylum**—once known as the **Genesee County Poor Farm**. Established in **1827**, this place provided refuge—and sometimes imprisonment—to society's **forgotten souls**: the mentally ill, orphans, the elderly, and those deemed unfit by society. Throughout its long history, thousands passed through its halls, and many **never left alive**.

This was not just a shelter—it was a place of suffering, hardship, and often death. Many who died there had no family, no identity, and were buried in **unmarked graves** on the grounds.

Echoes of the Forgotten

Today, Rolling Hills Asylum is considered one of the **most haunted locations in New York**. Its halls are filled with paranormal activity, as reported by countless visitors:

- **Apparitions** of former residents, including a **seven-foot-**

tall shadowy figure known as "Roy", are frequently encountered wandering the dark hallways.

• Visitors report hearing **the cries and whispers** of spirits who seem desperate to be remembered. These voices come from empty rooms, often calling out in anguish.

Over 1,700 souls were laid to rest here... some never left.
(Picture Wikimedia Commons)

• Visitors frequently describe encountering the apparition of **a nurse**, silently walking the halls as if still attending to patients long gone.

• Perhaps the most eerie is the presence of **children's laughter and giggles**, echoing faintly in the asylum's empty corridors, even though no children are present.

At Rolling Hills, it feels as though **the past never left**, and the building itself is a **monument to those forgotten**—their spirits trapped and longing to be remembered.

Morris-Jumel Mansion: Spirits from New York's Revolutionary Past

(Manhattan, NY – History and Hauntings in Manhattan's Oldest Mansion)

Standing proudly on a hilltop overlooking **Upper Manhattan**, the historic **Morris-Jumel Mansion**, built in **1765**, is Manhattan's oldest surviving residence. Initially constructed for British officer **Roger Morris** and later home to the wealthy **Stephen and Eliza Jumel**, the mansion saw both Revolutionary War strategy meetings (George Washington himself once used the mansion as headquarters in **1776**) and the dramatic, luxurious parties hosted by the infamous socialite **Eliza Jumel**.

But beneath its elegant exterior and historical grandeur lies a **sinister side**. Rumors of paranormal activity date back over a century, centered primarily around the mansion's most famous resident: **Eliza Jumel**, who lived and died within its walls.

Haunted by History

Visitors to the mansion frequently report experiences that suggest **Eliza Jumel's spirit** has never left the home she loved so dearly:

- **The apparition of a woman dressed in 19th-century attire**—believed to be Eliza—has been seen pacing the halls or staring out windows, as though awaiting visitors who never arrive.

- Staff have described encounters with a ghostly figure on the mansion's staircase—dressed elegantly and silently ascending before vanishing entirely.

- **Unexplained voices and whispers** echo through empty rooms, especially in the parlor and Eliza's bedroom, as though the past continues its conversations long after death.

- Many guests experience sudden **cold drafts and chills**, even on warm days, as though Eliza herself passes by them, invisible yet unmistakably present.

One particularly haunting story tells of schoolchildren visiting the mansion who saw a **woman dressed in period clothing** standing at the upstairs window, gazing down at them. Upon investigation, staff discovered the mansion was empty—but many were certain they had glimpsed **Eliza herself**, still observing her home from beyond the grave.

New York is a place where history and hauntings blend, where the **spirits of the past** still walk, talk, and interact with those who dare to enter their domain. If you ever find yourself at these haunted locations, remember:

You are stepping not just into **history**—but into the very presence of the **restless dead**.

North Carolina

The Brown Mountain Lights: Spirits in the Mist

(Brown Mountain, NC – The Ghostly Orbs That Defy Explanation)

For over a century, curious travelers, locals, and paranormal investigators have journeyed to the ridges of **Brown Mountain** in western North Carolina, hoping to catch a glimpse of the **famous ghostly orbs**. The Brown Mountain Lights are strange, glowing balls of light that mysteriously appear, dance, and disappear along the mountain's slopes. **Scientists, historians, and believers** alike have tried—and failed—to fully explain their origins, leaving the mystery intact.

Ancient Legends

The legend of the Brown Mountain Lights has its roots deep in local folklore. According to Native American stories, these luminous orbs are the **spirits of Cherokee maidens** still searching through the mountain mist for their lost loved ones

—warriors who vanished in battle long ago. Others claim they are the lanterns of **searchers** who never found their way home.

For centuries, the glowing orbs have appeared... are they lost spirits searching for their own way home.

Unexplained Encounters

Those who visit Brown Mountain often report eerie experiences:

• Witnesses describe seeing **luminous balls of red, blue, or white** floating above the treetops. Some lights hover gently, others move erratically, and some appear to chase those brave enough to approach.

• Visitors frequently describe feeling a profound sense of awe and sadness, as though they're witnessing something deeply emotional or sacred.

• Some travelers say the lights respond directly to human presence, dimming or brightening as if aware they are being observed.

Over the decades, numerous scientific explanations have been proposed—from marsh gas to reflections and atmospheric anomalies—but none have satisfied everyone. Today, the Brown Mountain Lights continue to haunt and fascinate those who witness their ethereal glow, forever dancing in the darkness as a poignant reminder of North Carolina's mysterious past.

The Devil's Tramping Ground: A Circle of Evil

(Bear Creek, NC – Where Nothing Grows and Evil Walks)

Hidden deep in the woods near the quiet rural community of Bear Creek, North Carolina, lies an eerie anomaly known as the **Devil's Tramping Ground**—a mysterious, barren circle about forty feet wide where absolutely **nothing grows**. The soil is mysteriously sterile, and any attempts to plant or sow grass have failed, puzzling scientists and locals alike for generations.

Nothing grows here... nothing stays here... but something is always watching.

A Circle Where Evil Walks

Local legends claim this bizarre circle is **the Devil's personal walking path**, a place where he appears each night, pacing restlessly, plotting his dark schemes against humanity. This chilling explanation has persisted through generations, supported by unnerving experiences and reports:

• Visitors have placed objects—stones, sticks, even furniture—inside the circle overnight, only to find them **mysteriously moved outside the circle by morning**, as if something—or someone—had cleared the space.

• Campers daring enough to stay overnight report hearing the unsettling sound of **footsteps circling their tents**, and feeling as though someone is watching closely, even when no one is visible.

- Dogs brought near the circle frequently act strangely, whining, barking uncontrollably, or refusing to enter the mysterious barren space altogether.

Despite attempts to scientifically explain the phenomenon—soil samples, radiation tests, geological analysis—no definitive cause for the barren circle has ever been discovered. Thus, the legend endures, leaving many convinced that this mysterious ring of deathly earth is truly where the Devil himself treads each night, forever marking his territory in North Carolina's soil.

The Carolina Theatre: Haunted by Fire and Tragedy

(Greensboro, NC – Ghostly Echoes from the Past)

In downtown Greensboro stands the grand **Carolina Theatre**, an elegant building steeped in history, built in **1927** as one of the city's premier entertainment venues. The theater, beautifully ornate and opulent, was beloved by audiences and performers alike for decades, until tragedy struck on a cold night in **1981**. A devastating fire swept through the theater, damaging much of the building and claiming the life of a woman who was tragically unable to escape the blaze.

A Tragic Haunting

Ever since that terrible night, strange occurrences have plagued the restored Carolina Theatre. Staff, performers, and visitors have shared chilling experiences they attribute to the theater's tragic past:

- The apparition of a woman has frequently been seen wandering the halls or seated silently in the empty auditorium, gazing sadly toward the stage. Many believe this ghostly figure is the woman who perished in the fire, still reliving her final moments.

- Staff members have reported hearing inexplicable sounds of footsteps, whispers, and even faint cries for help, especially in areas where the flames once burned fiercest.

- Lights flicker, doors open and close on their own, and cold drafts suddenly fill rooms—even during warm summer performances—leaving visitors feeling watched by unseen eyes.

In an attempt to understand and perhaps appease the lingering spirit, paranormal investigations have taken place at the Carolina Theatre, with investigators documenting **strange temperature fluctuations** and **unexplained electrical disturbances**.

Today, the Carolina Theatre continues to operate, hosting performances and events—yet the **ghostly presence** remains a part of its story, forever linked to the tragic events of that night. Visitors can't help but wonder whether the woman who perished still remains, silently watching over the place she loved, her presence a haunting reminder that **not all history fades with time**.

In North Carolina, these haunting locations are more than mere stories—they're windows into the **state's hidden past**, where the supernatural remains close, the mysteries persist, and the **past still walks among us**.

North Dakota

Liberty Memorial Building: Home of the Stack Monster

(Bismarck, ND – A Ghostly Presence in the Archives)

Located near the heart of North Dakota's capital city, the Liberty Memorial Building in Bismarck is not only a historic landmark, but also the site of a haunting that employees speak of in hushed whispers. Constructed in 1924 as a tribute to World War I veterans, this majestic building houses the North Dakota State Library and Archives—an ideal place for history to manifest into something far more unsettling.

The Legend of the Stack Monster

For years, former employees and archivists working late into the night have described eerie encounters with a mysterious presence they've nicknamed the **"Stack Monster."** These encounters typically occur deep within the archival stacks, a maze of shelves filled with countless historical records and forgotten memories.

• Employees have reported sudden, unexplained drops in temperature while working alone, accompanied by a powerful feeling of dread—as if an invisible presence is standing right beside them.

• Others have heard heavy footsteps echoing down empty corridors, rustling papers, and quiet whispers that seem to come from nowhere.

• Some archivists swear they've glimpsed a shadowy figure darting between shelves, just out of clear sight, vanishing before they can investigate.

Deep within the archives of the Liberty Memorial Building, footsteps echo where no one walks. The 'Stack Monster' watches in silence, hidden among the shelves. (Image Public Domain)

Despite extensive research into the building's past, the identity of the "Stack Monster" remains unknown. Could this spirit be that of a long-forgotten archivist, still watching over the records? Or perhaps it's someone who was drawn to the powerful history preserved within these walls. Either way, the Stack Monster continues to haunt those who delve too deeply into the archives, reminding them that history is never truly past—it lingers, always watching.

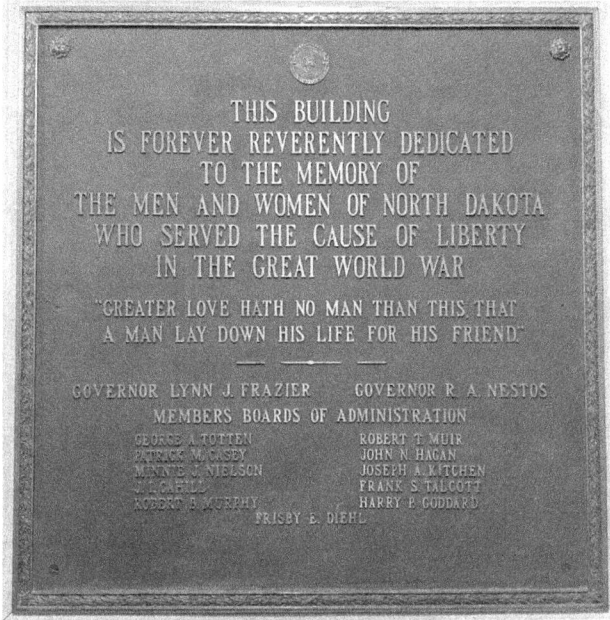

Names etched in stone... but some say the past still whispers within these walls. (image Public Domain)

Saint Anne's Guest Home: The Ghost of Sister Mary Murphy

(Grand Forks, ND – A Nun's Tragic End and Restless Spirit)

Saint Anne's Guest Home, a Catholic care facility nestled in the community of Grand Forks, seems warm and inviting at first glance. Founded with compassion and care, the facility has provided shelter and solace to many residents. Yet beneath its calm exterior lies a haunting story of tragedy and loss.

The Tragedy of Sister Mary Murphy

Its walls offer care and comfort... but some say a restless spirit still walks the halls. (Picture Wikimedia Commons)

In 1978, Sister Mary Murphy, a dedicated nun known for her gentle nature and compassion, experienced personal anguish that drove her to despair. On a quiet evening, she climbed to the top of the building's bell tower and tragically took her own life. This heartbreaking event left a lasting imprint, and it wasn't long before strange occurrences began.

• Residents and staff alike have reported seeing the apparition of a nun dressed in traditional habit, silently wandering the halls, as though lost or searching for something she cannot find.

• Many visitors claim to experience an overwhelming sadness or heaviness when near the bell tower—some even reporting hearing the faint sound of sobbing or the distant tolling of bells.

• Staff members working night shifts frequently encounter sudden chills, unexplained footsteps, and doors opening or closing on their own—believed by many to be Sister Mary Murphy's restless spirit still caring for the place she once loved deeply.

To this day, residents of Saint Anne's Guest Home often feel comforted rather than frightened by the nun's ghostly presence. Her spirit, though restless, seems gentle, as if she's still trying to offer comfort in the halls she walked during life, trapped perhaps by sorrow or a lingering sense of duty.

Gravity Hill: Defying the Laws of Nature

(Near Sentinel Butte, ND – An Unexplained Phenomenon)

Out near Sentinel Butte in the remote and starkly beautiful landscapes of western North Dakota lies a place that challenges the very laws of physics: Gravity Hill. At first glance, it seems like an ordinary road, winding gently uphill through the lonely countryside. But those who stop here experience something astonishing—cars placed in neutral inexplicably roll uphill, defying gravity itself.

Cars roll uphill... but no one knows what unseen force is pushing them.

Mystery of Gravity Hill

Scientists and skeptics have tried to explain Gravity Hill as an optical illusion—a trick of perspective that makes an uphill slope appear downhill—but locals whisper different explanations.

• According to local legends, the phenomenon is paranormal in nature, a sign that the area is haunted by spirits who manipulate reality itself. Some say it's the ghosts of Native Americans who once inhabited these lands, drawing attention to sacred or forgotten places.

• Visitors who test the hill often report feeling an odd, almost magnetic pull as their vehicle begins its bizarre upward journey. Others describe an eerie sensation of being watched or guided by an unseen presence.

• Paranormal enthusiasts, curious travelers, and families all gather at Gravity Hill to experience the strange occurrence firsthand—only to leave perplexed and fascinated, wondering whether what they've experienced was simply a clever illusion, or something genuinely supernatural.

Despite rational explanations offered by science, Gravity Hill's allure remains strong. For those who've visited, the experience becomes a cherished memory, a glimpse into the unknown, and a reminder that in North Dakota, mysteries can still be found in the most unexpected places.

In North Dakota, history is never just history—it's alive, restless, and waiting. These haunting places prove that even in the quietest corners, the past refuses to stay buried.

Ohio

Ohio is a land steeped in history, filled with beautiful landscapes, bustling cities, and **haunting echoes of the past**. Yet beneath its tranquil facade lies a world of mystery and the supernatural, where restless spirits still roam. In the eerie darkness of the **Ohio countryside**, along abandoned hallways of historic prisons, and behind the ornate facades of Victorian mansions, Ohio's haunted legends have taken root. From the mysterious lantern-bearing specter of **Moonville Tunnel**, to the anguished souls within the forbidding walls of **Ohio State Reformatory**, and the secrets lurking behind the ornate windows of **Franklin Castle**, these chilling stories captivate those brave enough to explore them.

The Ghostly Lantern-Bearer of Moonville Tunnel

(Moonville, OH – A Ghostly Warning from Beyond the Grave)

Deep within the rugged woods of southeastern Ohio lies a crumbling relic of the past—the **Moonville Tunnel**, a ghostly reminder of a long-abandoned mining town. Once bustling with coal miners and railway workers in the late **1800s**, Moonville was a small community dependent on the railroad. Today, the town itself is gone, reclaimed by the forest, but the **Moonville Tunnel** remains—dark, moss-covered, and steeped in eerie silence.

They say if you enter the tunnel at night, you might see the lantern... but never the man holding it

The Haunting Legend

According to legend, in the late 1800s, a brakeman or signalman working along the railroad met a tragic fate inside the Moonville Tunnel. As he stood holding his lantern, signaling trains, he was struck and killed, unable to escape an oncoming locomotive. Since that night, the tunnel has become a paranormal hot spot, where his spirit is said to linger, forever trying to warn travelers of the danger he could not avoid himself.

Travelers venturing through the Moonville Tunnel today report chilling encounters:

- **The phantom lantern**: Visitors often see a flickering, ghostly light moving through the tunnel, held aloft by an unseen figure. Witnesses describe the eerie sight as the glow of an old railroad lantern—yet no one is ever there when approached.

- **Ghostly figure sightings**: Many visitors swear they've glimpsed the silhouette of a shadowy man standing within the tunnel, silently watching before disappearing entirely.

- **Sudden temperature drops**: People who enter the tunnel frequently experience sudden chills and an oppressive sense of dread, as if stepping into another era—into the last moments of the brakeman's tragic death.

- **Whispers in the darkness**: Some who venture through the tunnel alone have heard quiet whispers echoing along its brick-lined walls, warning them to leave before another tragedy occurs.

To this day, Moonville Tunnel remains a destination for thrill-seekers and paranormal investigators, hoping to catch a glimpse of the **lantern-bearing ghost**, forever trapped between life and death.

Ohio State Reformatory: Echoes of Pain and Despair

(Mansfield, OH – Where the Past Never Truly Leaves)

The **Ohio State Reformatory** in Mansfield is an imposing structure built between **1886 and 1910**, once serving as a prison renowned for its harsh conditions, suffering, and violence. Behind its massive Gothic facade, prisoners endured cruel treatment, isolation, and even death, leaving behind a lasting spiritual imprint. Closed since 1990, the reformatory's violent history still lingers, making it one of the most notoriously haunted locations in America.

Listed by the Travel Channel and countless online sources as one of the most terrifying and haunted places in America, the Ohio State Reformatory is where restless spirits still roam, and whispers of the past echo through its decaying halls. (Picture Wikimedia Commons)

Restless Souls Behind Bars

Today, visitors and paranormal researchers report deeply unsettling experiences within the old prison walls:

• **Shadowy figures** roam the cellblocks and solitary confinement wings, often glimpsed darting quickly between cells, as though hiding from unseen guards.

• **Echoing footsteps and doors slamming shut**: Guests have reported these phenomena frequently—sounds of heavy prison doors slamming echo through empty corridors, long after the building has closed to visitors.

• **Whispers and screams**: Soft whispers, pleas for help, and anguished cries fill the darkness, as though the spirits of inmates long past are still reliving their suffering.

• **The Cell of Solitary**: Perhaps the most haunted area of the prison is solitary confinement—where guests have reported a sense of oppressive dread, nausea, and even the feeling of being touched by unseen hands.

The Ohio State Reformatory has become a magnet for paranormal enthusiasts, who believe the souls of prisoners remain trapped here, forever reliving their darkest hours, unable to find rest or forgiveness.

Franklin Castle: Cleveland's Most Haunted Mansion

(Cleveland, OH – Mystery, Tragedy, and the Ghosts Within)

Standing tall and forbidding amidst the busy streets of Cleveland, the ornate Victorian mansion known as **Franklin**

Castle is notorious not just for its elaborate architecture, but also for its disturbing history. Built in **1881** by Hannes Tiedemann, a wealthy German immigrant, the mansion has witnessed tragedy after tragedy. Tied closely to rumors of murder, betrayal, and heartbreak, Franklin Castle has earned a reputation as **one of the most haunted buildings in America**.

A History of Heartache

The original owner, Hannes Tiedemann, suffered immense personal loss, as several of his family members—particularly his young children—died mysteriously or under questionable circumstances inside the home. Whispers of Tiedemann's cruelty circulated, suggesting he may have been involved in their tragic deaths. Over the years, rumors of secret passageways, hidden rooms, and violent events have further darkened its legacy.

Hauntings in the Castle

Those who dare to step inside Franklin Castle today report disturbing experiences that confirm the mansion's dark past:

- **Ghostly apparitions**: The spirits of women and children are frequently seen walking the halls, sometimes crying, sometimes merely staring silently at visitors.

- **The sound of a crying child**: Visitors often hear the heart-wrenching sobs of a child echoing through empty rooms—believed to be the ghost of Tiedemann's daughter, Emma, who died tragically young.

- **Moving objects and footsteps**: Doors slam, footsteps echo, and shadows move through rooms untouched by living hands. On occasion, personal belongings disappear, only to reappear elsewhere in the mansion hours later.

- **Cold spots and eerie whispers**: Visitors often feel a sudden, inexplicable chill, as though someone or something has passed through them. Whispers heard clearly in empty rooms add to the sense that Franklin Castle's tragic history remains vividly alive.

The castle has changed hands many times over the years, yet each owner leaves quickly, unsettled by experiences that defy explanation. Today, the castle still fascinates paranormal researchers and historians alike, all hoping to unlock the secrets hidden behind its walls—and perhaps understand why its spirits remain bound to the property, forever trapped by their tragic past.

In Ohio, history doesn't merely reside in books and museums—it breathes, moves, and whispers in the darkness, forever reminding us that some chapters of the past remain eternally unfinished.

Oklahoma

The Stone Lion Inn: A Haunting Legacy of Innocence Lost

(Guthrie, Oklahoma – Echoes from Beyond the Grave)

In the picturesque town of **Guthrie, Oklahoma**, sits a grand Victorian mansion known as the **Stone Lion Inn**, built in 1907 by wealthy local businessman **F.E. Houghton**. Originally constructed as a luxurious home for the Houghton family, the sprawling Victorian mansion, with its stately façade, intricate woodwork, and elegant rooms, quickly became one of Guthrie's most admired residences. But behind its refined appearance lies a deeper, more mysterious story—one touched by tragedy and shadowed by spirits that still linger in its ornate halls today.

In the early 1900s, the mansion was a lively place filled with laughter, children's games, and family gatherings. But when tragedy struck in 1917, the home would forever be changed. Augusta Houghton, the playful and beloved eight-year-old daughter of the Houghton family, became gravely ill with whooping cough—a deadly disease at the time. Despite the family's desperate attempts to save her, young Augusta passed away, leaving behind grief and sorrow that would linger through the generations.

A Child's Spirit Still Plays

Almost immediately after Augusta's death, strange events began to occur in the Stone Lion Inn. Family members and visitors alike claimed they could hear soft laughter, faint giggles, and the footsteps of a child running through the hallways and bedrooms. But when they investigated these mysterious noises, they found nothing but silence and empty spaces.

Today, the Stone Lion Inn operates as a charming bed-and-breakfast and is widely recognized as one of the most haunted locations in Oklahoma. Visitors travel from all over the country, drawn by the promise of a paranormal experience. Augusta's presence remains the inn's most frequently reported haunting, her spirit seeming to prefer playful interaction to frightening encounters:

• Guests frequently describe hearing **soft laughter and whispers**, often echoing in empty hallways or behind closed doors, as if Augusta is playing hide-and-seek with the living.

• Doors throughout the inn open and close mysteriously, sometimes gently and other times dramatically, as if a child is running playfully through the halls.

• Many visitors have reported feeling the sensation of **small, cold fingers tugging gently on their clothing**—especially in the bedrooms that once belonged to the Houghton children—

an experience that leaves guests both startled and touched by Augusta's lingering spirit.

Mysteries of the Attic and Beyond

While Augusta remains the most prominent ghost, she is not alone. The inn's attic, once a lively play area for the Houghton children, is said to harbor its own eerie secrets. Guests who venture there late at night have described hearing **disembodied laughter**, footsteps pacing back and forth, and the sound of **toys moving as if a child is playing quietly alone**.

Other unexplained phenomena include:

- **Doors and windows opening and closing spontaneously**, often witnessed by multiple people simultaneously.

- **Disembodied voices**, including children's conversations and occasional laughter, which echo softly through the quiet halls late at night, leaving guests uneasy yet fascinated.

- **Footsteps**, particularly small and playful ones, are frequently heard running through corridors, even when the building is otherwise empty.

Ghostly, Yet Gentle

Unlike many haunted locations, the Stone Lion Inn's atmosphere is rarely described as frightening or oppressive. Instead, visitors and paranormal researchers often describe an overwhelming feeling of warmth, nostalgia, and gentle curiosity—almost as though Augusta and the other spirits still lingering within its walls are merely reaching out, seeking company or comfort from the living.

This uniquely comforting haunting makes the Stone Lion Inn both beloved and cherished, a place where history blends seamlessly with mystery, and where the tragic loss of a child has become a story that touches the hearts of those who visit.

More Than a Haunting—A Reminder of Guthrie's Past

Today, the Stone Lion Inn continues to host guests, as well as popular murder mystery weekends that embrace its reputation for ghostly encounters. Whether drawn by history or by paranormal fascination, visitors are invariably left touched by the gentle spirit of Augusta, forever eight years old, whose ghostly laughter still echoes softly through the halls of this stately Victorian mansion.

In Guthrie, Oklahoma, history is never just a distant memory—it lives and breathes within the **Stone Lion Inn**, where the past still walks gently beside those brave enough to listen.

Cain's Ballroom: Tulsa's Haunted Musical Landmark

(Tulsa, OK – A Dance Hall for the Living and the Dead)

Built in **1924**, **Cain's Ballroom** is a cornerstone of Tulsa's music history, famously known as the "Carnegie Hall of Western Swing." Yet beyond its lively performances and legendary concerts, Cain's Ballroom harbors something more mysterious—a lingering energy from performances past.

The music never really stops... some say ghostly dancers still move across the floor.

Ghostly Performances

Staff and visitors have reported numerous ghostly experiences:

• Musicians rehearsing in the empty ballroom often hear faint applause or whispers coming from the darkness, as if unseen audiences from the past still linger, applauding a performance long ended.

• Employees working late at night describe seeing shadowy figures moving through the empty venue, quickly vanishing when approached.

• The ghostly silhouette of a performer dressed in period clothing has been spotted standing on stage, silently holding an instrument—then disappearing into thin air.

- Instruments have mysteriously moved, speakers crackle inexplicably, and faint, old-fashioned music can sometimes be heard playing softly when the ballroom is deserted.

Cain's Ballroom continues to draw music lovers and ghost hunters alike, both hoping to experience the intersection of music and the supernatural. Visitors wonder if the ballroom's famous performers are so attached to the venue they've refused to move on, forever reliving their greatest shows.

Gilcrease Museum: Spirits Among the Artifacts

(Tulsa, OK – Where Art and Ghosts Intersect)

Perched atop the scenic Osage Hills near Tulsa, the **Gilcrease Museum** holds the world's largest collection of Western American art. Founded by oilman Thomas Gilcrease in **1949**, the museum boasts masterpieces, historical manuscripts, and Native American artifacts—yet there's more to the museum than just impressive artwork.

The Haunting Presence

Many staff, security guards, and visitors have claimed to encounter supernatural events within the walls of the Gilcrease Museum:

- A shadowy figure believed to be Thomas Gilcrease himself has been seen strolling through the galleries late at night, inspecting his beloved collection long after his death.

- Visitors frequently experience unexplained cold spots, even on the hottest Oklahoma days, particularly in the rooms housing Gilcrease's favorite pieces.

- Security cameras and alarms often malfunction inexplicably, capturing shadows or unexplained movements when no one is present.

- The scent of tobacco smoke occasionally drifts through the museum, though smoking is strictly prohibited—an eerie reminder that perhaps Gilcrease's spirit still lingers, quietly observing from beyond.

Perhaps Gilcrease's love for his art collection binds him to this world, unwilling or unable to leave behind the treasures he carefully gathered in life.

In Oklahoma, history whispers from the shadows, ensuring that the past never fully fades away—especially in places where the boundary between life and death remains thin.

Oregon

Oregon—a state of lush forests, winding rivers, and breathtaking mountain ranges—also holds secrets hidden beneath its scenic beauty. Here, history and legend intertwine, creating a tapestry of mysterious occurrences that linger in the shadows of beloved landmarks. From the enigmatic forces at the **Oregon Vortex**, to the grim history of Portland's **Shanghai Tunnels**, to the unsettling memories of the **Hot Lake Hotel**, Oregon's haunting tales come alive, forever captivating those who dare to explore the unknown.

The Oregon Vortex: A Place Where Reality Bends

(Gold Hill, OR – Mysteries That Defy Explanation)

Hidden deep within the lush, wooded hills of southern Oregon, just outside the tiny community of Gold Hill, lies the **Oregon Vortex**—a peculiar roadside attraction open to curious visitors since **1930**. At first glance, it might seem like a mere roadside curiosity, but step inside this circular area, and reality itself seems to twist and bend.

A Place Where Physics Fail

First discovered by prospectors in the early 1900s, the Oregon Vortex quickly gained notoriety for the bizarre phenomena experienced within its boundaries. Its strange occurrences defy conventional scientific explanations, drawing visitors and skeptics alike to witness firsthand what many believe to be genuine paranormal events:

• Visitors report intense feelings of **vertigo and dizziness**, as though gravity is pulling them off-balance. Some claim to feel pulled or pushed by unseen hands, as if gravity itself has shifted.

• **Visual distortions** occur frequently within the vortex. Two people standing face-to-face may appear dramatically different in height, a puzzling phenomenon visitors swear must be witnessed to be believed.

• Animals avoid the area entirely, instinctively steering clear of what some say is a supernatural force field.

Many theories have emerged to explain the vortex—magnetic anomalies, optical illusions, gravitational anomalies—but none has fully explained the strange events. For those who visit, the sensation that they've stepped beyond reality itself leaves a lasting impression, blurring the line between natural wonder and supernatural mystery.

The Shanghai Tunnels: Beneath Portland's Dark Streets

(Portland, OR – A Sinister Underground World)

Beneath the lively streets of downtown Portland lies a hidden and chilling network known as the **Shanghai Tunnels**. Built in the mid-1800s, these dark, winding tunnels originally connected various waterfront bars, hotels, and businesses, providing a convenient way to move goods—but also hiding a sinister secret.

Beneath Portland's streets, lost souls still whisper... once taken, few ever escaped. (Picture Wikimedia Commons)

Portland's Shadowy History

The tunnels gained notoriety during the city's dark era of maritime kidnappings, a practice known as "shanghaiing." Sailors and unsuspecting visitors were abducted, drugged, or otherwise incapacitated, then transported through these underground passages onto waiting ships. By the time victims awoke, they were already at sea, forced into labor aboard sailing vessels bound for distant ports.

Echoes of the Lost

Today, the Shanghai Tunnels are said to be haunted by the restless spirits of those who died or disappeared beneath Portland's bustling streets:

- Visitors touring the tunnels report hearing **phantom footsteps** and **desperate whispers** echoing from empty corridors, believed to be the souls of kidnapped men and women still seeking escape.

- Ghostly apparitions, often appearing battered, confused, or frightened, have been glimpsed wandering through the dark passageways, silently crying out for help that will never come.

- Visitors report a profound sense of dread or sorrow when exploring the tunnels, as though the sadness and fear of those abducted so long ago remain embedded in the very bricks and earth.

The tunnels serve as a haunting reminder of Portland's sinister past—where the suffering of countless forgotten souls still lingers in shadowy corridors beneath the city, eternally trapped by tragedy.

The Hot Lake Hotel: Ghosts of Healing and Horror

(La Grande, OR – A Historic Resort with a Haunting Past)

Nestled within the peaceful and scenic Grande Ronde Valley near La Grande, Oregon, the historic **Hot Lake Hotel** stands quietly alongside the steaming hot springs from which it draws its name. Built in 1864 as a charming Victorian resort, the building promised visitors relaxation, luxury, and the healing powers of natural mineral waters. Over the decades, however, this majestic resort would witness far more than leisurely vacations—it became the backdrop to countless stories of hope, heartbreak, and haunting tragedy.

A History Soaked in Hope and Despair

In its early days, Hot Lake Hotel was a destination for wealthy travelers seeking rejuvenation in its natural mineral springs. By the early 20th century, the hotel expanded dramatically, transforming into an elegant sanatorium and hospital. Patients flocked from across the country, desperate to be healed by what was believed to be miraculous water. The reputation of the springs was so strong that the hotel flourished, filled with individuals suffering from ailments like tuberculosis, arthritis, and other debilitating illnesses.

But where there was hope, there was also tragedy. During the devastating influenza epidemic of 1918, the hotel struggled to accommodate the influx of patients, many of whom succumbed to illness. Surgeries and treatments of the era were primitive and often painful, and many patients never made it home. A profound sadness became woven into the building's very foundation.

Later, for a brief and unsettling period, the hotel served as a mental institution, housing individuals who suffered from severe psychological ailments. Stories of harsh treatment and neglect became whispered about the valley, further darkening the building's legacy.

Ghostly Echoes from a Painful Past

Today, the Hot Lake Hotel's hallways echo with more than the sounds of guests and staff. Visitors frequently share chilling experiences suggesting the souls who suffered here may never have truly left:

• **Apparitions from Another Time**: Guests often report seeing spectral figures dressed in **Victorian gowns** or **hospital attire from the early 1900s**, wandering slowly through halls or standing motionless at windows. Many guests have vividly described an apparition of a woman, pale and sad, staring out toward the lake, lost in memories of loved ones never reunited.

• **Unexplained Sounds and Sorrowful Echoes**: Late at night, guests have heard unsettling noises—the faint sound of **sobbing, moaning, or whispered conversations** drifting from empty rooms. Some visitors claim they hear the soft sounds of hospital carts rolling down deserted hallways, a lingering echo of the hotel's painful past.

• **Doors and Lights With a Mind of Their Own**: Guests and staff frequently report doors opening and closing spontaneously, slamming shut with startling force. Lights mysteriously flicker or shut off completely, leaving rooms suddenly plunged into darkness. When investigated, there is never a logical explanation for the disruptions.

The Surgery Wing: A Spirit Trapped in Despair

Perhaps the most disturbing reports come from the area that was once the surgical wing. Here, the apparition of a man dressed in traditional 1920s hospital attire has repeatedly been seen. He stands silently, often staring sadly at guests, as though pleading for help or relief. Those who've encountered him feel overwhelming sadness or anxiety, describing him as a soul eternally trapped, forever reliving his suffering.

In one harrowing account, a visitor exploring the hallway near the surgery rooms turned suddenly cold, overcome with a sharp feeling of dread. When she turned around, the man was standing behind her, close enough to touch. He vanished moments later, leaving only a lingering sense of melancholy and unanswered questions.

A Place Both Beautiful and Haunting

Today, Hot Lake Hotel remains open, attracting history lovers, paranormal investigators, and the merely curious. Its rooms and halls echo with the laughter and conversation of the living—but beneath it all remains the quiet whisper of those lost souls, whose history is forever entwined with the building's own.

If you visit Hot Lake Hotel, remember this: you aren't merely checking into a picturesque resort. You're stepping into a place where history and spirits remain inseparable, where past tragedies linger in the shadows, where hope and healing once stood side by side with pain and loss—and where the echoes of those who came seeking solace might still be heard, waiting for their stories to finally be told.

In Oregon, the past doesn't simply fade away. It breathes and whispers, quietly waiting in hidden tunnels, dark passageways, and grand halls—inviting us all to step closer, and discover that the boundary between past and present is far thinner than we ever imagined.

Pennsylvania

Gettysburg Battlefield: Ghostly Soldiers Who Never Left

(Gettysburg, PA – The Spirits of America's Bloodiest Battle)

The serene fields of Gettysburg, Pennsylvania, seem tranquil now, rolling gently beneath picturesque skies. But beneath this peaceful landscape lies a tragic and violent history, forever marked by blood and courage, sacrifice and sorrow. On July 1st through 3rd, 1863, this quiet farmland transformed into a living hell as Union and Confederate armies clashed in one of the most savage, brutal, and pivotal battles of the American Civil War. Over the course of those three terrible days, more than **50,000 soldiers were killed, wounded, or went missing**—a human cost so staggering it permanently scarred the land and echoed through history itself.

The echoes of war never faded... ghostly soldiers still march through the mist. (Picture in Public Domain)

Today, Gettysburg stands not only as a hallowed monument to sacrifice and bravery but also as a site where the past remains vividly alive. Many visitors to the battlefield feel as if they have stepped through a thin veil separating the present from the tragedies of the past. For in Gettysburg, they say, history never sleeps.

Echoes of the Fallen: The Battlefield's Haunting Legacy

Gettysburg has become legendary, not just among historians, but among paranormal investigators and tourists alike, who frequently experience encounters that defy rational explanation:

• On calm, moonlit evenings, visitors often hear the unmistakable sounds of battle: **the phantom roar of cannon fire**, the **sharp crackle of musket shots**, and distant shouts of officers commanding unseen troops. Numerous witnesses have sworn to hearing drums beating to the rhythm of ghostly regiments long after the sun has set and the tourists have departed.

- One of the most chilling accounts comes from visitors who have walked through the woods near Little Round Top or Devil's Den at twilight. Here, entire **regiments of spectral soldiers** are reported to have been seen marching silently through fields, their ghostly forms illuminated briefly by moonlight. Visitors describe these apparitions vividly: soldiers dressed in ragged Confederate uniforms or tattered Union blues, rifles at their sides, eyes hollow, marching into a fight that ended more than a century ago.

- On **quiet nights**, when fog drifts eerily across Cemetery Ridge, visitors have reported hearing **phantom cannon fire** and distant explosions so vivid and realistic they rush to seek cover—only to find the fields utterly silent and peaceful moments later. Park rangers and battlefield guides often quietly confirm these tales, recounting their own unsettling experiences as proof the battle is far from over for the spirits who remain.

- Perhaps the most famous haunted spot is **Devil's Den**, a rocky outcropping where Confederate sharpshooters once hid. Countless visitors to this area have experienced inexplicable camera malfunctions, cold spots, sudden sensations of being touched by invisible hands, and sightings of a lone Confederate soldier who silently observes visitors, then vanishes into thin air.

- The infamous **Triangular Field** nearby is another paranormal hotspot, known for causing electronic equipment —cameras, phones, and recorders—to malfunction inexplicably, as though the ghosts themselves refuse to be documented. Visitors who stand quietly here often describe a feeling of overwhelming sadness, as though the despair and desperation of the soldiers who fought and died here still linger palpably in the air.

The Phantom Voices of Soldiers in Pain

The most emotionally haunting experiences at Gettysburg involve the anguished cries of wounded soldiers. Nighttime visitors frequently report the soft, mournful sounds of men crying out in agony—pleading for help that never arrives. On quiet, misty nights, some visitors swear they can hear **drums beating solemnly** or even the distant tunes of Civil War-era bugles, as though the soldiers remain frozen in those tragic days of 1863.

Ghostly Encounters at Gettysburg's Most Haunted Spots

- **Devil's Den**, the boulder-strewn terrain where intense fighting occurred, is haunted by apparitions so vivid visitors have mistaken them for reenactors—until they fade or vanish before their eyes.

- At **Little Round Top**, tourists claim to have been approached by soldiers dressed in uniform who warn them to leave quickly. Moments later, these figures disappear, leaving the visitors shaken yet unharmed.

- The **Farnsworth House Inn** near the battlefield, which served as a makeshift hospital during the battle, reportedly echoes with cries of wounded soldiers. Guests have reported seeing apparitions of nurses and soldiers moving silently through the rooms at night, still attending to their long-dead patients.

Gettysburg: Where History Refuses to Fade

Gettysburg remains America's ultimate intersection of history and haunting. To walk its grounds is to step into the memories of America's darkest days. Each ghostly apparition, each unexplained sound, serves as a powerful reminder of the human tragedy that unfolded here. These restless souls are not merely remnants—they are guardians of memory, forever wandering the place where they fell, unable or unwilling to leave their brothers behind.

Visitors who journey to Gettysburg quickly realize they've stepped onto sacred ground, where the veil between life and death grows thin, and where history is anything but silent. They sense the heavy weight of the past on their shoulders—the sorrow, the valor, and the sacrifice—and perhaps the spirits of Gettysburg linger to ensure we never forget.

Eastern State Penitentiary: Echoes of Madness and Despair

(Philadelphia, PA – Where Solitary Confinement Became Eternal)

In the heart of Philadelphia stands a massive, haunting fortress of stone, its towering walls and gothic spires casting long shadows over the neighborhood below. This is the infamous **Eastern State Penitentiary**, an institution established in 1829 with a vision that was revolutionary and tragically flawed. Intended to reform criminals through complete isolation, it was the first penitentiary to use solitary confinement as its primary means of punishment—a practice meant to encourage reflection, penitence, and redemption. But the idealistic plan quickly turned into a nightmare.

Walls Built from Sorrow

Life within Eastern State Penitentiary was one of bleak solitude. Prisoners were housed in single cells, sealed off from any human contact, and even outdoor exercise took place in solitary, walled courtyards. Guards enforced absolute silence; inmates were hooded whenever they were moved, deprived even of a glimpse of another human face. This relentless isolation proved devastating, driving countless prisoners toward madness and even death. Suicide and mental breakdowns became frighteningly common.

One tragic case was prisoner number **1102**, a man named **James Clark**, who, after prolonged isolation, began screaming uncontrollably, claiming invisible beings were tormenting him. Others tried desperately to communicate by tapping on pipes or scratching messages into the stone walls—tiny rebellions against the crushing loneliness.

Some inmates never left... their whispers still echo through the empty cells

The Haunting Remains

Eastern State Penitentiary closed its doors in 1971, but many say the prisoners who suffered within its walls have never truly left. Today, the prison stands empty, its cold corridors and crumbling cells open to visitors who come seeking history—and often encounter something far more chilling.

The spirits imprisoned within Eastern State still make their anguish felt. Visitors and staff regularly report deeply unsettling phenomena:

• **Shadowy apparitions** stalk through empty cell blocks, their movements frantic or sorrowful. One frequently sighted apparition is a figure who paces continuously, vanishing just as visitors approach—believed to be an inmate still trapped in his torment.

- **Cell Block 12**, infamous for its history of violence, has earned the reputation as the prison's most active haunt. Here, visitors have felt sudden, inexplicable waves of sadness, despair, and even physical nausea. Cold spots move through the halls, and heavy cell doors sometimes swing open or slam shut with no apparent explanation.

- **Mysterious laughter and anguished cries** echo from sealed cells that haven't housed a living prisoner in decades. Many who visit feel as though they're overhearing the past replaying itself, captured eternally by the stone walls that imprisoned so many for so long.

- Perhaps most disturbing is the story of **"The Locksmith's Cell."** Once occupied by a locksmith named Joseph Taylor, who reportedly died under mysterious circumstances, visitors claim they hear **ghostly tapping noises** emanating from the cell—a chilling echo of desperate attempts at communication from a man long gone.

Cell Block 12: A Haunting Heart of Despair

Of all the penitentiary's eerie spaces, Cell Block 12 stands out for its intense paranormal activity. Its walls have witnessed murders, violence, and relentless cruelty. Today, the atmosphere in Cell Block 12 is oppressive, suffocating even the bravest visitors with dread. Some people have abruptly fled in terror, convinced they were chased or touched by invisible hands. Paranormal investigators often leave this cell block shaken, convinced they've encountered spirits who remain trapped, consumed by bitterness and despair.

Beyond the Bars: Ghostly Touches

Guests frequently describe physical sensations:

• Feeling unseen hands touch their shoulders or tug at their clothing, as though prisoners long-dead are desperate to communicate.

• Being pushed or scratched lightly, leaving visitors with more questions than answers.

These interactions leave many visitors both frightened and fascinated—forever marked by their encounter with the supernatural.

A Prison for Eternity

Today, Eastern State Penitentiary is a popular historic attraction, with tours that openly embrace its dark legacy. Yet, beyond the educational displays and historical reenactments, there remains something intangible and unsettlingly real—a reminder that suffering, loneliness, and anguish have imprinted deeply into its very walls. For the spirits of Eastern State Penitentiary, solitary confinement has become eternal.

Those who visit should prepare themselves to face the echoes of madness and despair, as history in this grim fortress is never silent—and never truly past.

Rhode Island

Fleur-de-Lys Studios: The Tragic Muse of Providence

(Providence, RI – Where Art and Tragedy Meet)

Amidst the charming, cobblestone streets of Providence's historic district stands Fleur-de-Lys Studios, a strikingly ornate, fairy-tale-like building constructed in **1885**. Designed by renowned painter Sydney Richmond Burleigh, the building quickly became a sanctuary for artists, poets, and dreamers, its halls echoing with creativity and inspiration. Within these ornate walls, creativity flourished, ideas blossomed, and beautiful masterpieces came to life. Yet, beneath this vibrant surface lay hidden a haunting tale—a story of talent, sorrow, and loss that still resonates through the halls to this day.

Angela O'Leary: An Artist's Unfinished Dream

In the early 1900s, among Fleur-de-Lys Studios' residents was a gifted young watercolor artist named **Angela O'Leary**.

Angela was known for her remarkable talent and quiet intensity, creating hauntingly beautiful paintings that revealed an extraordinary depth of emotion. But Angela's gifts came at a price; she battled an internal darkness—an invisible struggle with depression and self-doubt.

Despite her outward grace and success, Angela was increasingly tormented by loneliness and sorrow. Friends and fellow artists noticed her growing isolation, her gentle laughter giving way to somber silences, her paintings turning progressively darker, filled with shadows and melancholy.

One cold, dreary evening, Angela's battle with despair reached its tragic conclusion. Alone in her studio, surrounded by unfinished canvases and faded dreams, Angela O'Leary ended her own life, leaving behind a poignant legacy of unfinished masterpieces, unanswered questions, and heartbreaking loss.

Angela's brushstrokes faded long ago... but some say her spirit still lingers, watching from the shadows. (Image Public Domain)

A Ghostly Presence Among Artists

From the day of Angela's death onward, Fleur-de-Lys Studios became known not only as a center of creativity, but also as a place haunted by the gentle, yet restless, spirit of Angela herself. Many believe she never truly departed, her spirit forever tethered to the building that once symbolized her hopes, dreams, and ultimately, her despair.

Artists, visitors, and caretakers have described numerous

encounters with Angela's apparition, particularly on the upper floors, where her studio once stood:

- **Silent Observations**: Artists working late into the night have reported seeing the ethereal form of a pale woman standing silently in doorways or corners of the studios, watching intently, as if intrigued by their work. Her apparition typically fades slowly when approached, leaving behind an overwhelming sense of melancholy.

- **Cold Spots and Whispers**: Even on warm summer evenings, visitors frequently encounter chilling cold spots—areas of sudden, icy air that defy explanation. Some say these cold drafts are often accompanied by a faint, mournful whisper or a gentle sigh, as if Angela's spirit still grieves or longs for comfort.

- **Misplaced Art Supplies**: Brushes, paints, or unfinished canvases often move inexplicably from their original locations. Some artists attribute these strange incidents to Angela's gentle yet mischievous spirit, subtly reminding them of her presence, or perhaps inspiring them to complete the work she left behind.

A Muse from Beyond the Grave

Curiously, artists who have experienced Angela's presence rarely describe feeling fear. Instead, many have reported a sense of empathy, melancholy inspiration, or even comfort, as if Angela's spirit continues to guide or encourage their creativity from beyond. One artist described waking suddenly at night, compelled to begin painting, only to produce some of her most beautiful and deeply emotional work—believing Angela had quietly guided her hand.

Visitors drawn by the stories often leave feeling both inspired and saddened, reflecting upon the fragility of artistic genius and the hidden struggles that too often accompany it.

Fleur-de-Lys Studios: Art and Haunting Entwined

Today, Fleur-de-Lys Studios remains a cherished space in Providence's artistic community, where creative spirits—living and departed—continue to mingle. Angela's spirit has become a beloved ghostly muse, quietly wandering halls where creativity once blossomed and despair tragically triumphed.

This ornate building is not merely haunted; it is an enduring reminder of how closely art and tragedy can be entwined, a place where the past remains forever present, reminding all who pass through its doors that genius, like life itself, can be fleeting and fragile, yet hauntingly beautiful.

The Conjuring House: Fear in the Rhode Island Countryside

(Harrisville, RI – Where Nightmares Became Reality)

Tucked away deep within the dense forests and rolling hills near Harrisville, Rhode Island, stands an unassuming, weathered farmhouse built in **1736**. Known simply as **The Conjuring House**, this historic building looks peaceful—almost charming—at first glance. But beneath its aged beams and quiet facade lurks an unspeakable history of torment and terror, making it one of America's most infamous haunted locations.

Though the home gained international notoriety from the chilling **Hollywood blockbuster *The Conjuring***, the true events that occurred within these walls surpass even the darkest cinematic imaginings.

An Idyllic Beginning Turns Terrifying

In **1971**, Roger and Carolyn Perron purchased this isolated farmhouse, dreaming of tranquility and simplicity in the peaceful Rhode Island countryside. Along with their five daughters, the Perrons imagined their lives in the old home would be filled with family warmth and happiness.

Yet, almost immediately, something sinister made its presence known.

The Perron family left... but something stayed behind, still watching, still waiting

A Spirit Known as Bathsheba

Among the many spirits rumored to inhabit the property, none was more notorious—or terrifying—than that of **Bathsheba Sherman**, a woman who lived nearby in the mid-1800s. Local legends whispered dark tales about her life: accusations of witchcraft, rituals performed in secrecy, and rumors of her involvement in a child's mysterious death. Although historical records remain unclear, Bathsheba's ominous reputation was enough to haunt the imaginations of townsfolk for generations.

Soon after settling into their new home, Carolyn Perron began experiencing frightening encounters that would come to define their lives for nearly a decade:

• She often felt as if **an unseen presence watched her constantly**, day and night, making her deeply uncomfortable, never able to shake the feeling of being stalked in her own home.

• At night, Carolyn described feeling **cold, invisible hands tugging at her blankets**, and waking up with **mysterious bruises** and scratches on her body. The attacks grew increasingly violent and personal, leaving the family terrified to sleep.

• The Perron children reported seeing apparitions regularly—**ghostly figures silently roaming through bedrooms and hallways**, including a spectral woman dressed in a dirty gray gown. They later identified this figure as Bathsheba Sherman, her eyes filled with hatred and malice.

Tormented by Unseen Forces

As months went by, paranormal occurrences escalated from mere sightings to outright attacks:

- **Heavy footsteps** would echo loudly through empty rooms above their heads, as if invisible intruders moved freely through their home.

- Loud bangs, disembodied whispers, and chilling laughter filled the night, leaving the family sleep-deprived and overwhelmed with fear.

- Family photographs and treasured belongings would vanish inexplicably, later appearing in impossible locations—often violently shattered or damaged.

Even visiting friends and guests became victims of the home's dark forces. Multiple visitors recounted terrifying encounters, such as furniture suddenly sliding across rooms or doors violently slamming shut. Some guests swore they felt **invisible hands shoving them aggressively** toward staircases or walls.

Enter the Warrens

As these terrifying events continued, the Perron family desperately sought help, ultimately turning to renowned paranormal investigators **Ed and Lorraine Warren**. During their investigation, Lorraine Warren—an experienced clairvoyant—claimed to sense the oppressive presence of a deeply malevolent spirit within the home. She believed Bathsheba's restless, angry spirit was indeed responsible for the attacks, intent on driving the Perrons from the property.

During one of their attempts to cleanse the house, a chilling séance went terribly wrong. Carolyn Perron, who participated, was suddenly and violently thrown from her chair, screaming hysterically as an unseen force assaulted her in front of her terrified family. The Warrens later described the event as one of the most terrifying moments they ever encountered, even in their extensive careers dealing with the paranormal.

A Haunting That Never Ended

Despite their attempts at spiritual intervention, the Perron family remained trapped in their own personal nightmare for years, unable to afford to relocate. They endured a decade of constant fear, finally leaving the home in 1980. But even then, the farmhouse's haunting legacy endured.

Today, the Conjuring House continues to attract visitors, paranormal enthusiasts, and historians fascinated by its chilling past. Numerous subsequent owners and guests continue to report chilling phenomena:

- Apparitions still appear, silently watching from dark corners or moving slowly from room to room.

- Unexplained whispers and footsteps persist, keeping residents awake through long, sleepless nights.

- Visitors frequently feel sudden, overpowering sensations of dread, nausea, or anxiety when touring the home—signs, they believe, that Bathsheba or other tormented spirits still linger, eternally trapped in a cycle of torment.

More Than Just a Ghost Story

The Conjuring House remains far more than a haunted farmhouse—it stands as a stark reminder of how past tragedies and dark histories can manifest in terrifying ways. For those who dare to visit, it offers a harrowing glimpse into a world of spirits who refuse to rest, forever reminding the living that some secrets refuse to stay buried.

Visitors beware: at the Conjuring House, history never dies— and neither, perhaps, does the danger.

South Carolina

Hilton Head's "Blue Lady": Guardian Spirit of the Lighthouse

(Hilton Head Island, SC – A Tragic Legacy of Love and Devotion)

On the storm-battered southern shore of Hilton Head Island, the old lighthouse stands like a silent sentinel—its worn stone walls, cracked with age, watch quietly over the rolling waves of the Atlantic. Once, it was a beacon of safety, faithfully guiding sailors home through violent storms and treacherous seas. Today, however, its faded lantern room stands empty, and its windows are dark—yet the lighthouse is far from abandoned. Within its shadowy corridors and winding stairs, a gentle but persistent spirit remains: the legendary "Blue Lady," a ghostly figure whose devotion to saving lives long outlived her own.

A Storm, a Promise, and a Daughter's Love

In the turbulent autumn of **1893**, as fierce winds roared and angry waves pounded Hilton Head's rocky coastline, the island's lighthouse keeper, **Adam Fripp**, desperately climbed the lighthouse stairs to keep the beacon burning. Amidst the brutal chaos of the storm, tragedy struck—Adam collapsed suddenly, his heart failing as he struggled to keep the flame alive. In his final breath, he turned to his young daughter, **Caroline**, who had rushed to his side, and with dying words pleaded for her to keep the lighthouse burning.

Bound by love, loyalty, and grief, Caroline promised her father she would fulfill his dying wish, no matter the cost.

Night after night, Caroline stood vigilant at the lighthouse lantern, tirelessly tending the flame to guide mariners safely through the storm's fury. Islanders watched in awe and worry as the lighthouse remained steadfastly lit, night after stormy night, Caroline's silhouette clearly visible through the windows, her beloved blue dress illuminated by the soft glow of the lighthouse lantern.

Days turned into nights, and nights into days, yet Caroline never left her post, refusing sleep or rest despite the pleas of worried neighbors. She understood the lighthouse was the difference between life and death for sailors battling the stormy sea. Exhausted and heartbroken from losing her father, Caroline pushed herself beyond human limits, driven by an unbreakable promise.

Finally, one fateful evening, the light faltered, flickered briefly, then dimmed entirely. Islanders rushed to the lighthouse, fearing the worst. Inside, at the base of the winding staircase, they found Caroline—her lifeless body crumpled beneath the final steps. Still dressed in her cherished blue gown, her gentle face now peaceful in eternal rest, Caroline had given her life honoring her father's final wish.

Some say a ghostly keeper still tends the light... even though no one is there. (Image Wikimedia Commons)

The Spirit Who Refused to Rest

From that night forward, Caroline's spirit became forever bound to the lighthouse she had faithfully tended. Sailors and islanders alike began reporting sightings of a young woman dressed in blue standing watch at the top of the lighthouse—especially during the most severe storms. Quickly, they realized that even death could not end Caroline's devotion.

Over the decades, her spirit earned the affectionate name **"The Blue Lady,"** and her ghostly appearances became both legendary and frequent:

- **Sailors** battling fierce storms have sworn to see the apparition of a young woman dressed in a flowing blue gown clearly visible through the lighthouse windows, her silhouette outlined by flashes of lightning, faithfully tending the long-extinguished lantern. Her presence, mariners claim, guides them safely around hidden reefs and dangerous shores, as though Caroline's spirit still refuses to allow harm to befall them.

- Visitors brave enough to approach the lighthouse after dusk have heard the unmistakable sound of **soft footsteps**echoing quietly up and down the winding staircase—a gentle reminder that Caroline remains steadfastly on duty, eternally climbing the stairs she climbed during her final, desperate days.

- Others recount feeling a gentle breeze or hearing soft, sorrowful sighs as they wander the lighthouse grounds, sensing that Caroline still mourns her father's death, yet feels compelled to protect anyone who visits.

Guardian Angel of Hilton Head

The Blue Lady is beloved by residents and visitors alike, never viewed as threatening or malevolent. Instead, she is seen as a comforting protector, a guardian angel whose love and loyalty transcend even death itself. Her gentle yet unwavering presence reassures islanders, reminding them that Caroline's selfless devotion continues to shield Hilton Head from harm.

Even today, as hurricanes approach the island and skies darken with storm clouds, locals look toward the silent lighthouse, hoping to catch a glimpse of Caroline's ghostly figure—a sight many consider a blessing, a comforting signal that the Blue Lady stands watch once more, determined to guide sailors safely home.

For those who believe, the old Hilton Head Lighthouse is more than just a historic landmark: it is the eternal home of a courageous young woman whose love and devotion shine brightly, illuminating even the darkest storm, and whose spirit gently reminds us all that true devotion is everlasting.

Caroline still waits by the lighthouse... but for whom, no one knows.

South Dakota

Hotel Alex Johnson: A Bride's Tragic Fall

(Rapid City, SD – The Spirits Who Never Checked Out)

In the bustling heart of Rapid City stands the elegant, Germanic-style **Hotel Alex Johnson**, built in 1928. This historic hotel, filled with ornate details and classic charm, has hosted presidents, dignitaries, and even Hollywood celebrities. But hidden behind its grandeur lies a tragic, unsettling past, and some guests who checked into this luxurious landmark have never truly checked out.

Guests report flickering lights, phantom footsteps, and a woman in white who never checked out. (Picture Wikimedia Commons)

The Mystery of Room 812

The hotel's most chilling legend revolves around Room 812 and the tragic story of a young bride who met a mysterious and untimely death. It was the 1970s, and the young woman, glowing with happiness, checked into the hotel with her new husband. Shortly afterward, tragedy struck: the bride was found dead on the sidewalk below her eighth-floor window. The circumstances of her fall remain shrouded in mystery, sparking decades of whispers—was it suicide, an accident, or something far darker?

Since that night, guests staying in or near Room 812 have experienced disturbing phenomena:

• **The Ghostly Bride** has been frequently spotted wandering the hallways on the eighth floor, dressed in a flowing white wedding gown. Witnesses have described her melancholy expression, as if forever searching for answers—or justice—for her tragic end.

- Visitors staying in Room 812 have awoken in the night to a sense of an invisible presence at their bedside, whispers, or gentle sobbing emanating from nowhere. Objects have mysteriously shifted or disappeared entirely, while windows have inexplicably opened in the night, bringing in chilling gusts of air as though reliving the bride's tragic fall.

- Staff and guests frequently report sudden cold drafts, phantom footsteps, and mysterious knocking on doors, even when no one else is present. Elevators have been known to stop randomly on the eighth floor, doors opening to reveal no one inside—at least, no one visible.

The Hotel Alex Johnson continues to welcome travelers, but be warned: those who check in to Room 812 may find themselves sharing the night with the sad, eternal presence of the bride who never left.

Bullock Hotel: Deadwood's Sheriff Still on Duty

(Deadwood, SD – Seth Bullock's Eternal Vigil)

Amidst the rustic streets of Deadwood, South Dakota, stands the stately and historic **Bullock Hotel**, built in 1895 by Seth Bullock himself, the town's first sheriff. Bullock was known as a tough, principled lawman, determined to bring order to a town infamous for violence and vice. Even after death, it seems Bullock refuses to leave his beloved hotel unguarded.

The Sheriff Who Never Left

Since his passing in 1919, staff and guests have reported numerous sightings of Seth Bullock's stern yet comforting presence throughout the hotel:

- Bullock's apparition—always impeccably dressed in period attire—has been spotted by guests and employees, silently standing in hallways, as if still keeping watch over the establishment he built and loved.

- Visitors have reported objects moving on their own, glasses sliding off the bar counter as if pushed by invisible hands, and doors mysteriously locking or unlocking themselves.

- Particularly eerie are reports of **phantom footsteps** pacing the halls, audible even when the hotel is otherwise silent. Guests have described waking to find an apparition looming near their beds, quietly observing them, or feeling a firm yet invisible hand nudging them awake—as if Bullock himself is ensuring guests remain safe, even in death.

Those who stay at the Bullock Hotel quickly realize they're not alone. Sheriff Bullock's spirit remains a guardian of the law—and perhaps, forever, of Deadwood itself.

Mount Marty College: Spirits Who Still Walk Campus

(Yankton, SD – Paranormal Education in the Dorms)

Founded in 1936 by Benedictine Sisters, Yankton's Mount Marty College is known for its welcoming atmosphere and serene campus. But beneath this peaceful surface, the college conceals chilling tales of paranormal activity and spectral visitors who remain bound to its history.

Campus Hauntings: The Ghostly Staff and Students

Students, faculty, and maintenance staff have long whispered stories about the eerie happenings throughout the campus:

- **The Ghostly Nun**: Numerous students have reported seeing a spectral figure of a nun quietly walking the halls of Whitby Hall late at night, her gentle footsteps echoing softly before she fades into thin air. Those who've seen her describe a comforting yet deeply melancholy presence, believed to be a departed sister who once cared deeply for the students and the school.

She walks the halls in silence... but if you listen closely, you might hear her pray

- **The Bell Tower's Shadow**: The spirit of Sister Mary Murphy, who tragically died by leaping from the bell tower, has been witnessed by several staff members and students. They describe seeing a woman dressed in nun's habit standing atop the tower, silently watching the campus below, as though forever mourning an untold sorrow.

- **Ghostly Students and Staff**: Dorm rooms, lecture halls, and corridors frequently echo with the sounds of disembodied voices and footsteps. In Marian Auditorium, students rehearsing late-night performances claim they've felt a sudden chill and glimpsed ghostly figures watching from empty seats—an unsettling audience of spirits eager to relive past performances.

- **Phantom Encounters in Corbey Hall**: In the oldest part of campus, students describe unsettling incidents: doors slamming shut on their own, lights inexplicably flickering, and shadows darting across hallways. Maintenance workers report sudden, inexplicable electrical malfunctions, and some have even felt gentle, ghostly touches or whispers in empty rooms.

At Mount Marty College, history quietly continues to repeat itself, with spirits seemingly drawn to campus life, unable or unwilling to leave their memories—or perhaps their friends—behind.

In South Dakota, the boundaries between life and death blur, as ghosts of the past continue to reach out, inviting you into their eternal world. But be careful—once you cross into their realm, you might find it difficult to leave.

Tennessee

Bell Witch Cave: The Witch Who Terrorized Tennessee

(Adams, TN – The Haunting That Inspired American Folklore)

In the quiet countryside of Adams, Tennessee, tucked away in dense woods near the Red River, lies the infamous **Bell Witch Cave**—one of America's most chilling paranormal landmarks. The cave itself is modest and unassuming, yet beneath its shadowy limestone surface lies a dark legend known throughout the nation.

The Bell Family Nightmare

It began in **1817**, on the farmstead of John Bell, a respected farmer and family man. The Bell family's peace was shattered one night by unexplained knocking sounds and strange noises in the darkness outside. Initially dismissing it as pranksters or animals, the family soon realized they faced something far more sinister.

They say the Bell Witch still whispers from the darkness... if you listen, she might whisper back. (Picture Wikimedia Commons)

The activity escalated rapidly, turning violent and terrifying:

• The Bells endured relentless torment by an invisible entity that pulled hair, slapped faces, threw objects across rooms, and spoke in a loud, shrill voice. The voice claimed to be "Kate," identifying itself as a vengeful witch who sought to destroy John Bell.

• John Bell himself was viciously targeted. He experienced physical attacks, choking sensations, and mysterious illnesses, ultimately leading to his mysterious death in **1820**—an event many attributed directly to the Bell Witch's deadly curse.

• Witnesses, including neighbors, church leaders, and even **President Andrew Jackson**, who visited the Bell farm to investigate, reported experiencing the terrifying entity firsthand. Jackson famously declared, "I would rather face the entire British Army again than spend another night with the Bell Witch!"

A Portal to the Supernatural

The haunting eventually subsided, but locals soon came to believe the Bell Witch's malicious spirit retreated into a cave located near the Bell farm—a cave that would forever carry her name. Visitors to the **Bell Witch Cave** have experienced strange phenomena ever since:

• Visitors report hearing disembodied voices whispering their names or laughing mockingly from the dark corners of the cave.

• Strange, glowing lights have appeared within the cave, flickering and dancing mysteriously before vanishing suddenly, leaving visitors disoriented and afraid.

• Numerous guests have reported physical sensations of being touched, scratched, or even pushed by unseen hands. Cameras and other electronics frequently malfunction or stop working entirely when brought near the cave entrance, as though the Bell Witch herself refuses to allow proof of her existence.

• Local legend holds that visitors who take stones from the cave as souvenirs experience terrible misfortunes, illnesses, or accidents—leading many frightened tourists to return their souvenirs to break the curse.

Today, the Bell Witch Cave stands as one of America's most enduring supernatural mysteries—a haunting reminder of the terrifying power of unseen forces and the dark legend of a witch whose wrath lingers centuries later.

The Orpheum Theatre: Memphis's Eternal Audience Member

(Memphis, TN – The Little Ghost Who Loves the Theatre)

In bustling downtown Memphis, Tennessee, stands the beautifully ornate **Orpheum Theatre**, built in 1928, renowned for its grandeur, elegance, and stellar performances. Yet beneath its dazzling chandeliers and lavish velvet curtains resides a more mysterious, otherworldly guest—one who arrived nearly a century ago and never departed.

The Tragic Tale of Mary

According to theatre legend, Mary was a spirited young girl who, in the **1920s**, tragically lost her life in a car accident directly outside the theater. Since that heartbreaking day, her playful yet poignant presence has become an inseparable part of the Orpheum's story.

Mary quickly made herself known to theatergoers and staff alike, her ghostly spirit drawn to the energy and excitement of the performances. Witnesses describe her as a small, delicate girl dressed in a white gown, her dark hair adorned with a ribbon. But her innocent appearance belies a mischievous streak:

• Performers have reported glimpses of Mary dancing joyfully in the shadows backstage, giggling softly before disappearing when approached.

• Audiences seated in the balcony have described feeling a sudden, inexplicable chill or sensing a child's presence brushing past their knees during performances.

- Theater staff frequently find doors opening and closing by themselves, lights flickering mysteriously, or props and costumes inexplicably rearranged—playful tricks attributed to Mary, forever delighting in the magic of theater.

- Perhaps most famously, seat C-5 on the balcony is considered "Mary's seat." Patrons sitting in this particular seat often sense a childlike presence beside them, gently laughing, whispering, or humming along to the performance. Some have even glimpsed Mary herself, sitting quietly in the empty seat, intently watching the show.

Rather than being feared, Mary has become beloved by the Orpheum community, warmly welcomed as a permanent audience member, the theater's eternal child who refuses to leave the performances she adores. Some performers even seek her approval, believing a glimpse of her spirit is good luck—a sign the show will succeed.

Today, Memphis's Orpheum Theatre embraces Mary as a treasured part of its history, reminding all who enter that some spirits remain behind not out of malice—but out of love.

Tennessee's Haunting Legacies: Where History and Spirits Collide

- At Adams's legendary **Bell Witch Cave**, the ghostly presence of a vengeful witch named Kate still torments those who dare enter her shadowy cavern, warning visitors that dark legends can become terrifyingly real.

- In Memphis, the beautiful **Orpheum Theatre** remains eternally home to young Mary, whose playful ghostly presence continues to captivate audiences, reminding everyone that spirits sometimes linger simply because they cannot bear to leave the places they love.

In Tennessee, history lives on through haunting legends, mysterious caves, and charming theaters—and visitors soon discover that in this state, the past remains as vividly alive as the spirits who continue to wander, watch, and whisper from beyond.

Mary never got to see the show... but some say she still waits outside, watching in silence

Texas

The Driskill Hotel: Haunted by Ambition, Loss, and Lingering Spirits

(Austin, TX – Where Elegance Meets Eternity)

In the bustling heart of downtown Austin, amidst music-filled streets and vibrant nightlife, stands the majestic Driskill Hotel. Built in **1886** by wealthy cattle baron Colonel Jesse Driskill, the hotel was intended to be the most luxurious and impressive establishment west of the Mississippi. With its soaring columns, lavish ballroom, polished marble floors, and ornate stained glass windows, it quickly became the crown jewel of Texas hospitality, welcoming dignitaries, politicians, and wealthy patrons from across the nation.

Yet beneath the splendor and grandeur of the Driskill lies a deeper story of ambition, loss, and lingering spirits who refuse to depart, leaving behind a legacy far more mysterious than Colonel Driskill could have ever imagined.

Colonel Driskill's Ambition and Loss

Jesse Driskill poured his fortune, ambition, and soul into the hotel, determined to create a legacy that would immortalize his name. But misfortune struck soon after its grand opening. In 1888, overwhelmed by debts, Jesse was forced to sell his beloved hotel, an event from which he never recovered. In **1890**, Colonel Driskill passed away, his dreams dashed, his heart broken.

Yet even death, it seems, could not keep Colonel Driskill from the halls of his beloved hotel.

The Eternal Proprietor

Almost immediately following his death, guests and employees began experiencing unusual phenomena tied directly to Colonel Driskill himself:

• Guests have encountered the unmistakable apparition of Colonel Driskill, impeccably dressed in 19th-century attire, roaming quietly through the grand hallways, lobby, and bar area. His ghost is often seen standing silently in the lobby, observing guests with a watchful gaze, as if he still proudly oversees the comfort and hospitality of the establishment he built.

• Staff report unexplained occurrences late at night: elevators arriving mysteriously without being summoned, lights flickering and dimming inexplicably, and doors gently opening or closing as if guided by unseen hands—actions perhaps intended by the Colonel to remind them of his lingering authority and watchful eye.

- Many guests describe feeling an overwhelming sense of being watched or accompanied, though no one visible is nearby. Some have even felt the comforting touch of an unseen hand on their shoulder—a sign, perhaps, of Colonel Driskill warmly welcoming visitors to his hotel even after death.

The Tragic Tale of a Little Girl's Spirit

Colonel Driskill isn't the only ghostly presence tied to this elegant hotel. Another well-documented haunting involves the tragic spirit of a playful young girl who died in a heartbreaking accident in the late 1800s:

According to historical accounts, the child—visiting the hotel with her family—was playing with her ball near the grand staircase when she tragically lost her footing and fell to her death. Her spirit has haunted the Driskill ever since, eternally reliving her final, tragic moment.

- Visitors and employees have frequently heard childlike laughter and playful footsteps echoing along empty hallways, often accompanied by the soft bouncing of a small ball. Her apparition has appeared numerous times, smiling gently before vanishing suddenly around a corner.

- Staff report finding small, child-sized handprints inexplicably appearing on windows and mirrors—prints that seem impossible to clean, reappearing just as mysteriously.

- Numerous guests claim to have witnessed her ghostly form darting playfully through corridors, forever chasing her beloved ball, her innocent laughter echoing gently through the halls before fading into silence.

You may sleep peacefully... but in room 525 something else is awake, tidying up while you dream. (Picture Wikimedia Commons)

A Mysterious Presence in Room 525

One of the Driskill Hotel's most notoriously haunted locations is **Room 525**. Here, the veil between past and present feels especially thin:

• Guests staying in this particular room have frequently awoken in the dead of night to find their personal belongings mysteriously rearranged, sometimes neatly placed on the bedside table or carefully aligned along the floor, as though a caretaker had quietly visited in their sleep.

• Sudden, inexplicable drops in temperature, faint whispers in the dark, and gentle touches from invisible hands have left guests unsettled yet fascinated—certain they are not alone.

• Some visitors report feeling an invisible yet comforting presence, almost parental in nature—others are left uneasy, certain they have encountered the lingering energy of someone who refuses to depart the hotel's grandeur.

Music from Another Time

Adding to the hotel's eerie charm is the beautiful antique grand piano in the lobby, which, though seemingly untouched, frequently emits soft music in the deepest hours of the night. Security guards, alone in the silence, have sworn that they heard delicate notes drifting from the empty lobby, as if played by invisible fingers—perhaps a final serenade by Colonel Driskill himself, forever proud of the hotel he once cherished.

Where Guests Become Witnesses

The Driskill Hotel remains a favorite haunt—literally and figuratively—for visitors from around the world. Guests continue to check in, eager to experience the hotel's elegance and charm, yet often leave with unsettling stories of encounters they cannot fully explain. They've glimpsed Colonel Driskill watching silently from balconies and hallways, felt the playful presence of the tragic little girl, and been serenaded by an unseen pianist in the night.

At the Driskill Hotel, history doesn't just linger—it breathes, moves, and speaks to those who dare to listen. It's a place where the past remains eternally intertwined with the present, where luxury and tragedy merge to create an atmosphere both captivating and haunting. Visitors discover that Colonel Driskill's dream remains alive, forever anchored to his beloved creation, and that some spirits, bound by ambition or tragedy, never truly leave.

The Alamo: Spirits of Texas's Legendary Last Stand

(San Antonio, TX – Echoes of Courage and Sacrifice)

In the heart of bustling downtown San Antonio, amidst the vibrant crowds and lively streets, stands one of America's most hallowed—and haunting—historic landmarks: **the Alamo**. Originally built as a humble Spanish mission, this quiet mission became the site of one of history's most famous battles—a fierce and desperate siege that would forever symbolize bravery, sacrifice, and the indomitable Texas spirit.

At the Alamo, the battle never truly ended—listen closely, and you might still hear the faint echoes of cannons and the whispers of heroes who chose death over surrender.
(Picture Wikimedia Commons)

In February of **1836**, nearly 200 brave defenders, including legendary frontiersmen **Davy Crockett**, **Jim Bowie**, and Colonel **William B. Travis**, barricaded themselves behind the Alamo's weathered stone walls. For thirteen agonizing days, they endured a relentless siege by Mexican General

Antonio López de Santa Anna's overwhelming army. Despite being vastly outnumbered, the defenders refused to surrender, determined to protect their home or die in the attempt.

On the morning of March 6, the Alamo finally fell. Every defender perished in fierce hand-to-hand combat, their courageous stand etched forever into American history. The Alamo's defenders had fallen—but according to countless reports over nearly two centuries, their spirits never departed.

Echoes of a Battle Long Past

Today, visitors to the Alamo still encounter phenomena so vivid and unsettling that many believe the siege's tragedy left behind an indelible supernatural imprint:

• **Phantom Soldiers**: Staff, visitors, and security personnel have frequently reported seeing ghostly soldiers marching in formation across the courtyard or standing watch silently upon the fortress walls. These spectral figures appear briefly yet clearly, often dressed in authentic period uniforms. Witnesses have described these soldiers disappearing slowly, fading into nothingness as if history itself claimed them once more.

• **The Sounds of Battle**: Perhaps the most chilling paranormal phenomenon at the Alamo are the sounds that visitors often hear. In the stillness of night, phantom echoes of gunfire, musket blasts, distant cannon fire, and anguished screams have terrified and fascinated generations of visitors. Security guards and tourists alike have reported rushing toward sounds of fierce combat, only to discover silence and empty spaces, leaving them awed by history seemingly repeating itself in ghostly form.

- **Apparitions of Legendary Heroes**: Visitors have reported seeing clear and unmistakable apparitions of figures who closely resemble historical descriptions of famous defenders. **Jim Bowie**, bedridden and ill during the battle, has reportedly appeared to startled visitors near the old barracks, his face marked by determination and pain. Others have described sightings of **Davy Crockett**, calmly pacing the grounds, seemingly lost in thought before abruptly vanishing.

- **Whispers from the Shadows**: Visitors frequently recount hearing faint whispers in Spanish and English drifting gently through empty hallways and corridors. Some report hearing quiet prayers, anguished moans, or even softly spoken commands—like distant echoes from a battle that ended long ago, yet remains vividly present in spirit.

- **Ghostly Footsteps and Mysterious Encounters**: Staff who lock up at night report hearing steady footsteps pacing empty rooms, shadows moving in the corners of their eyes, and doors mysteriously opening and closing as though ghostly sentinels still patrol the halls, eternally guarding their beloved mission.

History Alive in the Heart of Texas

Today, the Alamo remains a sacred landmark, attracting millions of visitors eager to connect with its storied past. But those who linger after dusk sometimes discover something even more compelling—firsthand encounters with the ghosts of Texas's past, still faithfully keeping watch over the fortress they died to defend.

At the Alamo, history is never distant or abstract—it's alive, breathing, and vividly real. The spirits of its fallen defenders continue to stand guard, reminding visitors that bravery and sacrifice never fade, forever echoing through the corridors, walls, and grounds of this iconic battlefield. Those who dare to visit at twilight might find themselves stepping beyond the pages of history—and into a world where the battle still rages, where the courage of the defenders echoes eternally through the shadows, warning visitors that here, history never truly dies.

Utah

Fear Factory: Salt Lake City's Factory of Fright and Restless Spirits

(Salt Lake City, UT – A Place Where the Dead Refuse to Clock Out)

In the heart of Salt Lake City's industrial district stands a looming relic of the past—a collection of rusted pipes, decaying catwalks, towering smokestacks, and crumbling walls. Known today as **Fear Factory**, this old cement plant has become Utah's most infamous haunted attraction, drawing thousands of thrill-seekers every year. But beneath the staged scares and special effects, Fear Factory holds a far more sinister reputation.

The site, originally the **Portland Cement Works**, was a hub of industry and progress in the late 1800s and early 1900s, but its history is steeped in tragedy. The factory's unforgiving machinery claimed the lives of numerous workers, and its dangerous working conditions cast a dark shadow over its success.

Long after its closure, the factory remained silent, abandoned—a skeletal remnant of Salt Lake City's industrial past. Yet, those who dared venture inside knew something lingered in the ruins. Strange lights flickered in empty corridors, disembodied voices whispered in the darkness, and unseen forces sent chills down the spines of those who walked through its rusted gates.

Today, as one of Utah's premier haunted attractions, Fear Factory capitalizes on its terrifying history. But visitors quickly realize that not all of its frights are manufactured. Some are real.

A Factory Built on Blood and Tragedy

The Portland Cement Works, built in the late **1800s**, operated for decades as one of Salt Lake City's most important industrial sites. With its massive kilns, towering smokestacks, and maze-like corridors, the factory produced the cement used to build much of the city's infrastructure. However, behind the walls of progress lurked deadly hazards.

The factory was a dangerous place to work. Machinery malfunctioned, industrial fires broke out, and human error often resulted in horrific accidents. Many workers suffered severe injuries—or worse, met gruesome deaths within its walls.

The Most Notorious Deaths at the Factory

The factory gained an infamous reputation due to the **numerous deaths** recorded over its years of operation. The most chilling accidents include:

• **The Coal Grinder Incident:** One of the most infamous deaths involved a worker named **George Howe**, who was tragically **pulled into a coal grinder** while performing maintenance. His coworkers could do nothing but listen to his screams as the massive machine crushed him. To this day, many visitors report hearing **grinding noises and phantom screams** echoing from the lower levels, where the accident occurred.

Once a factory of industry... now a factory of whispers and shadows

• **The Silo Collapse:** In the early 1900s, **a cement storage silo collapsed**, burying three workers alive beneath tons of crushing debris. Their bodies were never recovered. Staff and paranormal investigators claim that these lost workers haunt the factory, appearing as **shadowy figures** or **causing equipment malfunctions** when people enter certain areas.

• **The Elevator Shaft Fall:** Several workers reportedly fell to their deaths in one of the factory's elevator shafts. Some were construction workers, others maintenance men, but all met the same fate—**plunging into darkness**. Many employees who work at Fear Factory today report **feeling unseen hands pushing them** near the old shaft, as if the ghosts of past victims are trying to warn—or claim—new souls.

• **Machinery Malfunctions:** Workers were frequently **crushed, burned, or electrocuted** due to faulty machinery. Many deaths were poorly documented, but their eerie presence remains. Paranormal investigators have recorded **disembodied voices**, and visitors claim to have been **touched or pushed** by unseen forces while standing near the massive, rusting equipment still present in the building.

After multiple deaths and injuries, the factory was eventually shut down. It sat abandoned for decades, its skeletal remains looming over Salt Lake City's industrial district. But even as it decayed, the stories of ghostly encounters only grew stronger.

The Haunted Factory Awakens

Even before it became a haunted attraction, urban explorers, thrill-seekers, and ghost hunters were drawn to the **deserted, crumbling ruins** of the old cement plant. What they experienced convinced them that the building was far from empty.

- **Mysterious Lights and Shadows:** Explorers frequently saw **unexplained glowing lights** flickering in dark corridors, only to disappear upon approach. Others reported **tall, shadowy figures** moving in the periphery of their vision.

- **Unnerving Sounds:** Visitors reported hearing **metal clanging, footsteps echoing from empty rooms, and whispers in the darkness**. Some even claimed to hear the faint sound of machinery starting up, as if the factory were still running—though no power had been connected for decades.

- **Phantom Workers:** Several people claimed to have seen **full-bodied apparitions** of factory workers, covered in dust and grime, standing silently in the hallways before vanishing into thin air.

These reports only intensified after the site was reopened as **Fear Factory** in 2011, when staff members and visitors began experiencing eerie encounters even before the attraction was fully operational.

Fear Factory: A Haunted Attraction with Real Ghosts

Today, Fear Factory is one of the most famous **commercial haunted houses** in the United States, known for its elaborate special effects, terrifying actors, and high-adrenaline scares. But many guests quickly realize that not all the horrors within the factory are part of the show.

- **The "Phantom Worker" Encounters:** Staff members often glimpse a **ghostly figure of a man in overalls** walking along the catwalks—only for him to vanish before their eyes. Security cameras have even caught movement in areas that were supposed to be empty.

- **Disembodied Voices:** Guests and actors frequently hear **whispers, moans, and even laughter** coming from rooms where no one is stationed. Some have even reported being **touched or grabbed** by unseen hands in the darkness.

- **Equipment Malfunctions and Cold Spots:** Paranormal investigators have noted unexplained **battery drains, flickering lights, and electrical surges**, often in the exact locations where fatal accidents occurred. Employees working late at night often report sudden cold spots or the feeling of someone breathing down their neck.

A Factory of Fear—Then and Now

While Fear Factory embraces its eerie reputation, its haunted past remains **more than just a marketing gimmick**. Those who visit expecting only **staged scares** often leave convinced that they've encountered **something much more real**—the ghosts of workers who never left, forever trapped within the walls of a factory that took so many lives.

For some, the thrill of Fear Factory is its Hollywood-style effects, elaborate mazes, and terrifying actors. But for others—those who hear phantom whispers, feel icy fingers brush their skin, or catch a fleeting glimpse of a shadowy figure watching them from the catwalk above—Fear Factory is more than just an attraction.

It is a **portal to the past**, a place where history still breathes, where restless spirits linger, and where the echoes of long-forgotten tragedies whisper through the darkness, waiting for new visitors to hear them.

Enter if you dare—but know that you may not be alone.

Vermont

The Ghosts of Lake Bomoseen: Shadows Beneath the Waters

(Castleton, VT – A Lake with a Forgotten Past)

Tucked away in western Vermont's scenic countryside, **Lake Bomoseen** is a serene and peaceful retreat, drawing visitors who come to hike, camp, and enjoy its pristine waters. But as beautiful as the lake is during the day, **something eerie lingers beneath the surface**—a restless history that has given the lake a haunted reputation.

A Town Drowned by Time

In the 19th century, the land surrounding Lake Bomoseen was home to **thriving slate quarries** that provided stone for construction throughout New England. Workers, many of them Irish immigrants, toiled in harsh conditions, cutting and hauling slabs of slate. Small **mining villages** popped up along the shores, housing families and laborers who relied on the lake for transportation and survival.

But as industries changed, the quarries shut down, and **the villages were slowly abandoned**, swallowed by time and nature. Some say parts of these settlements **remain beneath the waters**, hidden reminders of lives lost to history. When the lake is particularly still, boaters have claimed to see **shadowy outlines of buildings** beneath the surface—remnants of homes and businesses long forgotten.

Ghostly Encounters Along the Shoreline

Many who visit **Lake Bomoseen State Park** report **strange occurrences**—the feeling of **being watched**, **whispered voices drifting across the water**, and **phantom footsteps crunching through the woods** where no one is present.

- **Fishermen and campers** have reported seeing **ghostly figures walking along the shoreline**, only to disappear into the mist.

- Some boaters have claimed to see **a mysterious rowboat** gliding across the lake in the moonlight, **with no one aboard**—an eerie echo of the past.

- Hikers along the trails have reported hearing **unexplained splashes** in the water, as if someone—or something—is moving just beneath the surface.

Whether it's the spirits of long-gone quarry workers, echoes of forgotten villages, or something far older, **Lake Bomoseen holds onto its ghosts**—and those who visit often leave with stories they can't explain.

Emily's Bridge: A Tragic Love Story That Refuses to Fade

(Stowe, VT – The Ghost of a Heartbroken Bride)

Deep in the heart of **Stowe, Vermont**, nestled in a quiet wooded area, lies **Gold Brook Covered Bridge**, more famously known as **Emily's Bridge**. By day, it appears to be a charming, picturesque relic of the 19th century—but by night, the bridge **takes on a much darker presence**.

The Legend of Emily

The most common tale surrounding the bridge tells the tragic story of **Emily, a young woman betrayed by love**. In the mid-1800s, Emily was said to have **fallen deeply in love with a man her family disapproved of**. Determined to be with him, she planned to elope. The couple made plans to meet at the bridge and run away together, leaving behind the judgment of their families.

But **Emily's lover never arrived**.

Heartbroken and humiliated, Emily **took her own life** by **hanging herself from the bridge's rafters**, her despair forever tied to the lonely wooden structure.

A Haunting That Won't Fade

Ever since, **Emily's spirit** has remained bound to the bridge, her sorrowful presence still felt by those who dare to cross it.

- **Unexplained scratches appear on cars** that drive through at night, as though unseen hands are clawing at the vehicles.

- **Disembodied screams** and **soft crying** echo through the covered bridge, sending shivers down the spines of those who pass through.

They say Emily still waits on the bridge... but she's not waiting for you. (Picture Wikimedia Commons)

- Some **pedestrians report feeling invisible hands pushing them**, as if Emily is still there, warning them to leave.

- Paranormal investigators have recorded **strange whispers and EVPs (electronic voice phenomena)** near the bridge, with voices saying phrases like "*Help me*" or "*Why did he leave?*"

Locals warn **not to visit Emily's Bridge alone at night**, as many who do report feeling an **overwhelming sense of sadness or dread**—as if Emily herself is watching, waiting, forever seeking the love she lost.

The Equinox Hotel: The Ghost of Mary Todd Lincoln

(Manchester, VT – A Former First Lady's Lingering Spirit)

Few hotels in Vermont boast the same level of **historic prestige** as **The Equinox Hotel** in Manchester, which has stood for over **250 years**. A luxurious retreat for presidents, socialites, and business tycoons, this grand inn has played host to some of the most powerful figures in American history. But **one guest, it seems, never checked out**—and that guest is none other than **Mary Todd Lincoln**, the wife of President Abraham Lincoln.

A Place of Presidential Legacy

The Equinox Hotel became a fashionable **summer retreat for the wealthy** during the 19th century, attracting dignitaries from across the country. Mary Todd Lincoln, devastated by the assassination of her husband, sought solace at the Equinox in **1865**, hoping the peaceful Vermont mountains would bring her comfort.

However, tragedy and loss continued to follow her, and she became obsessed with **spiritualism**, holding séances in an effort to contact her deceased husband. **Whether her efforts were successful remains unknown—but many believe she never truly left the hotel.**

Ghostly Encounters at The Equinox

To this day, guests and staff at The Equinox report **paranormal activity**, much of it linked to Mary Todd Lincoln:

Mary Todd Lincoln checked in... but some say she never truly left. (Image Public Domain)

• Visitors claim to see **a woman in period clothing, wandering the hallways**, vanishing before they can approach.

• Some **feel an unshakable presence in certain rooms**, particularly in areas where Mary Todd Lincoln is believed to have stayed.

• The sounds of **faint whispers** and **rustling fabrics** have been heard late at night, though no source is ever found.

• **Unexplained cold spots** occur in rooms that were once used for séances, as if the energy of her spiritual attempts still lingers.

Though The Equinox remains a luxurious and sought-after retreat, many who visit leave with the unsettling feeling that they have **brushed against the past**—perhaps even encountering the lingering sorrow of the woman who once called it home.

In Vermont, **the past is never truly gone**—it lingers in whispers, footsteps, and fleeting glimpses of those who refuse to be forgotten.

Virginia

The Martha Washington Inn: A Haunted Haven of War and Music

(Abingdon, VA – A Grand Hotel with a Ghostly Violinist)

Nestled in the historic town of **Abingdon, Virginia**, the **Martha Washington Inn** has stood as a symbol of Southern hospitality since **1832**. Originally built as a grand family estate, the building later served as a **women's college**, a **Civil War hospital**, and eventually a **luxurious inn**. While its elegant exterior and welcoming atmosphere have made it a popular destination, guests often leave with chilling stories of ghostly encounters—particularly those linked to the **mournful strains of an unseen violin**.

The Spirit of Beth: A Ghostly Nurse and Her Violin

During the **Civil War**, the inn was repurposed as a **hospital for wounded soldiers**, where nurses tended to the dying and tried to ease their suffering. Among these compassionate caregivers was **Beth**, a young nurse who sought to bring comfort to the soldiers by playing her **violin**. As death loomed over the makeshift hospital, her music became a source of solace for the wounded, echoing through the halls as a gentle farewell to those who would not survive.

During the Civil War, the wounded found comfort in Beth's violin... some say her music still drifts through the halls at night. (Picture Wikimedia Commons)

Beth's story took a tragic turn when **one of the soldiers she cared for—her rumored lover—was killed**. Heartbroken, she continued playing her violin even as illness claimed her own life. But death did not silence her music.

Ghostly Encounters at the Martha Washington Inn

To this day, guests and staff **still hear the soft strains of a violin** drifting through the halls—particularly at night. The sounds seem to come from nowhere and vanish just as suddenly, leaving behind a haunting presence.

- Guests in **Room 403**, rumored to be Beth's former quarters, have reported hearing **soft weeping** at night and feeling an unseen presence watching over them.

- **Shadowy figures** have been seen gliding silently through the hallways, as though lost in time.

- **Cold spots and flickering lights** occur without explanation, particularly in the areas where Civil War soldiers once lay dying.

Whether Beth continues to search for her lost love or simply plays her violin to comfort those who visit the inn, one thing is certain: **her spirit never left.**

The Peyton Randolph House: Williamsburg's Most Haunted Mansion

(Williamsburg, VA – A House of Unrest and Unexplained Deaths)

Williamsburg, Virginia, is one of the most famous colonial towns in America, but among its preserved 18th-century homes, one stands out as particularly eerie: **The Peyton Randolph House**. Built in **1715**, this stately mansion was home to **Peyton Randolph**, a prominent politician and the first President of the Continental Congress. But beneath its distinguished history lies a disturbing reputation—it is widely considered **one of the most haunted houses in Virginia**.

A House Marked by Death

From the outside, the **Peyton Randolph House** appears to be a picture-perfect colonial estate, yet those who have lived or worked there describe an unsettling energy. Over the centuries, an **unusual number of deaths have been recorded on the property**, leading to speculation that something sinister lurks within its walls.

- **Unexplained fatalities:** The house has been linked to multiple untimely deaths, including family members, enslaved individuals, and later occupants. **Many of these deaths were sudden and mysterious**, with no clear medical cause.

- **Unrest among the enslaved:** Williamsburg's colonial history includes the tragic reality of slavery, and **enslaved individuals who suffered and died on the property** may still roam the grounds, their spirits seeking justice or release.

Voices whisper in empty rooms... some say the spirits of the past never left. (Image Public Domain)

Paranormal Phenomena at the Peyton Randolph House

The stories of hauntings at the Peyton Randolph House are **so numerous** that even ghost hunters hesitate to spend the night.

- **Apparitions of colonial-era figures** have been seen walking through the house, sometimes appearing in period clothing before vanishing into thin air.

- **Unexplained voices and whispers** echo through empty rooms, sometimes calling out names or carrying on ghostly conversations that seem trapped in time.

- **Guests have reported being physically touched or pushed** by unseen hands, particularly in rooms associated with past tragedies.

- **Furniture moves on its own, doors slam shut, and lights flicker violently**, as if unseen forces are still at war within the house.

Even in broad daylight, visitors report feeling **intense unease**—as though the spirits of the past are watching from the windows, waiting for their stories to be heard.

The Ferry Plantation House: A Gathering Place for Ghosts

(Virginia Beach, VA – A Haunted Plantation with Many Spirits)

Standing along **the Lynnhaven River in Virginia Beach**, the **Ferry Plantation House** is **a paranormal hotspot** known for **its multiple hauntings**. The current structure, built in **1830**, sits on a site with a much **older** and **darker** history. Before the existing plantation home, there was **a 17th-century courthouse**, a **colonial tavern**, and even a **ferry station**, where travelers crossed the river.

Over the centuries, **tragedy and misfortune** struck many who passed through, and **their spirits seem to have remained behind**.

The Many Ghosts of Ferry Plantation House

Unlike some haunted locations with a **single famous spirit**, the **Ferry Plantation House is haunted by at least eleven distinct ghosts**, each tied to the property's long and turbulent history.

The Lady in White

One of the most famous apparitions at the Ferry Plantation House is the **Lady in White**, a sorrowful specter seen roaming the grounds near the river. Some say she was **a young woman who drowned nearby**, forever searching for her lost love. Witnesses describe seeing her **drifting through the trees**, **gliding down staircases**, and sometimes **appearing in windows**—always wearing her signature white gown.

The Ghost of Sally Rebecca Walke

During the Civil War, **Sally Rebecca Walke**, the daughter of a plantation owner, suffered devastating loss. Her beloved fiancé was killed in battle, and **her grief drove her into seclusion**. She is believed to still linger in the house, appearing to visitors in **a tattered wedding dress**, mourning the life that was stolen from her.

Other Unexplained Paranormal Activity

With so many tragic souls lingering on the property, **Ferry Plantation House is a beacon for ghostly activity**:

- Visitors often report **cold spots, eerie whispers, and shadowy figures moving throughout the house**.
- **Objects move on their own**, particularly in rooms associated with the plantation's history of slavery.

They say at least eleven spirits roam these halls... some still waiting to be heard. (Picture Wikimedia Commons)

- Staff members have described **phantom footsteps**, furniture shifting at night, and **ghostly laughter** drifting through the halls.

- The sounds of **horses and carriages** are sometimes heard outside, as if colonial travelers are still arriving at the ferry station.

The Ferry Plantation House stands as **a living museum**—not just to history, but to the souls who refuse to leave it behind.

Washington

The Sorrento Hotel: The Ghost of Alice B. Toklas

(Seattle, WA – A Grand Hotel with a Literary Spirit)

Perched atop Seattle's **First Hill**, the **Sorrento Hotel** stands as a beacon of old-world luxury, an architectural masterpiece built in **1909**. The hotel's grand mahogany interior, elegant chandeliers, and Italian Renaissance Revival charm have made it a timeless retreat for the rich and famous. Over the years, it has hosted **politicians, celebrities, and literary giants**—but according to guests and staff, **one guest never checked out**.

Her name? **Alice B. Toklas.**

While many haunted hotels are known for **ghostly lovers, tragic brides, or restless souls of the murdered**, the Sorrento Hotel holds a unique distinction: it is said to be haunted by a **literary icon**, a woman whose presence in history is as legendary as her spectral appearances in the hotel's corridors.

Who Was Alice B. Toklas?

Born in **San Francisco in 1877**, Alice B. Toklas became famous as the **lifelong companion of modernist writer Gertrude Stein**. The pair were inseparable, living in Paris and becoming central figures in the **early 20th-century literary and artistic movements**, hosting salons attended by **Pablo Picasso, Ernest Hemingway, F. Scott Fitzgerald, and Henri Matisse**.

Alice B. Toklas still lingers in the shadows... some say she watches, waiting to be remembered. (Image Public Domain)

But before Toklas ever set foot in **Europe**, she had **strong ties to the Pacific Northwest**. Raised in California, she spent time in **Seattle**, where she had extended family. Some historians believe she **either stayed at or had connections** to the Sorrento Hotel before leaving for France**, although why her spirit would return to Seattle rather than Paris remains a mystery.**

Toklas is best known for writing *The Alice B. Toklas Cookbook*, which, aside from its famous recipes, contained **an infamous "hashish fudge" recipe** that became an early reference to edible cannabis in literature.

Hauntings of the Sorrento Hotel: Why Does Alice B. Toklas Linger?

While **Alice B. Toklas never died in Seattle,** paranormal researchers and guests alike report that **her presence lingers within the Sorrento Hotel**, particularly **near Room 408**. Why she remains is unknown—was this a place of **joy, sorrow, or unfinished business**?

Many theories suggest her spirit may be drawn to **Seattle as a place of early memories,** or perhaps **to a specific event tied to the hotel itself**. Some believe **her ghost is searching for something lost, wandering the hallways in an eternal pursuit of resolution.**

Regardless of the reason, the Sorrento has gained a reputation as **one of Seattle's most haunted locations**, thanks to eerie encounters with **an unseen but unmistakable presence.**

Strange Happenings at the Sorrento Hotel

Guests and staff at the **Sorrento Hotel** have described numerous chilling experiences, many of which seem directly linked to **Alice B. Toklas's lingering spirit.**

1. Floating Apparitions

The **most famous paranormal sighting** at the hotel is that of **a woman dressed in early 20th-century clothing**, seen **floating down the hallways** before disappearing into thin air.

- Witnesses describe the figure as **graceful, with an air of sophistication**, often seen moving toward Room 408 before vanishing.

- Some guests have woken in the middle of the night, **seeing a translucent woman standing at the foot of their bed**, watching silently before fading away.

- **Hotel staff closing up for the night have reported catching glimpses of a dark figure out of the corner of their eye**—only to find no one there when they turn around.

2. Room 408: The Sorrento's Paranormal Hotspot

If the Sorrento Hotel has a **most haunted room, it is undeniably Room 408**. Many of the **strangest and most unsettling experiences** have occurred within this specific suite.

- Guests have reported **feelings of intense unease**, as though someone is **watching them from the shadows**.

- Some have described **waking up to the sensation of someone sitting on the edge of the bed**, though no one is there.

- Objects—particularly books and **small personal belongings—mysteriously move** from one place to another with no explanation.

- Housekeeping staff have noted that **lights in Room 408 flicker and televisions turn on by themselves**, as if an unseen guest is still present.

Interestingly, **Toklas was known to be deeply superstitious**, often speaking of ghosts, spirits, and unexplained energies. If she was **drawn to the supernatural in life**, perhaps she **found herself tethered to it in death**.

3. Lights That Flicker at Will

Throughout the Sorrento, particularly in hallways leading to **Room 408**, lights are notorious for **flickering inexplicably**.

- Hotel employees have witnessed lights **turning on and off at random**, even when there is no electrical issue.

- Some claim the **chandelier in the main lobby will sway slightly**, as though touched by an invisible force.

- One common theory is that **Toklas is making her presence known**, using subtle energy to communicate with those who **pay attention**.

4. The Sound of Unseen Footsteps

One of the eeriest reports at the Sorrento Hotel involves **the unmistakable sound of high-heeled shoes clicking against the wooden floors**.

- Guests and staff frequently hear **the soft, deliberate steps of a well-dressed woman walking down the halls**—even when the corridor is empty.

- The sound often originates **from the upper floors**, particularly in **areas Toklas is believed to haunt**.

- Paranormal investigators believe this could be a **residual haunting**, meaning the ghost of Alice B. Toklas is **stuck in a repeating loop, forever pacing through the grand halls of the Sorrento**.

Why Alice B. Toklas? Why the Sorrento?

While **Toklas is not known to have died in Seattle**, her spirit seems inexplicably drawn to the **Sorrento Hotel**.

Theories for her haunting include:

1 A place of fond memories – Perhaps she stayed at the Sorrento during **her younger years**, forming a connection that lasted beyond death.

2 An unfinished story – Did an event in the Sorrento **leave an emotional imprint** on her spirit?

3 Her deep ties to the supernatural – Toklas was fascinated by **ghost stories, séances, and the spirit world**. It's possible she became **part of the very world she once studied**.

Whatever the reason, guests who visit the Sorrento often leave with an **unsettling feeling that they are not alone**—and some believe they have truly **crossed paths with the ghost of Alice B. Toklas**.

The Sorrento Hotel: A Grand Destination with a Literary Haunting

Seattle's **Sorrento Hotel** remains a **landmark of elegance and history**, a place where **the past lingers just beneath the surface**. Whether **Alice B. Toklas still wanders the** halls in search of something lost, or simply remains as a **spectral storyteller**, her presence is undeniably felt.

For those daring enough to book **Room 408**, a night at the Sorrento may offer more than luxury—it may offer **a glimpse into the past**, where history, literature, and the supernatural **intertwine in the shadows**.

Would you stay the night?

The Harvard Exit Theatre: The Woman Who Weeps in the Shadows

(Seattle, WA – A Haunted Theater in the Heart of Capitol Hill)

Seattle's **Harvard Exit Theatre**, once a beloved landmark in the city's **Capitol Hill neighborhood**, was famous for its cozy, independent films and vintage charm. But for those who worked there late at night or attended films in its dimly lit auditorium, the experience often came with an unsettling presence—a **spirit trapped within its walls, eternally grieving for reasons unknown.**

A Haunted Legacy

Built in **1925**, the Harvard Exit Theatre originally served as the home of the **Women's Century Club**, an organization dedicated to empowering women in the early 20th century. The grand brick building exuded history and elegance, but as time passed, reports of **ghostly activity** began to surface.

The most **famous spirit** associated with the Harvard Exit is a **mysterious woman** seen wandering the halls, always **crying softly**. Witnesses describe her as **dressed in an early 20th-**

century gown, her figure barely visible before she fades into the shadows.

Terrifying Encounters

- **Phantom Weeping** – Employees and patrons have frequently reported the **sound of a woman crying** in empty hallways or hidden corners of the building, yet no one is ever found.

- **Chilling Cold Spots** – Some guests have felt **sudden drops in temperature**, often accompanied by the feeling of someone standing nearby, unseen but undeniably present.

She lingers in the empty theater, softly weeping for reasons only she remembers

- **Locked Doors and Moving Objects** – Staff members arriving to open the building in the mornings would sometimes find **doors mysteriously locked from the inside**, lights flickering, and **chairs inexplicably moved.**

- **A Spectral Audience Member** – On multiple occasions, projectionists and late-night moviegoers reported **glimpsing a woman sitting alone in the theater**—only to realize moments later that she was never really there.

Despite its closure as a movie theater in **2015**, the building remains one of **Seattle's most haunted locations**, and those who pass by at night sometimes report feeling an eerie presence **watching them from the darkened windows.**

West Virginia

Lake Shawnee Amusement Park: The Cursed Carnival of the Dead

(Princeton, WV – A Tragic Playground Turned Paranormal Hotspot)

Deep in the **wooded hills of Princeton, West Virginia**, hidden behind overgrown trees and rusting relics of a bygone era, **Lake Shawnee Amusement Park** sits eerily abandoned. The skeletal remains of its **Ferris wheel loom against the sky**, the faded carousel stands frozen in time, and the once-thrilling swings **creak hauntingly in the wind**.

But despite its long closure, many believe **the park is far from empty**. Those who step onto its grounds often **sense something watching them**, feel an inexplicable chill in the air, or hear **the echoes of children's laughter from an era long past**.

Some places are abandoned. Others are **cursed**.

A Land Cursed by Blood

Before the **screams of thrill-seekers** filled the air, the land beneath **Lake Shawnee Amusement Park** was already steeped in **violence and tragedy**.

In the **late 1700s**, this area was settled by **Mitchell Clay**, a frontiersman hoping to build a new life for his family. But his dream turned into a **nightmare** when a **Shawnee war party attacked the homestead in 1783**, seeking vengeance for encroachment on their land.

- Two of **Mitchell Clay's children were brutally killed** in the attack.

- A third child was **captured and burned alive** by the Shawnee.

- In retaliation, **Clay and other settlers hunted down and slaughtered several Shawnee warriors**.

The **blood spilled on this land** left behind an **unsettled energy**, and many believe **the spirits of both the murdered settlers and the slain Shawnee warriors still linger**, bound forever to the soil beneath the park.

The rides have stopped, but the laughter never left... echoes of the past still haunt these abandoned grounds. (Picture Wikimedia Commons)

The Amusement Park's Tragic History

In the **1920s**, an ambitious businessman **purchased the land** and transformed it into **Lake Shawnee Amusement Park**, featuring:

A Ferris wheel

A carousel

A roller coaster

A swimming pond

For decades, **the park buzzed with life**, providing thrills and excitement to families from miles around. But **death soon returned** to claim new victims.

At least **six tragic deaths** occurred while the park was in operation, each one further **cementing its dark reputation**.

The Little Girl on the Swing

One of the most **chilling deaths** involved a **young girl who died tragically on the swing ride**.

- A **delivery truck** accidentally **backed into the ride while she was still swinging**, killing her instantly.

- **Her spirit is said to still haunt the swings**, appearing as a **ghostly figure in a pink dress**, sometimes with **blood stains on the fabric**.

- Visitors report seeing the **swings move by themselves**, even when **there is no wind**.

The Drowned Boy

The amusement park's **swimming pond**, once a favorite attraction, became the site of another tragedy.

- A **young boy drowned in the murky waters**, lost beneath the surface before anyone could save him.

- Even today, **visitors hear the sounds of splashing** when the pond is dry, and **ghostly cries** echo near the water's edge.

As more deaths occurred, rumors of the park's **haunted and cursed nature** began to spread. By the **1960s**, the tragedies became too much, and **Lake Shawnee Amusement Park was abandoned**—left to rot, consumed by nature, and **overtaken by its ghosts**.

Hauntings at Lake Shawnee

Decades after its closure, the spirits of **Lake Shawnee Amusement Park** have **not gone silent**. Paranormal investigators, urban explorers, and locals **continue to report disturbing encounters**, leading many to believe the site remains **a portal for restless souls**.

Terrifying Paranormal Activity

Ghostly Apparitions – Multiple visitors have captured **photos and videos of shadowy figures**, often of **children** running between the rusting rides.

Moving Swings – The **swing ride moves on its own**, even when the air is completely still. Some visitors claim to see **an invisible force pushing the swings**.

Eerie Voices – Electronic voice phenomena (EVPs) recorded in the park contain **whispers, giggles, and the words "Play with me"**—even when no one is around.

Unexplained Touches – Some investigators have **felt invisible hands tugging on their clothing**, as if a child is **trying to get their attention**.

Mysterious Fog – A **thick, unexplainable mist** has been known to **suddenly engulf the park**, particularly near the swing set.

But perhaps the **most unsettling discovery** came in the **1990s**, when archaeologists began to excavate the land.

A Hidden Burial Ground Beneath the Park

In the **1990s**, an excavation crew arrived to survey the site. What they found confirmed **everyone's worst fears—Lake Shawnee was built directly on top of an ancient Native American burial ground.**

- **Bones of Native American children and adults** were uncovered beneath the park.

- Some **remains were buried in a way that suggested ritual sacrifice or warfare**.

- The discovery **reinforced the belief that Lake Shawnee is cursed**, and that disturbing the land had **angered the spirits**.

Rather than remove the remains, archaeologists and historians decided to **leave the graves undisturbed**, fearing that further disruption could **intensify the hauntings**.

Lake Shawnee: A Place of Mystery and Terror

Today, the **abandoned amusement park** is one of **America's most infamous paranormal hotspots**.

- The site has been featured on **Ghost Adventures, Most Terrifying Places in America, and Paranormal Lockdown**.

- Paranormal investigators continue to **gather chilling evidence** of **ghostly presences and unexplained activity**.

- The park's owners **allow special night tours**, where brave visitors can **walk among the haunted ruins**—but **many leave with an overwhelming sense of dread**.

Those who visit **Lake Shawnee** report an eerie sensation:

A feeling that **someone— or something—is watching them**.

A presence that **lurks just beyond the trees**.

A whisper that **calls out, inviting them to stay… forever**.

Would you dare **step onto this haunted land**, knowing that the past still lingers, waiting for the next soul to join its eternal carnival?

Trans-Allegheny Lunatic Asylum: The House of Madness

(Weston, WV – Echoes of the Lost and Forgotten)

Standing like a **gothic fortress in Weston, West Virginia**, the **Trans-Allegheny Lunatic Asylum is one of the largest hand-cut stone buildings in America**. But **its beauty masks a chilling past**—one of overcrowding, neglect, and **patients trapped in unimaginable suffering**.

A Place of Healing That Became a Place of Horror

Built in **1864**, the asylum was meant to be **a sanctuary for the mentally ill**, following the "Kirkbride Plan"—a revolutionary treatment approach focusing on **fresh air, sunlight, and moral therapy**. However, as decades passed, **the asylum became a nightmare**.

By the **1950s**, over **2,400 patients were crammed into a building designed for 250**, leading to **horrific conditions**:

- **Patients slept on the floors, covered in filth.**

- **Lobotomies were performed using crude, inhumane techniques.**

- **Violent and mentally unstable patients were shackled or locked in solitary confinement.**

- **Many died from neglect, abuse, and botched treatments.**

The asylum finally **closed in 1994**, but **the tortured souls left behind never moved on.**

Ghostly Encounters at Trans-Allegheny

Today, the asylum is considered **one of the most haunted places in the world**. Paranormal investigators have documented:

- **Apparitions of former patients wandering the halls**, some screaming in agony.

- **Shadow figures darting across doorways and down hallways.**

Thousands were committed here... some never left.
(Picture Wikimedia Commons)

- **Disembodied voices, moaning, and laughter** recorded in empty rooms.

- **Objects moving on their own, doors slamming shut without explanation.**

One of the most **infamous spirits** is a **little girl named Lily**, believed to have died in the asylum. Her laughter is often heard in the children's ward, and visitors have reported **toys moving on their own**.

Would you walk through the asylum's empty halls, where the cries of the lost still echo?

West Virginia Penitentiary: A Prison of Eternal Punishment

(Moundsville, WV – A Place of Death and Darkness)

For **129 years**, the **West Virginia Penitentiary** housed **some of the state's most violent criminals**—and many **never left, even in death**. Built in **1876**, the imposing stone prison witnessed **murders, suicides, executions, and brutal treatment of inmates**.

A Brutal History

- The prison's **death row housed the worst of the worst**, leading to **94 executions by hanging or electrocution**.

- **Hundreds of inmates were murdered** by fellow prisoners, often in violent stabbings.

- **The "Sugar Shack" torture chamber** was a dimly lit

recreation room where inmates were **beaten, assaulted, and sometimes killed.**

Paranormal Activity at West Virginia Penitentiary

After its **closure in 1995**, investigators found the prison **still full of energy—and spirits**. Reports include:

• **Shadow figures lurking in the hallways** of cell blocks.

• **Screams and cries of former inmates** echoing through the corridors.

The walls still echo with the screams of the forgotten... some inmates never left. (Image Wikimedia Commons)

• **Unexplained cold spots and sudden nausea**, particularly in the "Sugar Shack."

• **Apparitions of prisoners and guards** appearing in the execution chamber.

One of the **most terrifying spirits** is "The Shadow Man"—**a tall, dark figure** seen standing in doorways and watching visitors, only to vanish when approached.

For those brave enough to visit, West Virginia offers more than history—it offers **glimpses into the afterlife**.

Would you dare explore these haunted locations, where the dead still walk among the living?

Wisconsin

The Pfister Hotel: Milwaukee's Grand Haunted Landmark

(Milwaukee, WI – A Luxurious Hotel with a Ghostly Reputation)

Opened in **1893**, the **Pfister Hotel** in **downtown Milwaukee** is one of the most elegant and historic hotels in the state. Known for its **opulent décor, grand chandeliers, and Victorian-era charm**, it has hosted **countless dignitaries, celebrities, and professional athletes** over the years.

But while the **Pfister is a symbol of luxury**, it also carries a chilling reputation: it is widely considered **one of the most haunted hotels in America**.

The Spirit of Charles Pfister

The most **frequently reported ghostly presence** is believed to be **Charles Pfister himself**, the original hotel founder. A proud and meticulous man, Charles poured **his fortune and

passion into building the Pfister, wanting it to be the most magnificent hotel in Milwaukee.

Even in death, it seems **he refuses to leave**.

• Guests and hotel employees **report seeing a distinguished-looking apparition in Victorian clothing**, often wandering the lobby or standing at the grand staircase.

• His presence is often **felt in the hotel's upper floors**, where many claim to **hear soft footsteps, faint whispers, and even feel an invisible presence brushing past them**.

• Some say Charles **watches over guests, ensuring they have a proper stay**—but those who don't respect the hotel's traditions sometimes experience eerie disturbances.

The Haunted Sports Hotel

The Pfister's **paranormal reputation skyrocketed** when numerous **Major League Baseball and NBA players** staying at the hotel began **reporting terrifying experiences**.

• **Bryce Harper**, the MLB star, refused to sleep alone after hearing **disembodied laughter in his room and furniture moving by itself**.

• **Carlos Gómez**, a former Milwaukee Brewers player, ran out of his room after hearing **a knock at his door—only to find no one there**.

• **Giancarlo Stanton**, another MLB player, described **lights flickering, the radio turning on by itself, and strange tapping noises** keeping him awake at night.

• **NBA teams**, including the Miami Heat and Oklahoma City Thunder, have **openly discussed their players experiencing** nightmares, waking up to strange noises, and even seeing **apparitions in their rooms**.

Some visiting athletes **now refuse to stay at the Pfister**, instead **booking other accommodations when playing in Milwaukee**.

Whether the spirit of **Charles Pfister still oversees his guests** or something even **darker lingers in its halls**, one thing is certain: **the Pfister Hotel is alive with more than just history**.

The Rave / Eagles Club: A Concert Hall with a Dark Past

(Milwaukee, WI – Music, Memories, and the Spirits Who Never Left)

Once an **elite athletic club in the 1920s**, the **Eagles Club** in Milwaukee has transformed into one of the **city's most famous concert venues**, now known as **The Rave**. Its **grand ballroom, underground bars, and hidden passageways** make it a **favorite among musicians and fans**—but beneath the loud music and bright stage lights, **something else lingers**.

A Venue with a Haunted Legacy

Over the years, **performers and employees alike** have reported **strange occurrences** at The Rave, many of which point to **multiple spirits still haunting the building**.

• **A Ghostly Little Girl** – The most well-known spirit is that of **a young girl**, often seen **running through the basement and lower levels**. Some claim she was a **child who drowned in**

the old athletic club's abandoned pool, her presence forever tied to the building.

• **Unexplained Sounds** – Employees frequently **hear voices, giggling, and footsteps** when no one else is around.

• **Apparitions in the Balcony** – Musicians performing on stage often report **seeing shadowy figures watching them from the upstairs balcony**, only to find the area completely empty.

• **The Spirit of a Former Employee** – A worker who allegedly **died in the building** is still believed to haunt the venue, making his presence known by **moving objects, turning lights on and off, and making eerie whispering noises**.

Bands and musicians who have performed at The Rave often **refuse to go anywhere alone**, with many claiming that they **feel watched or hear unexplainable sounds in the hallways**.

For visitors, The Rave remains **one of Milwaukee's most exciting concert venues**—but for the ghosts who linger, it remains **a place where the music never stops**.

Boy Scout Lane: The Road of Vanishing Footsteps

(Stevens Point, WI – A Mysterious Road Where the Scouts Never Returned)

Deep in the **isolated woods of Stevens Point, Wisconsin**, there is a road that seems **ordinary at first glance**—a simple dead-end stretch surrounded by dense forest.

But this road has a **dark legend** attached to it, one that has kept **locals terrified for decades**. Known as **Boy Scout Lane**, the road is said to be haunted by **an entire group of missing Boy Scouts**—their restless spirits still wandering the trees, searching for a way home.

Faint lanterns glow in the trees... but no one is carrying them

The Legend of the Lost Scouts

There are **multiple versions** of the legend, but they all end the same way: **none of the Scouts ever made it back**.

1 Murder by the Scout Leader – One tale claims that a group of Boy Scouts went on a camping trip in the woods, only for their **leader to snap and murder them all**.

2 Death by Fire – Another version states that **a lantern tipped over, sparking a deadly fire** that trapped and killed the Scouts in their tents.

3 A Vanishing Without Explanation – Some believe that the group simply **disappeared without a trace**, as though **swallowed by the forest itself.**

Despite **no official records confirming these deaths**, visitors to **Boy Scout Lane continue to experience chilling phenomena,** leading many to believe **something supernatural is at play**.

Paranormal Encounters on Boy Scout Lane

- **Phantom Lanterns** – Visitors walking the road at night report seeing **distant glowing lights**—as if the missing Scouts are **still trying to find their way back to camp.**

- **Ghostly Footsteps** – Many have heard **the sound of boots crunching through the leaves**, but when they turn around, **no one is there.**

- **Disembodied Whispers** – Some hikers claim to hear **the hushed voices of young boys calling out**, sometimes whispering their names.

- **Sudden Drops in Temperature** – Even in warm weather, **cold spots appear** along the road, giving travelers an **unshakable feeling of being watched**.

Some **who dare to walk the road at night** report an overwhelming **sense of dread**, as though unseen eyes are **watching from the trees**—waiting, **just beyond the darkness.**

Wyoming

Wyoming Frontier Prison: The Haunting of the Old Pen

(Rawlins, WY – A Prison of Torment and Ghostly Retribution)

Prisons are often places of **suffering, violence, and despair**, and the **Wyoming Frontier Prison**, operational from **1901 to 1981**, was no exception. Nicknamed **"The Old Pen,"** this foreboding stone structure in **Rawlins, Wyoming**, housed some of the **West's most violent criminals**, and for many of them, **this prison became their final resting place**.

A Brutal Past That Refuses to Rest

The Wyoming Frontier Prison was **notorious for its harsh conditions**, including **overcrowding, extreme cold in the winters, and a total lack of proper plumbing for decades**. The prisoners lived in **misery**, and some **never left the prison walls—even after death**.

- The **death row execution chamber** witnessed **dozens of hangings** and **multiple botched executions** that left the condemned suffering for **minutes instead of seconds.**

- The **prison's gas chamber** was introduced in the **1930s**, claiming the lives of Wyoming's most dangerous criminals—including **convicted murderers who are rumored to haunt the building to this day.**

- Inmates **killed each other in violent prison fights**, and their restless spirits seem to **linger, trapped within the cold stone walls.**

Terrifying Paranormal Activity

Since its closure, the **Wyoming Frontier Prison** has become one of the state's **most haunted locations**, with countless **paranormal encounters reported** by visitors, ghost hunters, and former staff.

- **Disembodied voices and moans** are frequently heard, as if the tortured souls of former prisoners still echo through the halls.

- **Phantom footsteps** are reported **following visitors down dark corridors**, only to **vanish when they turn around.**

- **Shadowy figures** lurk in **Cell Block A**, where **the most violent criminals were housed.**

- The **execution chamber**, where the gas chamber and gallows still stand, is the most active area—visitors report **sudden feelings of intense dread**, **cold chills**, and **whispers in the air** when they step inside.

Whether it's the spirits of **hanged prisoners seeking justice**, or **the echoes of suffering forever trapped within the walls**, the **Wyoming Frontier Prison remains a chilling reminder of the past**—a place where **the dead never truly left**.

The Occidental Hotel: Spirits of the Old West

(Buffalo, WY – Where Cowboys and Ghosts Check In and Never Leave)

For travelers passing through **Buffalo, Wyoming**, the **Occidental Hotel** offers a glimpse into the **glory days of the Old West**—a time when **cowboys, gunslingers, and outlaws** roamed the streets. Established in **1880**, this grand and historic hotel hosted **famous guests like Butch Cassidy, Calamity Jane, and Teddy Roosevelt**.

But the Occidental Hotel has more than just history within its walls—**it has ghosts**.

She lingers at the stairs... watching, waiting, never leaving

The Lady in Blue

The most famous **resident spirit** of the Occidental Hotel is **a mysterious woman in a blue dress**, seen wandering the hallways at night.

- **Guests report waking up to the sound of soft footsteps outside their doors**, only to find the hallways empty.

- Some have glimpsed **a shadowy figure of a woman in blue standing at the end of the hallway**, disappearing when approached.

- Others claim to have seen **her reflection in mirrors**, even when **no one else is in the room**.

Who is she? Some believe she was a **woman who tragically died in the hotel**, while others think she may be **an elegant guest from the past who refuses to leave**.

More Hauntings at the Occidental

- **Disembodied voices and whispers** are often heard near the grand staircase.

- **Doors open and close on their own**, sometimes slamming shut with **no breeze or draft to explain it**.

- **A piano in the lobby has been known to play by itself**, as if an unseen musician is still entertaining guests from beyond the grave.

For those who check in, **they may experience more than just Old West hospitality—they may also encounter the spirits of those who never checked out.**

The Irma Hotel: The Spirit of Buffalo Bill Cody

(Cody, WY – A Hotel Built by a Legend, Still Haunted by One)

Wyoming's rugged frontier history is woven into every corner of **The Irma Hotel**, a place where **legends still walk among the living**. Built in **1902** by none other than **Buffalo Bill Cody himself**, the hotel was meant to be **the jewel of the West**, a luxurious stop for **cowboys, outlaws, and aristocrats alike**. With its grand Victorian-style architecture, **ornate cherrywood bar**, and Western charm, the Irma became an **icon of Wyoming's golden age**.

But **Buffalo Bill's dream didn't end with his death**—at least, not entirely. Guests and employees alike **continue to feel his presence** throughout the hotel. **Some claim to have seen him**, others **have heard his footsteps**, and many have **experienced chilling paranormal encounters** within these historic walls.

Could it be that **Buffalo Bill Cody never truly left**?

The Ghost of Buffalo Bill Cody

William "Buffalo Bill" Cody was more than just a **legendary showman and frontiersman**—he was a larger-than-life figure whose Wild West shows **captivated the world**, bringing the tales of **American cowboys, sharpshooters, and Native American warriors** to audiences across Europe and North America. His hotel, the **Irma**, named after his beloved daughter, was his pride and joy.

To this day, **many believe Buffalo Bill's spirit remains attached to the Irma**, watching over **his greatest legacy**.

Haunting Encounters with Buffalo Bill

🤠 **A Cowboy at the Bar** – The most famous paranormal sighting in the Irma Hotel is **a ghostly cowboy figure**, often spotted **sitting at the original cherrywood bar**, staring into the distance as if lost in thought.

Bartenders have seen whiskey glasses slide across the bar on their own, as if **an unseen patron is still drinking his usual.**

Visitors report an **unsettling sensation of being watched** while seated at the bar, only to **turn and see no one there**.

Buffalo Bill built the Irma... and some say he never left.

Some have described **seeing a cowboy in an old-fashioned duster coat, boots propped up**, only for him to vanish before their eyes.

His Presence in the Halls – Buffalo Bill's personal suite, located upstairs, is another hotspot for strange activity.

Guests staying in **his former room** have described **hearing heavy footsteps pacing the floorboards late at night**, as if he is still **restless in the afterlife**.

Some report waking up to **the faint smell of cigar smoke**, even though smoking has been banned in the hotel for years.

A few visitors have even claimed to see **his apparition standing near the windows**, looking out at the streets of Cody **as if still watching over his town**.

Furniture That Moves on Its Own – The original **ornate cherrywood bar**, a gift from **Queen Victoria of England**, is rumored to be **a paranormal hotspot**.

• Barstools have been seen **shifting by themselves**, as if someone unseen **has taken a seat**.

• **Cold drafts** are often felt around the bar, even when the room is warm and no doors are open.

Buffalo Bill may have passed on, but **his presence in the Irma remains strong**, ensuring his beloved hotel continues to thrive—even in the afterlife.

Other Hauntings at the Irma Hotel

Buffalo Bill isn't the only spirit that lingers within the Irma's walls. **Several ghostly figures have made themselves**

known over the years, their apparitions spotted by both guests and staff.

The Lady in White

One of the most famous ghostly figures at the Irma Hotel is **the Lady in White**—a mysterious, **elegant woman dressed in Victorian-era clothing**.

• She has been spotted **gliding down the hallways**, her white gown **flowing behind her**.

• Some guests have awakened in the middle of the night **to see a shadowy female figure standing at the foot of their bed**, watching them silently before disappearing.

• Others have **seen her reflection in the hotel's antique mirrors**, even though no one was standing nearby.

Who was she? Some believe she was **a former guest who died at the hotel**, while others think she may have been **a woman in love with Buffalo Bill**, still searching for him in the afterlife.

Unexplained Noises and Phantom Footsteps

Many guests and staff have reported hearing **strange, unexplainable noises** throughout the Irma Hotel:

Knocking Sounds in the Walls – Loud **knocking and tapping sounds** have been reported **in empty rooms**, as if someone is trying to get attention from beyond the grave.

Footsteps in Empty Hallways – The unmistakable **sound of boots walking on wooden floors** echoes through the hotel, especially **in the dead of night**—but when guests investigate, they find **no one is there**.

Whispers from the Past – Some visitors have heard **disembodied voices murmuring in empty rooms**, their words **just out of reach**, like echoes from a forgotten conversation.

The Phantom Smell of Cigar Smoke

One of the most **unsettling phenomena** at the Irma Hotel is the **lingering scent of cigar smoke**—even though **smoking has long been banned**.

- The smell is **most often detected near Buffalo Bill's former room and the bar**, where he was known to **enjoy a cigar after a long day**.

- Guests have described waking up in the night **overwhelmed by the strong aroma**, only for it to vanish **as quickly as it appeared**.

- Some staff members have even **felt a tap on the shoulder**, only to **turn around and find no one there**—as if Buffalo Bill himself is still watching over his hotel.

Buffalo Bill's Legacy Lives On

Today, the Irma Hotel remains **one of Wyoming's most beloved historic landmarks**, attracting visitors **from around the world**. Its **Western charm, rich history, and undeniable aura of the past** make it a must-visit destination—but for those who **stay the night**, the experience might be more than just a trip back in time.

The spirits of the **Old West** still roam these halls. Some are seen. Others are only felt.

And Buffalo Bill? He may still **be keeping watch over his greatest creation**, ensuring that the Irma Hotel **never fades from history**.

So, if you ever visit, raise a glass to the man himself. But don't be surprised if **you hear his boots walking behind you**, or **feel the unmistakable smell of his cigar filling the air**.

He's still here. **And he's not leaving anytime soon.**

Part 3

Conclusion: The Ghosts We Leave Behind

Reflections on America's Haunted Legacy

Why Ghost Stories Endure

For as long as humans have been telling stories, **ghosts have haunted our imagination**. From whispered campfire tales to the chilling accounts shared in old newspapers, **ghost stories have been passed down for generations**, embedding themselves into the very fabric of American folklore. They serve as **cautionary tales, historical echoes, and, in some cases, deeply personal experiences** that blur the line between legend and reality.

But why do ghost stories continue to **captivate, terrify, and intrigue us**—even in an age of scientific reasoning and modern technology? Why do we still seek out **haunted houses, historic cemeteries, and eerie urban legends**? The answer lies deep within our **psychology, our culture, and our fascination with the unknown**.

The Role of Ghost Stories in American Folklore

America, a land of **immigrants, pioneers, and revolutionaries**, has always been a country shaped by **stories**—tales of adventure, struggle, and survival. And within those stories, **ghosts have played a significant role**, often serving as reminders of **the people and events that history has tried to forget**.

• **Ghost stories preserve local legends** – Every small town and historic city has **its own ghostly lore**, whether it's a battlefield where soldiers still march at night or a haunted hotel where past guests refuse to check out. These tales often serve as a **living memory of past events**, ensuring that those who came before us are never truly lost.

• **They reflect the anxieties of their time** – Ghost stories tend to emerge **in response to cultural fears**. In colonial America, fear of the supernatural was linked to **witch trials and religious puritanism**. In the 19th century, ghost stories flourished in response to **the Civil War and rising interest in spiritualism**. Even today, ghost stories continue to **evolve alongside modern fears**, from haunted asylums to abandoned factories.

• **They connect generations** – Grandparents tell ghost stories to grandchildren, communities host **haunted history tours**, and books like this one continue to **document and retell** the spectral experiences of those who claim to have encountered something beyond this world.

Simply put, **ghost stories help us keep our history alive—even when history itself refuses to rest**.

The Paradox of Hauntings in a Scientific Age

Despite **advancements in technology, psychology, and science**, reports of hauntings **have not diminished**. If anything, **ghost hunting is more popular than ever**, with paranormal investigation shows, ghost-hunting apps, and digital ghost tourism creating **a new kind of modern folklore**.

But why, in an age of logic and reason, do so many still believe in ghosts?

1 Science has not disproven ghosts – While science provides **alternative explanations** for hauntings—such as electromagnetic fields affecting the brain or sleep paralysis causing ghostly visions—it has never **conclusively proven that ghosts do not exist**. As long as there is room for doubt, **people will continue to believe**.

2 Technology has fueled belief – Ironically, instead of diminishing ghost stories, **modern technology has amplified them**. From **thermal cameras capturing unexplained figures** to **EVP (Electronic Voice Phenomena) recordings of mysterious whispers**, technology has given believers **new ways to document the paranormal**.

3 Personal experiences override skepticism – No matter how much science explains hauntings away, **millions of people claim to have seen, heard, or felt something unexplainable**. For many, a personal encounter with the unknown is **far more powerful than scientific skepticism**.

Even **hardcore skeptics** find themselves **drawn to haunted places**, eager to see if something truly lies beyond the veil of life and death.

The Universal Human Desire to Explore the Unknown

At the heart of every ghost story is **a mystery**, and humans are **natural seekers of the unknown**. Whether through **science, religion, or folklore**, we have always sought to understand **what happens after we die**.

- **Ghost stories provide a bridge between the living and the dead** – They give us **glimpses of the past**, suggesting that those who came before us may still be here, in some form or another.

- **They offer comfort and fear in equal measure** – For some, the idea of ghosts is **terrifying**—proof that **unseen forces exist beyond our control**. For others, ghosts represent **the persistence of the human soul**, an assurance that death is not truly the end.

- **They allow us to experience fear in a safe way** – Just as people **ride roller coasters for the thrill**, we seek out **ghost stories, haunted houses, and eerie locations** because they allow us to experience **the rush of fear without real danger**.

Ghost stories endure because **they are more than just stories**—they are reflections of **our deepest fears, hopes, and the timeless question of what lies beyond life itself**.

Ghost Stories as a Window into American History

A ghost story is rarely just about a ghost. Behind every whispering spirit, flickering light, and shadowy apparition lies **a deeper, more human story**—one of **love, loss, war, tragedy, and unfinished business**.

America's most haunted places are not just **eerie destinations for thrill-seekers**—they are **living records** of the past, preserving history in ways that books sometimes cannot. While **some history is written in documents and monuments, other stories linger in the very walls of old buildings, in the echoes of forgotten voices, and in the chilling presence of those who refuse to be forgotten**.

In this chapter, we explore how **ghost stories and hauntings serve as powerful historical markers**, revealing **the tragedies, struggles, and triumphs of the past** and how they continue to shape America today.

The Haunting Echoes of War

The Civil War: America's Bloodstained Ghost Story

No war in American history left **more hauntings in its wake** than the **Civil War**. The battlefields where tens of thousands **fought and died** are now among the **most haunted places in the nation**, their echoes still heard **on foggy mornings and moonlit nights**.

War sites are especially prone to hauntings for several reasons:

1 **High Concentrations of Tragedy** – Sudden and violent deaths often lead to reports of **lingering spirits**.

2 **Strong Emotional Energy** – Fear, anger, sorrow, and determination **imprint themselves** on the land.

3 **Unfinished Business** – Many soldiers died **far from home**, leaving behind loved ones and **unspoken words that echo through time**.

These battlefields are not just places of **ghost stories**—they are **monuments to the past**, where history refuses to be forgotten.

Haunted Prisons and Asylums: The Spirits of the Forgotten

Not all ghosts are tied to war. Some hauntings are rooted in **pain, injustice, and cruelty**—stories of those who **suffered behind locked doors**, hidden away from society.

Prisons are **repositories of suffering**, filled with **centuries of fear, anger, and hopelessness**—emotions that some believe have seeped into the very walls.

Asylums and Sanitariums: The Hauntings of the Abandoned and Neglected

In the 19th and early 20th centuries, **mental institutions and tuberculosis sanitariums** were often **underfunded and overcrowded**, leading to **inhumane treatments**. Many **patients died nameless and forgotten**, their restless spirits **still seeking peace**.

Ghost stories from **prisons and asylums** serve as **harsh reminders of America's past failings**, warning against **the mistreatment of those cast aside by society**.

The Spirits of the Gilded Age: Haunted Hotels, Theaters, and Mansions

Not all hauntings stem from **suffering and violence**—some ghosts remain in places they **once loved, refusing to leave** behind the opulence and prestige of their past lives.

Historic Hotels: Where Guests Never Check Out

Hotels, once **symbols of wealth and luxury**, are **common haunts** for spirits who seem to enjoy the company of the living.

In these places, **history is not just preserved—it lingers**. Guests may **enter expecting luxury**, but some **leave with ghost stories of their own**.

Theaters: Spirits of the Stage

Theaters, filled with **dramatic energy and emotion**, are often **believed to attract lingering spirits**—actors who refuse to leave the stage, phantom audiences, and even mischievous ghosts who love to **play pranks on performers**.

Actors and stagehands have long shared **theatrical superstitions**, believing that **some spirits stay behind, ensuring the show must go on**.

Mansions and Estates: The Ghosts of the Elite

The grand homes of **America's wealthiest families** have often **outlived their original owners**, but in some cases, those owners **never truly left**.

In these homes, **the echoes of privilege, tragedy, and mystery remain**, and visitors often report **strange whispers, phantom music, and figures standing in the windows long after sunset**.

Ghost Stories Reflect Regional Identity

Across the United States, **different regions embrace their hauntings in unique ways**—some using them to **celebrate history**, while others attempt to **bury their ghostly past**.

The South: Haunted Elegance and Civil War Tragedy

The **American South** is steeped in **ghostly lore**, with hauntings tied to **plantations, battlefields, and tragic histories of war and slavery**.

The Impact of Haunted Tourism

Ghost stories are more than just **chilling tales told around a campfire**—they have become **a booming industry**, driving curiosity, tourism, and even economic growth. Across America, cities and small towns alike **capitalize on their haunted histories**, transforming local legends into **ghost tours, haunted hotels, and paranormal experiences**.

What was once **taboo or feared is now celebrated**, with **entire towns embracing their supernatural past** as a means to **preserve history, attract visitors, and fuel their economies**. Haunted tourism is not just about ghosts—it's about **the intersection of folklore, history, and entertainment**, all of which create a unique and profitable industry.

Ghost Tourism as a Major Industry

Haunted tourism has evolved from **a niche attraction to a mainstream industry**, generating **millions of dollars**

annually. The demand for **haunted experiences** spans across various platforms:

- **Ghost tours** – Walking tours of **historic sites, graveyards, and haunted houses** allow visitors to hear eerie tales while exploring **the actual locations tied to supernatural legends**.

- **Haunted hotels** – Many historic hotels, such as **The Stanley Hotel (CO) and The Myrtles Plantation (LA)**, market their paranormal reputation to **attract thrill-seeking guests**.

- **Paranormal investigation experiences** – Some locations allow **overnight ghost hunts**, providing visitors with **EMF readers, spirit boxes, and night-vision cameras** to experience the paranormal firsthand.

- **Haunted attractions** – Theme parks, **Halloween events, and immersive haunted experiences** recreate ghostly encounters for entertainment.

- **Television shows and documentaries** – Programs like *Ghost Adventures* and *The Haunting of Hill House* fuel the **public's obsession with haunted locations**, leading more people to visit these infamous sites.

- **Books, podcasts, and social media** – Stories of hauntings continue to **spread through modern media**, ensuring the legends never fade.

With **a growing number of travelers actively seeking supernatural encounters**, haunted tourism has become **a powerful force**, not just for entertainment but for **economic revival in historic towns**.

The Commercial Side of the Paranormal

Beyond individual locations, the **paranormal industry as a whole** continues to thrive, proving that **America's fascination with ghosts is stronger than ever**.

• **Television and Film:** Shows like *Ghost Adventures, The Dead Files*, and *The Haunting of Hill House* have **ignited public interest in hauntings,** leading more people to seek out real-life paranormal destinations.

• **Books and Podcasts:** From historical ghost books to true crime podcasts, the **demand for eerie tales has never been higher**.

• **Haunted Houses and Attractions:** Every October, haunted houses, corn mazes, and immersive horror experiences bring in **millions of visitors and dollars**, turning fear into a profitable business.

In the end, haunted tourism is not just about **scaring people**—it's about **telling stories, preserving history, and creating experiences that connect people to the unknown**.

When Ghosts Bring Prosperity

Ghost stories do more than **terrify and entertain**—they **revive towns, preserve history, and shape economies**. Across the U.S., **haunted tourism is breathing life into forgotten locations, turning tragedies into legends, and ensuring that America's ghosts remain very much alive**.

So the next time you step into **a haunted hotel, a historic battlefield, or an eerie old prison**, remember:

It's not just about the ghosts.

It's about the **stories that refuse to die—and the people willing to listen.**

The Psychological and Emotional Pull of the Paranormal

What is it about **ghost stories** that keeps us coming back for more? Why do we actively seek out **haunted houses, eerie cemeteries, and paranormal encounters**, even when we know they might send chills down our spines?

The **paranormal fascinates us** because it speaks to something **deeper than just fear**—it taps into **our emotions, our history, our curiosity, and even our search for meaning in life and death**.

For some, ghost stories are a **thrill**, a safe way to experience **fear and excitement** without real danger. For others, they are a **connection to the past**, a way of preserving **stories, legends, and history**. And for many, the paranormal represents something **far more profound**—a **potential glimpse into what lies beyond death**, a **search for answers about what happens to us when we die**.

No matter where we fall on the spectrum of **skepticism or belief**, one thing is certain: **ghost stories endure because they speak to the deepest parts of what it means to be human.**

The Thrill of Fear: Why We Love to Be Scared

One of the simplest explanations for why people seek out **ghost stories, haunted houses, and supernatural experiences** is **the adrenaline rush**.

- **Fear triggers a physical response** – When we feel scared, our bodies **release adrenaline and endorphins**, increasing our heart rate and heightening our senses. This **biological reaction** is the same whether we're running from real danger or simply watching a horror movie.

- **We enjoy controlled fear** – Ghost stories provide **a safe way to experience fear**—we can explore a haunted house or listen to a scary tale **knowing that we are not actually in danger**.

- **The thrill-seeking personality** – Some people **actively seek out** haunted locations and paranormal experiences, much like they enjoy **roller coasters, skydiving, or extreme sports**. The rush of **fear mixed with excitement** keeps them coming back for more.

This **love of being scared** is one reason why **haunted tourism** continues to thrive, why horror movies remain popular, and why people still gather to tell **ghost stories on dark, stormy nights**.

The Search for Proof: Do Ghosts Exist?

For many, the pull of the paranormal is not just about **fear**—it's about **finding answers**.

- **A desire to prove the afterlife** – Some people seek out ghostly encounters **as a way to confirm that life continues**

after death. If spirits exist, then **death may not be the end**—a deeply comforting thought.

• **Paranormal investigation has become mainstream** – Thanks to popular ghost-hunting shows, more people are **actively trying to capture evidence of hauntings** using **EMF meters, EVP recordings, and infrared cameras**.

• **Unexplained experiences fuel belief** – Many believers **did not start out believing in ghosts**—but after a personal encounter **that defied explanation**, they became convinced. Stories of **seeing apparitions, hearing voices, or feeling an unseen presence** have turned many skeptics into believers.

Even those who are skeptical **can't completely dismiss the unexplained**—some of the most **credible ghost stories** come from people who **never believed in ghosts until something happened to them**.

The Skeptic vs. Believer Debate: Psychology or Paranormal?

Not everyone believes in ghosts—but even skeptics can't deny that **the paranormal is a global fascination**.

• **Skeptics argue that hauntings are psychological** – Many scientists believe that ghostly experiences can be explained by **sleep paralysis, electromagnetic fields affecting the brain, or even the power of suggestion**.

• **Believers counter that some experiences defy explanation** – While some ghostly encounters can be debunked, many **remain mysterious**, with **credible witnesses** and **documented evidence** that suggest something beyond psychology.

- **Cultural and personal beliefs shape our views** – Some cultures embrace **ghosts and spirits as part of everyday life**, while others reject the idea entirely. Similarly, personal experiences often **determine whether someone believes or not**.

The **debate between skeptics and believers** will likely continue forever—but that's part of what makes the paranormal so compelling.

Final Thoughts: The Power of the Paranormal

Ghost stories endure because they **tap into something universal**—our **love of mystery, our fear of the unknown, our connection to history, and our hope that there is more beyond this life**.

- **For thrill-seekers**, ghosts are a **scary and exciting challenge**.

- **For believers**, ghosts are **evidence of life after death**.

- **For storytellers**, ghosts help **preserve history and tradition**.

- **For those grieving,** ghosts are a **comforting presence, proof that loved ones never truly leave**.

Whether **ghosts are real or not**, the stories we tell about them **are very real**, shaping our culture, our fears, and our search for meaning.

So the next time you hear **a floorboard creak when no one is there**, feel **a sudden chill in the air**, or wake up to **the sense that someone is watching**—

Ask yourself: **Is it just your imagination?**

Or are you standing on the edge of something **far greater than we understand**?

The Ghosts We Leave Behind

Ghost stories are more than just eerie tales whispered in the dark—they are **a living part of American culture**, deeply woven into **our history, our fears, and our fascination with the unknown**. Whether **fact or fiction, legend or reality**, hauntings continue to **captivate, terrify, and inspire**, reminding us that the past is never truly gone.

But what do these stories really tell us? Are hauntings **merely echoes of the past**, or are they **something more—something deeply connected to the human experience itself**?

The Eternal Presence of Ghosts in Culture

No matter how much **science and technology advance**, ghost stories **never disappear**—if anything, they grow stronger, **adapting to new generations, evolving with new fears, and taking on new forms in media, tourism, and folklore.**

Why do we continue to tell these stories?

- **They are a connection to history.** Every ghost story is tied to **a real place, a real event, or a real person**—whether it's the spirits of soldiers at Gettysburg, the lost souls of abandoned asylums, or the legends of cursed mansions, these tales help us **remember the past in a way that facts and textbooks never could.**

• **They reflect our changing world.** Ghost stories evolve alongside **cultural fears**—where early American hauntings were tied to **witch trials and puritan superstitions**, modern ghost stories often focus on **technological anxieties, lost identities, and unresolved injustices**.

• **They shape our communities and economies.** From **Salem's witch trials to Savannah's haunted streets**, entire cities have embraced their **paranormal past**, turning history into a **thriving industry of ghost tours, haunted hotels, and eerie attractions**.

Whether we **truly believe in ghosts or not**, these stories **persist because they matter**—because **they remind us of what came before, and what we may leave behind**.

Hauntings: Proof That History Never Dies

There's a reason why **certain places feel haunted**—because **they are still alive with memory, with sorrow, with tragedy, and with love**.

• **Abandoned prisons and asylums hold the echoes of suffering.** The walls of **Eastern State Penitentiary, Waverly Hills Sanatorium, and Trans-Allegheny Lunatic Asylum** seem to remember the **pain and despair of those locked away inside**.

• **Battlefields echo with the final moments of soldiers.** At **Gettysburg, Antietam, and Little Bighorn**, visitors still hear **phantom gunfire, marching footsteps, and whispered cries from the past**.

- **Hotels and mansions preserve the lives of those who never wanted to leave.** The spirits of **The Stanley Hotel, The Myrtles Plantation, and The Driskill** may simply be **holding onto the places they loved in life**.

Haunted places are often **historical places**, and perhaps ghosts are simply **history refusing to be forgotten**.

We do not fear the past itself—but we fear the idea that **history lingers, that memories can leave an imprint, that the energy of the dead can stay behind, unable to move on**.

In this way, hauntings serve as **a bridge between past and present**, reminding us that **our world is built upon the stories, struggles, and spirits of those who came before us**.

Are Ghosts Just Reflections of Ourselves?

Perhaps ghosts are not **spirits of the dead**, but **reflections of the living**—of our **fears, our desires, and our search for meaning**.

- **Ghosts embody our deepest fears.** They represent **loss, the unknown, and the fear of what happens after death**. They force us to confront **the question we all must face: What happens when we die?**

- **They reflect our longing for connection.** Many hauntings are **not malevolent, but sorrowful**—spirits trapped in places they once loved, unable to let go. These stories **mirror our own reluctance to say goodbye to the past**.

- **They fuel our endless curiosity.** Whether through **science, folklore, or personal experience**, we are **constantly searching for answers**—about ghosts, about death, about what lies beyond.

Perhaps, in seeking out ghosts, we are really seeking out **ourselves**—trying to understand **our place in history, our connection to the past, and what our own legacies will be when we are gone**.

Final Thoughts: The Stories We Leave Behind

Hauntings are more than **stories of the dead**—they are **stories of the living**. They remind us that **history is not just something that happened—it is something that lingers, something that breathes, something that shapes the world we walk through every day**.

- **Some ghosts are legends.** They exist in **stories passed down through time**, whispered in small towns and written in the pages of history books.

- **Some ghosts are memories.** They are **the energy of those who lived before us**, a presence that can be felt in the walls of an old house or in the stillness of a battlefield.

- **And some ghosts are just us.** The stories we tell about **hauntings, spirits, and the supernatural** are really about **our own fears, desires, and longing for answers that may never come**.

One day, the places we call home, the streets we walk, and the buildings we enter **will belong to another generation**. And who knows? Maybe they will feel our presence, sense our memories, hear our voices in the dark.

Because in the end, **ghost stories aren't just about the dead.**

They are about **the stories that refuse to be forgotten.**

And maybe, just maybe, that's because **some of us never truly leave.**

How to Explore Hauntings Safely & Respectfully

How to Explore Hauntings Safely & Respectfully

If you are ready to embark on **your own ghostly adventures**, there are a few **important guidelines** to keep in mind. The paranormal world is intriguing, but **it must be approached with respect—not just for spirits, but for the real history behind these sites**.

1. Research Before You Go

- Learn the history of the site—**who lived there, what happened, and why it might be haunted.**

- Read firsthand accounts, listen to paranormal investigations, and familiarize yourself with **any reported activity.**

- Know the rules—**is the location open to the public, or do you need permission?**

2. Visit with an Open but Cautious Mind

- Keep an **open mind**, but **don't let fear take over**—many experiences can be explained through **environmental factors, psychology, or even human error**.

- Pay attention to **your surroundings, your feelings, and any sensations that seem out of place**.

3. Join Guided Tours or Investigations

- Many historic haunted locations offer **tours led by experts** who can provide **historical context and paranormal insight**.

- Paranormal investigations often allow **hands-on use of ghost-hunting equipment**, like **EVP recorders, EMF meters, and night-vision cameras**.

4. Be Respectful of Spirits & History

- If ghosts exist, they were once **people**—treat them with the same **respect you would show the living**.

- Avoid **provoking or mocking spirits**, as many believe this can lead to **negative experiences**.

- **Never trespass or damage historic locations**—preserving these sites is just as important as exploring them.

5. Document Your Experiences

- **Keep a journal** to note **strange sensations, sounds, or unusual feelings**.

- Take photos—but remember, **not everything strange in an image is paranormal**.

- Record audio in empty rooms—some of the most **compelling EVP (electronic voice phenomenon) recordings** have captured ghostly voices responding to investigators.

Whether you encounter **a full-bodied apparition or simply the eerie weight of history pressing down upon you**, every visit to a haunted site is **an opportunity to explore, to learn, and to decide for yourself what you believe.**

www.ingramcontent.com/pod-product-compliance
Lightning Source LLC
LaVergne TN
LVHW011926070526
838202LV00054B/4509